W9-BPS-282

BEYOND
THE
WELFARE STATE

BOOKS BY IRVING HOWE

Celebrations and Attacks
Leon Trotsky: A Study
World of Our Fathers
The Critical Point
Decline of the New
Steady Work: Essays in the Politics of Democratic Radicalism,
1953–1966
Thomas Hardy: A Critical Study
A World More Attractive
The American Communist Party: A Critical History
(with Lewis Coser)
Politics and the Novel
William Faulkner: A Critical Study
Sherwood Anderson: A Critical Biography
The U.A.W. and Walter Reuther
(with B. J. Widick)

BOOKS EDITED BY IRVING HOWE

25 Years of Dissent
The World of the Blue-Collar Worker
Essential Works of Socialism
The Seventies: Problems & Proposals
(with Michael Harrington)
Voices from the Yiddish
(with Eliezer Greenberg)
A Treasury of Yiddish Poetry
(with Eliezer Greenberg)
The Idea of the Modern
The Basic Writings of Trotsky
The Radical Imagination
Edith Wharton: A Critical Collection
The Radical Papers
A Treasury of Yiddish Stories
(with Eliezer Greenberg)

BEYOND THE WELFARE STATE

Irving Howe

EDITOR

SCHOCKEN BOOKS
New York

First published by Schocken Books 1982
10 9 8 7 6 5 4 3 2 1   82 83 84 85
Copyright © 1974, 1978, 1979, 1980, 1981, 1982 by Dissent, Inc.
Library of Congress Cataloging in Publication Data
Main entry under title:
Beyond the welfare state.
1. Welfare state—Addresses, essays, lectures.
2. Socialism—Addresses, essays, lectures. I. Howe, Irving.
HB846.B49   1982   330.12′6   81–40408
AACR2
Manufactured in the United States of America
ISBN 0–8052–3787–9 hardback
0–8052–0685–X paperback

Contents

Irving Howe

———————⟫•◦•⟪———————

Introduction

IT MAY seem wildly optimistic to put together a book about going "beyond" the welfare state at the very time that there is a major attack in the United States against whatever little we have of a welfare state. But perhaps not. Perhaps the overheated reaction against the welfare state now dominating American politics will prove to be a last gasp of the American right, a final enraged turn backward to outmoded simplicities—after which we will enter an era marked by a new, sophisticated interpenetration between state and society, government and economy.

The idea of a blissful return to a laissez-faire economy (which in reality never existed) is either a reactionary utopia or a cynical slogan masking corporate interests. Whatever else, a modern industrial society must accept a large amount of governmental intervention into socioeconomic life. (As I write, spokesmen for the American automobile industry say that in order to make the enormously expensive conversion to small, fuel-efficient cars that might save a wounded industry, they will need a lot of financial help from Washington; these must surely be the same kinds of people who scream against "bureaucrats in Washington" as parasites on an otherwise-healthy "free economy.")

In the long run all that remains to be determined is whether this governmental intervention will occur in behalf of the underprivileged, the poor, the modestly paid workers, or the national and multinational corporations. It is amusing—but also infuriating—to note that together with the assault on the welfare state which takes the disguise of "get the government off our backs," the corporate sector has steadily profited from governmental succor in *its* behalf: think only of Lockheed, Penn Central, Chrysler, tax programs heavily beneficial to oil corporations. The all-but-certain long-range trend will be a further politicizing of economic policy.

That is why the contributors to this book hold two perspectives: first, immediately to defend our vulnerable and inadequate welfare state, and second, to raise the possibilities for far-ranging structural reforms that would extend, perhaps transform, the welfare state in the direction of greater egalitarianism and more democratic participation. About this latter theme I have nothing to add: the essays that follow speak for themselves and, I think, speak well. But it may help the reader if I first set down—briefly, schematically—a few notes about the welfare state itself.

What Is the Welfare State?

Suppose we draw up a preliminary model of the welfare state. Now a model is not a picture. It lacks, and to serve its purposes must lack, the complexities of reality. A model articulates skeletal structures, the bones of society. It seeks to isolate essential qualities. But it cannot describe how things change, nor can it bother with idiosyncratic traits.

The welfare state represents a phase in the development of capitalist society. Yes—but a capitalist society partly transformed and somewhat humanized through the pressures of internal, democratic insurgency. The welfare state preserves the essential traits of the capitalist economy in that the interplay of private or corporate owners in the market remains primary, but it also modifies the workings of that economy in that the powers of free disposal by property owners are regulated politically. Creating a certain tension between government and economy, the welfare state acts to save capitalism from its own self-destructive drives or excesses. It acts, so to say, as a brake on the spontaneous inclination of that economy to end up in the ditch of severe crisis. The welfare state helps capitalism; it limits the power of capital; it does the first by doing the second. A helpful extension of these remarks is provided by Henry Pachter:

The welfare state is a capitalistic economy which largely depends on the free market but in which the countervailing powers have been politicized and are consciously employed to balance the economy, to develop the national resources, or to pursue fixed goals of social policy. . . . The welfare state may achieve techniques of industry-wide planning, price-fixing and over-all control of development, but though it will nationalize the coal industry in France and England, erect a TVA in the United States and build a government steel mill in India, it stops short of expropriation. On the contrary, its proclaimed aim is to preserve the structure of property and to protect the formation of a free market. . . . The basic relationships of buyer and seller, employer and employee, owner and nonowner are no different from those prevailing under pure capitalism, but they are supplemented by state interference in two important areas: where classical capitalism is indifferent to the distribution of income, the welfare state at least tries to make income differential less steep; also, whereas under pure capitalism the development of resources is but an accidental by-product of the profit incentive, the welfare state sets itself definite goals of developing public and private facilities. . . .

Indisputably, the welfare state has eased, if not wholly liberated, the lives of millions of people. Social policies largely taken for granted by younger people, though in the early 1980s subject to renewed political attack, have provided major benefits: unemployment insurance, social security, old-age pensions, job-safety provisions, acceptance of the right of workers to organize unions. If these are today taken for granted that is because an earlier generation fought and sacrificed for them. Nor are they trivial matters, despite what extremists of right and left tend to say. Such gains rest on a new, if not yet adequate, sense of communal responsibility. They rest on an awareness that the older American creed of "individualism" which yielded—and can still yield —many precious values, no longer provides us with adequate norms of humane social life. And a crucial part of the new sense of communal responsibility ("Yes, I am my brother's keeper" as against "Screw you, Jack") has been the political acceptance and social institutionalization of new insurgent blocs: unions, blacks, women, even gays. All this has often created new, unforeseen problems, but they are problems that are a consequence of social advance.

Many of the criticisms traditionally made of capitalism hold for the welfare state, if now in subtler and more complex ways. Basic disparities in wealth and income remain. Major differences in political power, largely following from radical inequities of wealth and income, seem more striking than ever. The lack of democratic participation and control in our economic life persists. (That a Douglas Fraser, as head of the United Automobile Workers, is elected to the board of the Chrysler Corporation signifies less a readiness to follow the European policy of "codetermination" than evidence of how desperate this poorly run corporation has become.) And the absence of social planning—for instance, the failure to anticipate and prepare for the energy crisis—continues to plague us under the welfare state.

It is something, this welfare state, that is constantly being undermined, reconstructed, patched together. It is a result of social compromise and improvisation; certainly here in the United States it cannot be considered a planned construct. The model we advance for it may suggest an inner equilibrium, but the reality has frequent difficulties, conflicts, breakdowns. No sooner, for example, does the corporate sector regain its confidence as a result of the ministrations of the welfare state than it sets about vindictively trying to choke it to death.

If the welfare state ever could reach a point of internal perfection, the point at which it would approach its "ideal type," it would constitute a system of regulated conflicts making for pluralist balance and stability. So, in fact, some wishful liberal theorists sometimes describe it. But this point of perfection cannot of course be reached. For the welfare state makes its historical appearance in a context which ensures that it will be complicated by a multitude of problems. Problems, say, of a specific national past (racism, in the United States). Or problems of concurrent international conflict (the Cold War with the Soviet Union, our dependence on Middle East oil). Or a series of new modes of moral criticism which the welfare state is ill-equipped to deal with (the politics of the late 1960s, the styles of the counterculture).

The unavoidable inner tensions of the welfare state—especially those that pertain to the working class—are well described by Alisdair MacIntyre:

It was only gradually that people in Britain became conscious of themselves as living in a society where a right to minimal standards of welfare was presupposed. . . . Even a modern affluent working class, even a working class with a socialist tradition . . . has to learn that the welfare state is *essentially a realm of conflict* in which the real benefits of welfare are always in danger of being undermined . . . and thus a realm in which it needs a good deal of running even to keep standing in one place. So a working-class political self-consciousness about welfare as a point at which elementary rights have continually to be reclaimed seems to be one of the preconditions for the maintenance of welfare in an advanced capitalist society.

What Are the Sources of the Welfare State?

About the several theories regarding the sources of the welfare state I think it fair to say that none seems totally irrelevant and none totally persuasive. But some are more persuasive than others. Let me mention a few.

Economists who prefer to eliminate messy human passions from their theorizing have seen the welfare state as essentially an outcome of autonomous socioeconomic processes. A modern economy cannot function according to the simplistic prescriptions of Milton Friedman, if only because certain kinds of investment (defense, space, industrial reconstruction) are too massive for private capital to undertake and therefore require governmental action. Also, in a complex economy there have to be some regulating agencies to prevent chaos, just as the increase of air traffic requires expert controllers in airports.

A second approach to the welfare state comes from orthodox or sectarian Marxists, some of whom simplify the thought of Herbert Marcuse, itself not always free of excessive simplicity. They see the welfare state as a mode of government designed to keep the masses quiescent with bread and circuses (actually, bread and mass culture). In this view the welfare state arises mainly from the political foresight and shrewd manipulations of the business classes (though I must confess to having seldom noticed these qualities among them).

There is a third view, favored by liberals and socialists, which holds that the welfare state is a triumph—partial but substantial—achieved through struggles undertaken by masses of men in the labor, liberal, and socialist movements. Far from being the result of impersonal economic processes, or a sop thrown to the workers in order to thwart their rebelliousness, the welfare state is a *conquest* wrested from the dominant classes in capitalist society.

Most of us in this book would probably choose to stress the last of these opinions. And though it is an opinion regarded with suspicion by orthodox Marxists, it can easily be put into Marxist terms. The welfare state would then be seen as a result of class struggles which have proceeded up to a certain point and then, for a longer or shorter time, been blocked. The welfare state would be seen as a sort of intermediate stage in the prolonged historical contest between capitalism and socialism—a stage indicating the inroads made into capitalism by insurgent classes but also the ability of capitalism to redress itself and adapt to new circumstances.

In Europe there is an additional factor, and that is the special role of the social democracy, often the main political initiator of welfare states on the continent. Though still pledged formally to socialism, the European social democracy has not seriously tried to establish a democratic socialist society that would signify a decisive break with capitalism. What the social democratic parties have done is to consolidate the welfare state on a decidedly more generous basis than we have yet managed in the United States. But further than that the social democrats have not gone.

Why so? Because, their critics would say, they are characterized by a deep timidity, an unwillingness or inability to break decisively with the status quo. Because, more dispassionate observers might suggest, in no European country, not even Sweden, has the social democracy received an unambiguous mandate from the voters to move very far beyond the welfare state.

But there are other, perhaps deeper reasons. The old socialist faith in nationalization of industries has been severely shaken. Nationalization, where it occurs, seems no panacea: it seldom involves a break with inherited relations between rulers and ruled, and it often seems more of a device for bailing out portions of a sick economy than for creating a new one. Hence there is no longer the traditional certainty about what going "beyond" the welfare state might mean (a point discussed in a number of essays in this book). More important, as G. D. H. Cole has written: "The experience of one kind of totalitarian rule under Hitler and of another kind of totalitarianism under Stalin unavoidably put into the minds of reasonable persons a fear of placing too much power into the state's hands, even if the state professed to be socialist." This fear is of course shared by intelligent socialists too, but it necessarily makes them more uncertain and hesitant about their projected future. Indeed the single most absorbing topic of discussion among the more venturesome European social democrats, especially in France and Sweden, has been of strategies for moving toward a socialized (that is, commonly owned and democratically managed) economy while avoiding the blight of an excessive concentration of state power.

The Inner Dynamics of the Welfare State

A major achievement, or result, of the welfare state might be called the "desacrilization" of power. As Michael Walzer writes,

> The development of the welfare state has generated a pervasive enlightenment about the functions of political organization. For the first time in history masses of men have known with absolute clarity that the state ought to be doing something for them. They are rationalists-of-everyday-life, each one demanding, "What has it done for me?" Prewelfare theorists have generally denied the validity of this simple question, insisting that the state always *is* more than it *does*. They have described it as a closely knit body, dense and opaque, whose members were involved emotionally as well as materially, mysteriously as well as rationally, in the fate of the whole. The members ought to be involved, it was said, not for the sake of concrete benefits of any sort, but simply for the sake of communion. Since loyalty was a gift for which there was to be no necessary return, it could not be predicated on anything so clear-cut as interest. It depended instead on all sorts of ideological and ceremonial mystification. . . .
>
> The state still does depend on ideology and mystery, but to far less a degree than ever before. It has been the great triumph of liberal theorists and politicians to undermine every sort of political divinity, to shatter all the forms of ritual obfuscation, and to turn the mysterious oath into a rational contract. The state itself they have made over from a "body politic" into a machine, the instrument of its citizens (rather than their mythical common life) devoted to what

Bentham called "welfare production." It is judged, as it ought to be, by the amounts of welfare it produces and by the justice and efficiency of its distributive system.

A remarkable development, and from it comes a new social dynamic. What occurs characteristically during the early stages of the welfare state is a series of "invasions" by previously neglected or newly cohered groups demanding for themselves a more equitable portion of the social product. Such demands had of course occurred in earlier times, but one factor especially enabling for these new insurgents is that the welfare state provides a common ideology in the name of which they can legitimate their demands, press for a share of power, and even act against the welfare state as it exists. They feel *entitled.* And what makes them feel entitled is this new social ethos of the welfare state, itself a consequence of earlier struggles by disadvantaged groups.

Let me suggest a very rough distinction between what I would call the first and second stages of the welfare state. In the first stage conflicts and divisions seem relatively clear: we need elementary social benefits and rights, we need them in order to survive, we need them so as to have a half-decent old age. In the second stage things are by no means so clear. There is a pervasive sense of malaise, there are suddenly powerful new modes of discontent which seem all but unmanageable through political means, and there is a tendency for insurgencies to break up into smaller constituencies, sects, and one-issue movements. The sociologist C. Wright Mills once made a keen distinction between issues and troubles. Issues are precisely formulated; troubles are strongly felt but hard to dramatize into a slogan or formulate as a demand. In the first stage of the welfare state, which seems just about to be reaching its end, the liberal-left groups were able to articulate issues effectively. In the second stage we variously express our troubles but have still not succeeded in transforming them into clear or dramatic issues.

In its first stage the welfare state is subjected to "invasions" mostly by economic interest groups seeking to improve their conditions. First and foremost this means workers and their unions. By now, in the early 1980s, a substantial segment (though by no means all) of the American working class has found a place within the society. (Some leftists would grumble that it has been "coopted.") In the second stage of the welfare state there occurs a new series of "invasions" that are less precisely fixed in program and more far-reaching or grandiose morally than those of the earlier economic groups. Examples of such new "status" or "value" constituencies are the women's movement, the gays, the environmentalists, and various religiopolitical tendencies. All speak in terms that extend beyond, and sometimes claim to dismiss, mere economic interests. They speak in behalf of "larger" values, experimental lifestyles which will elevate or purify our experience. And meanwhile, straddling the two stages of the welfare state, there remain the efforts of racial communities such as the blacks, which rightly speak in behalf of both interests and values.

This course of "invasion" is far from completed in the United States; indeed it is scandalously frustrated by racial and social meanness. As long as there are groups trying to break in and powers intent on keeping them out, we can be certain that the welfare state will be marked by severe conflict. Nor is there any certainty that the welfare state will prove receptive to all the claims likely to be made by groups largely outside its system of dispensation. It is possible that the legitimate demands of the blacks will not be met and that this would in turn lead to a crippling of the welfare state as we know it. But if that were to occur it would not, I believe, be the result of an inherent dynamic or ineluctable necessity within the welfare state. It would rather be the result of a tradition of racism so deeply ingrained in America (though not found in other societies that have developed a welfare state) that it threatens to persist indefinitely.

Sooner or later invasions produce counterinvasions. During the past several years we have witnessed in the United States a remarkable thrust, almost as if by decision, among the defenders of the corporate system. They have decided to enter the welfare state *as if* they were the spokesmen for disadvantaged groups seeking redress. Grown more sophisticated, the American right seems to have decided that it can neither ignore the welfare state nor risk an effort to destroy it head-on. The right has therefore taken a leaf from the liberal and labor book: it organizes "political action committees," it turns out far more sophisticated propaganda than ever before (sometimes by hiring ex-radical intellectuals), and it presents itself not as a spokesman for American capitalism but as a beleaguered defender of personal liberty. If all this were not so serious, it would be very funny. Nevertheless there is a decidedly new twist here: the corporate forces which the welfare state was supposed to discipline now turn about and, by mimicking the tactics of insurgency, use the welfare state to damage it.

Inner Problems of the Welfare State

Its early achievements notwithstanding, the welfare state clearly has some dysfunctional characteristics. Are these inherent? Are they a result of the very successes of the welfare state? Would a further extension of this mode of society multiply or deepen the dysfunctional characteristics? We really can't say with any assurance, for we are speaking here not about a completed arc of history toward which we can attain a dispassionate perspective but about a social experience with which our lives are entangled every day.

Still, let me note a few of the problems that seem especially acute in the welfare state:

1. It must, almost by its very nature, arouse greater expectations than it can satisfy. It announces "open house" for everyone, but then it often shuts the door.

Successful "invasions" by one disadvantaged group spur others to similar kinds of assertion. But what worked for one may not work for the other. As a result the welfare state can become a target for attack by underprivileged groups which grow frustrated when their demands are not met. Furthermore, counterattacks from business interests keep the welfare state off-balance both in its capacity to fulfill the expectations it has aroused and in the moral and ideological claims it must continue to advance. At best, then, it is really a semiwelfare state, forced to neglect urgent needs, unable to live up to its earlier expectations, often driven to defensive postures. At worst it may even become an antiwelfare state. The dynamic of capitalist economy—sometimes helped along by governmental agencies staffed by friends of the very business interests they are supposed to regulate—can transform an attractive social program into something resembling its opposite. (Michael Harrington has documented how programs designed originally to provide housing for the poor have a way of turning into programs that provide housing for the affluent.)

And as for those in our society too feeble or demoralized to get themselves together in a coherent "invasion"—they often suffer shameful neglect. In the richest country in the world the welfare state allows a significant minority, the chronic poor, to be dumped beneath the social structure, all too often declining into a lumpen deposit of pathology and degradation.

2. Even as the welfare state may gratify the interests of one or another previously deprived group, it tends also to dampen concern with larger values such as justice, fraternity, equality, and community. The older individualistic ethic has a curious way of reasserting itself: instead of "Every man for himself and the devil take the hindmost," we now have "Every group for itself and who cares about the rest?" This may still be better than the earlier "rugged individualism," since some of these competing groups assert the claims of people who would otherwise be utterly helpless. Still, at least for the time, one consequence of the pluralist scramble encouraged by the welfare state is that fundamental issues of justice and power are muted. The system as such is seldom an issue in public debate, and that is a pity.

Yet we ought to beware of the sin of impatience. If the welfare state lulls previously militant groups into acquiescence—and this has happened with portions of the liberal and labor constituencies —it also enables them to gain a bolder sense of new, enlarged entitlements. And it grants succeeding generations the relative affluence to experiment with lifestyles and cry out against the slumbers of their elders. The notion that once a few needs are satisfied people will fall into permanent apathy, the idea that the welfare state creates a dormancy of modest satisfactions, may have a bit of truth at any given moment. But it does not seem to be true over the long run. New explosions of demand, new discoveries of need, new perceptions of right break through. Prolonged stasis seems highly improbable in the modern world.

3. In its own right the welfare state does not seem able to arouse strong loyalties. Perhaps this forms a minus to be put beside the plus of the demystification of the state described by Michael Walzer.

It seems easier, if not more intelligent, to die for the Stars and Stripes, or the Proletarian Fatherland, than for unemployment insurance and social security. There are fewer subrational loyalties, and perhaps no encompassing mystique, for the welfare state to exploit.

At the start the welfare state encourages political participation. Indeed without the arousal of large numbers of people moved to sudden political activity there could not be a welfare state to begin with. But then, apparently once some of these people have made social and economic gains, there follows a decline in political participation. People want to enjoy life a little: it's only natural. And in the United States at least, enjoying life is largely conceived in private terms.

The left-liberal-labor coalition on which the welfare state was built in this country starts to crumble: its various constituents go their own ways, forgetting the claims of solidarity, sometimes even clashing with one another. Evidently the earlier liberal hope that there would be a steadily mounting rate of political participation —if only because it pays off in direct socioeconomic benefits— turns out to be a delusion. It is one of those accursed paradoxes of history that even as, and perhaps because, the welfare state strengthens the fabric of socioeconomic life, it also undercuts the vitality of the democratic process. Are such moments of indifference, even apathy, mere intervals between flows of political and social energy? So one hopes.

4. One increasing difficulty of the welfare state is that it functions largely within the limits of the nation-state, so that it cannot cope with the growing number of socioeconomic problems that seem soluble, if at all, only on an international level. The example of the badly ailing steel and auto industries in the United States comes immediately to mind: what we are confronting here is a serious malady created by conflicts among national economies. There are other, more complex instances, a few of which are described by Richard Titmuss:

It is much harder today to identify the causal agents of change—the microbes of social disorganization and the viruses of impoverishment —and to make them responsible for the costs of "disservices." Who should bear the social costs of the thalidomide babies, of urban blight, of smoke pollution, of the obsolescence of skills, of automation, of the impact on the peasants of Brazil of synthetic coffee which will dispense with the need for coffee beans?

We are beginning to witness rather limited international or regional structures, like the European Common Market, which may presumably be able to cope with some of these problems. In time the European community might even form a kind of rudimentary welfare state on a transnational basis. But that remains a possibility for the future, and meanwhile the maladjustments which international economic conflicts and imbalances create for the welfare state are severe.

5. Within its limits, the welfare state finds it hard to provide avenues of fulfillment for many people whose conditions it has helped to improve. That is why there appear new social formations such as the subculture of the alienated young, responding less to acute economic need than a felt sense of the falsity of things, the moral emptiness of a society that places so obsessive an approval on the personal accumulation of wealth. Sometimes more, sometimes less visible, this subculture constitutes an antistatus rebellion, a shared wish to break loose from categories fixed by the society. And what complicates this situation, giving it a dangerous apocalyptic edge, is that even while the welfare state fails to provide such young people with goals and ideals that stir the moral imagination, traditional religious agencies are also coming to seem insecure and unexciting. Our society is therefore likely to experience a permanent unrest along its margins, partly sociopolitical in nature, partly religious, and partly a dubious mixture of the two.

6. It may be that we are starting to live through a *systemic* crisis in the welfare state, one due not to accidental or transient factors but to its intrinsic characteristics. The traditional economic crises of prewelfare capitalism had a self-regulating character—market glut, overexpansion, plunge into depression, reserve army of unemployed, "disciplining" of labor, depressed wages, gradual lowering of inventories, reopening of factories, a new boom, and

the same thing all over again. These did "purge" the economy, though at terrible human costs, and each time with a greater need for governmental medicine. Now under the welfare state there occurs a politicizing of crisis. As we have seen with the Carter administration, political decisions crucially affect whether there will be a recession, to say nothing of its extent and duration. Fiscal, monetary, banking, employment, and investment policies undertaken by the federal government turn out to be political equivalents to those aspects of the relatively autonomous workings of the economy which under prewelfare capitalism might hasten or slow, deepen or ease, a crisis.

To what extent is inflation an intrinsic cost of the welfare state? Has it been mainly the result of the increasing role of government in the economy, or has it been caused by a multitude of other factors such as the failure of the Johnson administration to raise taxes sufficiently during the Vietnam War, the enormous burdens placed on the economy by steadily rising OPEC prices and by military expenditures, the inflexibility of corporate-administered pricing, etc.? There are, so far as I am aware, no entirely clear or decisive answers to these questions as yet, but one intelligent economist, Robert Heilbroner, has noted that while the crises of earlier capitalism tended to have deflationary consequences, the crises of the welfare state seem largely inflationary. We thus end up with that strange mixture of unemployment, inflation, and economic stagnation called "stagflation." But it still seems too soon for us to say whether inflation is the inescapable price for the advantages of the welfare state, or how high that price has to be if it is inescapable. There is, meanwhile, the example of West Germany, a more "advanced" welfare state than our own, which nevertheless has succeeded in holding its inflation rate to about half of what it is in the United States.

THE welfare state has plenty of other difficulties but I have indicated enough of them to show that any thought of moving "beyond" it has to take into account, first of all, solving the problems within it. Perhaps, however, the only way to solve these problems is to move "beyond"—so a number of contributors to this book argue.

Better as it surely is than what we had in the past, or seem likely to have in the near future, the welfare state must still be regarded as inadequate, precarious, and improvisatory. Even a full realization of its promise would not usher in "the good society." The traditional socialist criticisms in respect to the maldistribution of power, property, wealth, and income would still hold. But to keep trying to realize the promise of the welfare state remains a moral and political obligation. And insofar as we fulfill that obligation, we may gain the experience, knowledge, and strength to go "beyond."

Michael Harrington

Why the Welfare
State Breaks Down

AMERICA is at a turning point. The radical nature of the period is recognized even by conservatives. When he was sworn in as secretary of the treasury in the summer of 1979, G. William Miller said that the nation had "inherited the most distressing economic environment in fifty years." Leaving aside the evasiveness of Miller's verb—it is a way to ignore the failure of more than two years of the Carter administration—his central point is quite true. If the times are not as dramatically miserable as the years between the stock market crash of 1929 and Franklin Roosevelt's inauguration in 1933, they are at least as confused and bewildering. Simultaneous inflation and chronic unemployment subvert all the theories, and theory-based policies, of the past generation.

Does the moment simply mark the reassertion of traditional capitalist contradictions? That would be the diagnosis of a vulgar radicalism and it is, as we shall see, quite wrong. But then are our difficulties the result of the welfare state, i.e., of the very reforms that were the response to the earlier crisis half a century ago? There are those on the right who think so: we went much too far along the road of government intervention, spending profligately, corrupting the people's moral fiber and productivity. There are also those on the left who see the welfare state as the problem: intervening timidly and inadequately, the liberals left the structural irrationalities of capitalism intact and subordinated Washington's actions to the priorities of giant, multinational corporations.

The rightist scapegoating of the welfare state is wrong, as Robert Lekachman has documented in the Fall 1979 *Dissent.* Obviously there is substantial truth in the democratic left's indictment of partial, often coopted, reforms that leave the basic system intact. But this does not take us far enough. One must also look at some of the unintended—social, psychological, cultural—consequences of the welfare state. These unintended consequences, it should be candidly admitted, were anticipated neither by the left nor by the center and right. In some areas we can be fairly specific about the changes that took us by surprise. In others it is necessary to speculate about a period that is postbourgeois yet not socialist, a time of in-between, the time of the "late welfare state."

Let us begin with the "old" and "objective" constituents of the crisis of American welfarism: *how traditional capitalist contradictions now manifest themselves, albeit in new and unprecedented ways.*

The most obvious factor here is the business cycle—which is now the political business cycle. During the euphoric period of "The Great Society" in the 1960s it was said that the fundamental rhythm of boom and bust had been eliminated from the economy. The nation, Lyndon Johnson said, is no longer at the mercy of a "relentless tide of ups and downs," and the Council of Economic Advisers immediately added that prosperity had become the "normal state" of the American economy. At the very moment when those claims were being made, in January 1969, the economy was starting to destroy them. In the decade since there have been three recessions, one of them as I write and perhaps the worst since the Great Depression and exacerbated by chronic inflation unknown in America in peacetime.

All three of these recessions were to some measure deliberately provoked, as we shall see shortly. But each of them also involved the resurgence of old-fashioned capitalist tendencies. Prosperity brings labor militancy, declining productivity, a loosening of industrial discipline, and soon the corporations begin to call openly for a downturn. Arthur Burns explained this antediluvian truth in 1978 to the American Enterprise Institute:

> Most people [Burns said] now realize that our economy is not recession-proof, and that our government's ability to deal with recessions—to say nothing of its ability to anticipate or forestall them—is quite limited. Most people also understand that however regrettable recessions may be, it is a mistake to view them as simply being pathological phenomena. In fact, recession often performs an unavoidable function by forcing managers to improve efficiency, by enabling interest rates to come down, and by wringing some of the inflation out of the economic system.

Thinkers as distant as Herbert Hoover—or Karl Marx—could agree with Burns. And although Burns (or Hoover) would not put it this way, it can be added that the process they describe is rooted in a system of unplanned, profit-maximizing production with a correlative structure of maldistributed wealth. For example, in 1977 the Congressional Budget Office said that a major reason for the "disappointing" recovery from the 1974 recession was "the stagnation of real income in recent years." The maldistribution of wealth, a basic element of capitalist—including welfare capitalist —society, thus functioned to perpetuate a crisis. This was one reason why joblessness at the peak of the 1978 "recovery" was higher than at the trough of the 1970–1971 recession.

In thus arguing that classic structural problems of the capitalist economy persist almost half a century after the creation of the American welfare state, I am not saying that these factors alone were the cause of the nation's troubles during the last decade. Such contradictions never assert themselves in "pure" form. They are always part of a process in which accidents unrelated to the deep workings of the system play a role. I will leave unicausal theories to the legion of academic and government economists who explain that our problems derive from such "one-time shocks" as the OPEC embargo of 1973–1974 and the subsequent quadrupling of oil prices.

Two comments are relevant to this thesis. First, inflation proceeded at a faster rate in the three quarters *before* the embargo in 1973 than in the quarter that experienced the embargo. This was a consequence of the effective end of price controls in January 1973, i.e., of allowing the "natural" economic forces to assert themselves. Thus America's domestic inadequacies would have brought on a crisis in 1973–1974 even if there had been no Yom Kippur War and OPEC cartel. Second, if it is undeniable that the quadrupling of oil prices exacerbated this "normal" downturn, it did so only because a wasteful energy system, built with federal subsidies according to corporate priorities, was there to make the very worst of a bad situation. That this central core of the American industrial system is so organized hardly seems the contrivance of Saudi princes and Libyan colonels.

Moreover this last point relates to a neoconservative theme often used by Jerry Brown and other, more conventional rightists. We are, it is said, bumping into inherent and natural limits. The welfare state, this argument continues, cannot distribute nonexistent wealth or ignore the fact that a period of growth based on cheap and abundant energy has come to an end. This is of course a generalization of the thesis that the 1973–1974 stagflation was created by OPEC and the notion—promulgated by the Carter White House in the summer of 1979—that the 1979–1980 recession is simply the result of the fall of the shah of Iran and the consequent "energy spasm" in the economy.

The Harvard Business School report *Energy Future* provides a marvelous, and empirically documented, refutation of this rationalization. It holds that "if the United States were to make a serious commitment to conservation, it might well consume 30 to 40 percent less energy than it now does, *and still enjoy the same or an even higher standard of living*" (emphasis added). I would extend this insight beyond the sphere of energy. A reduction by eliminating the wastefulness imposed by corporate priorities could improve the quality of life in this country; but this can only be done through democratic, anticorporate planning. This is not to deny that resources in the world are finite and that there are, in this ultimate sense, "limits." It is to say that the limits we have thus far encountered are primarily of human—and more specifically, of capitalist (or Stalinist)—construction rather than facts of nature. To return to the specific point at hand, the chronic recessions of the past decade result from the perverse workings of the system and are not accidents invented by foreigners.

So the business cycle, first exhaustively analyzed by Karl Marx, continues on its destructive way as we near the 100th anniversary of Marx's death. But there is indeed a new element in this old story: if the mysterious rhythms of boom and bust have not been brought under control, as the New Economics of the 1960s thought, they have been politicized. The 1970 recession was deliberately provoked by Richard Nixon in order to purchase a little price stability with a little unemployment. The problem was that the Phillips Curve, which said that prices and joblessness vary inversely with one another, broke down. Nixon got *both* politically intolerable levels of unemployment—which in those ancient times were reached at a point that is now called full employment by a good many experts—*and* what then seemed to be excessively steep price increases (which were, however, lower than anything seen under the Carter administration).

This was the background of Nixon's conversion to "Keynesianism," i.e., to his own reelection, in 1971. Arthur Burns, the Cotton Mather of the Federal Reserve, stoked up the money supply, fiscal policy became liberal, price controls were imposed, the president took credit for a Social Security increase imposed on him by a Democratic Congress, and so on. All these policies accomplished their aim: unemployment dropped, prices stabilized, and the improved economy helped to reelect Richard Nixon. Not so incidentally each of these policies also prepared the way for the extremely severe stagflation of 1973–1974.

Here again it would be wrong to counterpose the political and the economic, the conjunctural and the structural. The political management of the economy, which Nixon manipulated for his own purposes, had been created in response to the deep-lying trends in capitalism and cannot be understood without reference to them. Nixon's cynicism and dishonesty were not the work of history or of the system; but the context in which those vices operated, their ability to affect an entire economy, were the result of structures developed to counter basic capitalist drives. More to the point, if the welfare state is an attempt consciously to modify the workings and outcomes of that capitalism, then we see here the ability of capitalism to modify the welfare state.

Social Security is the most obvious case in point. It is, as Robert Lekachman has shown, the very centerpiece of the system.

"Welfare," taken in its narrow sense, is a very subordinate function of the welfare state. Indeed it is only one department of a social security apparatus that spends much more money on the nonpoor than on the poor. The crisis of that Social Security system first surfaced in the 1973–1974 recession. Pensions for the aging in the United States are not "funded," i.e., the government does not put the workers' contributions aside and then pay it back with interest when they retire. That is done in other countries like Sweden, and the monies collected are even invested in socially useful projects like cooperative housing. In this country, however, the current generation in the labor force provides the financing for the retirees through payroll taxes.

In 1973–1974 there was a drop in revenues in the Social Security system as unemployment rose to the highest levels since the Depression. At the same time costs were increased by stagflation, since the retirees' benefits are indexed. At this point there was concern that the system would literally run out of money in the not-too-distant future. This, it turned out, was an exaggerated fear. Still the Social Security tax—the most regressive federal levy—was increased. But then in the summer of 1979, as the economy was entering its third recession in a decade, a Joint Economic Committee report (prepared under the guidance of a sophisticated conservative, Senator Bentsen) came up with a gloomy projection of a stagflationist future in which Social Security would once again be in deep trouble.

A little earlier a cloud no larger than President Carter's hand appeared in the sky. In his 1980 Budget, released in early 1979, the president had admitted that "the present social security benefit structure cannot be financed over the long run under currently legislated tax rates." Therefore, he said, the administration will put forth proposals to "eliminate unnecessary benefits." The sum at issue was, as such matters go, derisory: $600 million out of a projected expenditure of $179.1 billion. But the symbolism was not unimportant. When, during the last recession, Gerald Ford had proposed to deal with this problem by "capping" the cost of living increases for the aging, i.e., by legislating a decline in their living standard, one could see that as a traditional exercise of

Republican social meanness. But now a Democratic president, in theory at least the heir of Franklin Roosevelt, was moving along the same path.

So the welfare state remains powerfully constrained by the inherent, and quite traditional, tendency of the capitalist economy to follow a rhythm of boom and bust. It also is profoundly affected by another classic capitalist mechanism: the concentration of corporate power. Indeed that trend is a key to the understanding of our newest economic puzzle, the simultaneous existence of both inflation and recession.

The theory that capitalist competition leads inevitably to monopoly was of course at the very center of Marx's analysis in *Das Kapital*. It is a prediction that becomes truer with each passing year. In the 1930s studies began to pinpoint one of the consequences of this development—administered prices. During the Great Depression, as Gardiner Means showed at the time, all prices fell, but the prices in concentrated industries declined much less than those in the competitive sector. Steel was an important case in point. Right after World War II, in the recessions of the 1950s, that same phenomenon became even more marked. Senator Kefauver held hearings that showed how giant enterprises like General Motors targeted rates of profit and rigged the market to yield the returns that were fixed in advance.

In the recent period, the stagflationist decade of 1969–1979, the phenomenon seemed to become so pervasive that a theory of monopoly price-setting seemed to be dubious. Now almost all prices remained high, even in times of economic downturn. Those anomalies can be resolved—there are sectoral causes of inflation in a nonmonopoly sector such as health care, there is centralized distribution that dominates the fragmented system of production in apparel, and so on. The decisive fact is that the American economy has become much more concentrated in the years since World War II. The 100 largest corporations, hearings under Ted Kennedy have shown, now own the same percentage of total assets as the 200 largest corporations did thirty years ago. Thus a venerable capitalist tendency contributes to our unprecedented inflation.

When demand contracts, as it did in 1973–1974, big business

does not lower its prices in order to increase volume, which is what it would do if it had any respect for Alfred Marshall: it raises prices in order to maintain profit levels on the basis of a lowered volume, which is what Karl Marx and Gardiner Means thought it would do. This is one of the reasons why Arthur Burns's theory that recessions "wring out" inflation does not work. It is a major cause of the demise of the Phillips Curve and, much more important, of all the public policies based on it. It also shows how corporations that still seek recessions no longer respond to them by lowering prices, i.e., it allows us to understand at least part of the genesis of stagflation.

In two extremely important areas, then, the traditional capitalist demons are at work: in the business cycle and in the trend toward monopoly. The current crisis of the welfare state cannot be understood apart from that fact—but then it cannot be explained by it alone. There are a number of other factors involved, some of them having to do with attitudes, psyches, even souls, and others more "objective" in character. Let us begin with the latter, less speculative category.

IT is well known that federal spending is a major source of the problem of stagflation. Arthur Burns says so, and Jerry Brown and Jimmy Carter do too. It is well known but wrong. Or more precisely, it is right only in terms none of the proponents of this thesis ever mention. If one measures federal spending as a percentage of "full-employment GNP" and computes it in constant dollars, then the government took 20.7 percent of output in 1955 and 19.1 percent in 1976.* Indeed the fluctuations during those twenty-two years are relatively minor. So the notion that accelerating outlay in Washington created stagflation does not

*One measures in terms of a hypothetical "full-employment GNP" (or as it is now put in this chastened era of chronic joblessness, a "high-employment GNP") in order to determine the trends produced by policy decisions as distinguished from those imposed on Washington by the economy. For instance, the enormous deficit in 1975 was the creature of stagflation more than of Gerry Ford's leadership. To compare federal priorities in different years (and therefore different economic environments), one reckons the direction and impact of Washington's actions within an assumed full-employment economy. That discounts the differing circumstances, and focuses on the trends that result from government action.

survive the most casual investigation. There was, however, a considerable shift in the *composition* of those expenditures. Defense outlays were 58.2 percent of the total in 1955 and 24.6 percent in 1976. Meanwhile transfer payments to individuals went from 18.9 percent to 45.7 percent, and social investments (in education, health, etc.) from 1.1 percent to 14.1 percent.

Given these patterns, one can only account for stagflation in terms of federal spending by arguing that social expenditures are more inflationary than military expenditures. The problem is, the opposite is much truer. Note that the largest single increase in spending occurred in payments to individuals (and Social Security was, of course, the mainspring of the trend, not "welfare"). In that extremely important instance the federal government does not spend the money itself—consumers do. This is inflationary only if it sends an excess of dollars into a market with insufficient goods (which is "demand-pull" inflation on the textbook model). Something similar happened when Lyndon Johnson refused to ask for a tax increase in order to finance an unpopular war. But since then, precisely in the stagflationist decade of 1969–1979, buying power has been lagging behind prices, not bidding them up.

More broadly, as a recent study by the Machinists (IAM) has documented, military spending creates fewer jobs than social spending. And it also pays people for producing goods not going on the market. Thus it tends to be more stagflationist than social outlays, contributing less to employment and more to inflation. So the thesis that federal social spending is the cause of our woes does not hold up any better than the notion that federal spending, pure and simple, is at the root of our difficulties. And yet there is a form of deficit-spending that has grown enormously in the postwar period and is rooted in the very nature of the system. It is corporate debt, and in the midst of all the jeremiads about federal prodigality, this federally facilitated private binge is rarely mentioned. Once it is described, it points the way to a larger proposition: that governmental subordination to boardroom priorities is a major source of the current crisis.

The maldistribution of wealth is, of course, a precondition for capitalism. Since a social class of private citizens has the function of making the key investment decisions on behalf of the society, that class must be much wealthier than all other classes. Moreover, unlike previous dominant classes (whose appetite for wealth was limited by their ability to consume), capitalists must get larger and larger profits over time. If they do not, they become a forgotten moment in the trend toward monopoly and concentration. The system, then, will not work without a basic substratum of injustice. At the same time this precondition periodically turns into a curse. The inherently limited consumption of the majority becomes a lack of effective demand for the output of giant enterprises. The welfare state was of course in considerable measure a response to just that problem.

By increasing the ability of the people to consume through transfer payments and other programs, a gentle inflation is supposed to stimulate full employment. In the almost half a century since Roosevelt improvised this tactic, it only really worked during two brief periods—the first that of the massive military spending in World War II, which came to about 50 percent of GNP, the second the Kennedy–Johnson years, which is another story. The point is that transfer payments are not charity but a structural necessity of the system. In a study designed to show that we had overestimated the number of poor people a few years back—i.e., a study that underplayed poverty whenever possible—the Congressional Budget Office reported that the normal workings of the economy, uncorrected by those federal programs, left one-quarter of the people poor.

The government in Washington then has to bring at least some of those people into the market or else the boom-and-bust cycle would be even more severe than it is now. *Deficit-spending is not a leftist aberration in late-capitalist society; it is a necessity of the system itself.*

This is a familiar story, even though the established wisdom does not tell it as I have. Not so familiar, but just as true, is the fact that corporations have become much more addicted to debt than the government. In 1946 public debt was equal to 129.4 percent of GNP; private debt, 73.6 percent. In 1974 (admittedly a banner year for private-sector borrowing) government debt had declined to 46 percent of GNP, corporate debt had risen to 152.8 percent. This was not an episode, or even a simple reflection of the business cycle. During good times in the 1960s corporations got about two-thirds of their funds from internal sources (profits and capital consumption allowances) and only about a third from credit markets or other external sources. In 1972 and 1973, even though profits soared the ratios had changed dramatically. In 1972 borrowed monies accounted for about 50 percent of the corporate total, in 1973 for around 60 percent. Since an extraordinary portion of that credit was short term, there was a near financial panic when the recession hit. Had the Federal Reserve not played an active role there might have been a number of dramatic bank failures.

Business learned very little from this experience. Corporate borrowing dropped dramatically in 1975 under the impact of the recession, but then began to climb again. In 1977 it was 45 percent of corporate funds; in the first three quarters of 1978 it was a slightly higher percentage. The standard establishment explanation of this trend is neo-Marxist: that a falling rate of profit deprives business of the chief internal source of monies for new investment, jobs, and productivity. This argument then rationalizes the central corporate political demands of recent years: that Washington legislate a higher profit rate by lowering corporate taxes and personal income levies on the rich, accelerate depreciation, relax environmental and occupational safety laws (which means imposing the private social costs of business on defenseless individuals), and so on.

There has been a fierce controversy over whether the rate of profit is falling. Part of the confusion arises because the existence or nonexistence of that "fact" depends on how it is defined and explained. Corporate profits are too low, someone like ex-Treasury Secretary William Simon would say, because business has been crowded out of credit markets by federal borrowing for social programs, because there is too much regulation, and so on. In short it is interference with the benign workings of capitalism, not capitalism itself, that is the substance of the "fact." This, as we have seen, is not true.

But the issue can be examined from another perspective. The system is in a secular as well as a cyclical slump and both trends are inherent, not accidental. Under these circumstances chronically poor economic performance in a time of structural changes that are systemically irrational, i.e., unplanned on principle, can pose some serious cash-flow problems for corporations. Where huge investments are needed, more often than not—one thinks of steel and energy—to pay for the antisocial and uneconomic results of past corporate policies, there can indeed be a shortage of capital, particularly when capitalists are speculating in land, jewels, and rare violins rather than putting their money into an uncertain economy. It is in this context that the private sector goes to Washington for its "risk" capital.

This analysis throws some light on a broader trend. The federal government facilitated a vast expansion of credit. Then when panic threatened in 1974 and 1975 it stepped in as a lender of last resort to banks—but not as an employer of last resort for workers. Arthur Burns, that supposed paragon of monetary probity, thus has the distinction of shaping an easy-money policy to help reelect his friend Richard Nixon, and of then organizing the rescue operation he himself had made necessary. Government in a capitalist welfare state then tends to promote the common good of the majority by first assuring the special interests of those at the very top. This is why the dole for the corporate rich is so much more generous than the handouts for the poor. That is not the result of the malevolence of the bureaucracy; it is an indispensable characteristic of the system itself.

A shocking case of congressional cowardice and hypocrisy in 1978 should help document this point. Five years of corporate propaganda about the capital shortage, low profit rates, and excessive government interference with the private sector came to a head in 1978 in the form of the Kemp–Roth and Steiger bills. Steiger provided for massive capital-gains reductions, Kemp–Roth for a huge, across-the-board tax cut in which the lion's share of the benefits would go to the very rich. Neither passed in their original form but both helped shape the Revenue Act of 1978. That law increased the deductions for capital gains from approximately $16.8 billion in 1978 to $22.3 billion in 1980. That $5.5 billion increment in welfare payments for the rich is roughly equal to 80 percent of the $6.7 billion in the federal welfare program, Aid for Families of Dependent Children. And the total value of the deduction is three-and-a-half times more than the outlays for AFDC.

As is so often the case in these matters, the rationale for this give-away was false. The Council of Economic Advisers pointed out in its 1979 Report that "lowering capital gains taxes is not an efficient means of promoting investment." Yet it is an excellent way of increasing the maldistribution of wealth. However, I do not want to focus on the fact of this scandal, which is rather commonplace, but on what it reveals about the attitude of the corporate rich. In essence they agree with my analysis: the system can only work on the basis of huge infusions of cash provided directly or indirectly by the government. They want corporations and the wealthy to be absolved of the responsibilities ordinary citizens must meet, and they justify this blatant demand for higher profits through federal subsidy on the grounds that it will make the economy more productive, which has not been the case at all. In capitalist society business wants government to provide it with "risk" capital, and that becomes a new source of stagflation.

In this example conservatives ignore the truly inflationary tendencies of subsidies to the private sector while talking sternly about the relatively minor inflationary impact of social spending. There is an analogous pattern in the attack on government regulation. There have been endless and angry protests from the executive suite in recent years against legal limits placed on the corporation's right to despoil the environment or to threaten the lives and limbs of working people. Yet as Steve Kelman documented in the *New Republic* more than a year ago, these new, socially conscious regulations do not cost nearly as much as the procorporate restrictions imposed by agencies under the control of those whom they are supposed to monitor.

Robert Eisner, the Northwestern University economist, made a partial list of those measures in a 1979 column in the *New York Times:*

> . . . price supports for milk as dairy prices skyrocket; trigger prices to "protect" our steel industry from foreign competition as profits of our steel industry soar; licensing agreements and route restrictions that drastically curtail competition in the trucking industry, laying the ground for repeated increases in prices and wages while trucks

suffer from idle capacity and small trucking firms go out of business; sugar quotas and price supports to maintain and raise sugar prices; acreage restrictions that reduce agricultural supply; import quotas, tariffs, and "orderly marketing agreements" that limit the import of cheaper and frequently better foreign automobiles, television sets, and textiles; and federal, state, and local restrictions in countless occupations and industries that reduce competition and raise prices.

Let me generalize. The problem of the welfare dependence of some of the poor has been widely recognized. *The problem of the welfare dependence, not simply of wealthy individuals but of the entire system of late-corporate capitalism, has normally been concealed.* Yet this is, as we have seen in just a few examples—and they could be multiplied almost endlessly—a structural source of the problem of stagflation, which now threatens to subvert the reforms of the past generation. There are then both old and new "objective" causes of the current crisis that are capitalist in character: business cycles, the tendency toward monopoly, the creation of a stagflationary welfare system for those whom we still call, out of habit, entrepreneurs. New factors are also at work in social relations and even in the sphere of culture.

THE state of nature, Hobbes said, was characterized by the war of each against all. The welfare state, we may now add, sometimes seems to be the war of each group against every other group. The resultant conflicts among and between the poor, the workers, and the middle class have in fact made the corporate rich more secure. But as befits this time of transition and uncertainty, they feel threatened by the very measures that have done so much for them. Note, then, that this is a period in which everyone has reasons for being unhappy, a reality President Carter skimmed over lightly in his talk about a "crisis of confidence."

First, there is the new group struggle created by the welfare state.

It would of course be foolish to contrast the present situation to an earlier time when seamless, homogeneous social classes without divisions confronted one another. In America, above all, the social classes have been marked precisely by extreme internal heterogeneity: workers were not simply workers but native-born and foreign; black, white, and Asiatic; skilled and unskilled; male and female; Catholic, Protestant, and Jew; and so on. Indeed it was the existence of these intraclass conflicts on a scale unknown in Europe that contributed mightily to the failure (thus far) of American socialism. These differences were sometimes reinforced by law—racial and sexual discrimination is the obvious example —but they were not the *creations* of law. What has happened under the welfare state is that groups have been constituted around legal rights and entitlements (or their absence).

Consider an example of this phenomenon from the history of the recent British Labour government. Under Prime Minister Callaghan's "incomes policy," inflation was successfully reduced in dramatic fashion. But as time went on under that policy some of the most nasty disputes had to do with pay differentials *within* the working class rather than *between* the working class and the corporate (or hereditary) rich. Trade unionists were concerned not with keeping up with the lords and ladies, but with keeping up with other trade unionists. They pressured a Labour government to that end and helped to bring it down. In America one union president noted a similar trend. Workers, he said, tend to view other workers as the prime cause of inflation.

Morris Janowitz makes some very perceptive comments on this phenomenon in his *Social Control of the Welfare State* (Chicago: University of Chicago Press, 1976). He writes that

> the influence of the welfare state on the social structure modifies and transcends the format of conventional interest-group politics. Political conflict becomes more than the struggle between competing occupational and interest groups. Each person and each member of his household must confront an elaborate set of contradictory or competing and often ambiguous issues in the pursuit of his self-interest—immediate or long-term. The new social and economic structure produces a fusion of claims and expectations about wages, property income, and welfare claims. A person's linkage to the mode of production under these conditions is based both on his occupation and on the institutions of social welfare.
>
> Of course, the claims and expectations of one's occupation remain central. However, the democratization of equity means that the return and stability of property rights, individual welfare plans, and the benefits of public social welfare are also crucial components for

the citizenry at large. The task of assessing one's self-interest becomes continuous and more complex, and pursuing one's personal or group goals almost defies programmatic articulation. . . . The complex social base of political participation under the welfare state conditions new patterns of political involvement—patterns characterized by high degrees of volatility, which do not really lead to stable and unified political preferences and alliances and which help account for the lack of clear-cut political majorities and the emergence of weak parliamentary regimes.

This is true enough—but it is a dangerous, potentially reactionary truth and has to be handled most carefully. Before getting to this point, however, a few more details should be filled in. In his book on postindustrial society, Daniel Bell made a similar point: that "situs" is becoming as important as status, i.e., the organization *where* one works is as significant as what one does *within* the organization. The united front of trade unionists and employers against some environmental regulations is an obvious case in point. Everyone in an industry, from the president to the janitors, feels a common interest in opposing measures that protect society. The active support of the UAW for a Chrysler bail-out is, however, a progressive departure from this pattern. The union is calling for roughly one-third control of the corporation by public and employee representatives in return for the government aid. It thus makes "situs" consciousness socially conscious.

A similar, but somewhat different, phenomenon was observable in the conflict between farmers and independent truckers during the diesel-oil shortage of 1979. Clearly—to everyone except the editorialists at the *Wall Street Journal*—a "free market" solution to the problem would have been economically chaotic as well as socially unjust. Therefore the government had to play a role in the crisis. But note that now there was no classic fight between the workers and the bosses or the poor and the rich. The independent truckers involved were self-employed workers, precarious entrepreneurs. The farmers were a more socially variegated group that contained a good many individuals who could not be dismissed as agribusinessmen. This is a dramatic example of the kind of new social conflicts arising out of the welfare-state apparatus itself. The focus of the dispute was government policy, not private capital, and both sides were made up of people who work. Second, there are new social problems of quantity and quality that affect the class structure.

There is a related, though quite different, point developed by Fred Hirsch in *Social Limits to Growth* (Cambridge, Mass.: Harvard University Press, 1976). So long as there was constant economic growth, the demands of the people for more reproducible goods could be met without any redistribution of wealth or change in the way economic divisions were made. The past ten years, however, have been anything but a period of constant economic growth, which is why this pillar of welfare-state consensus is being eroded. Even more problematical, when people begin to seek after "positional" goods—not washing machines and cars, which can be turned out in almost any volume, but exclusive neighborhoods, "fine" schools, quiet, unspoiled vacation spots —there is no way, even with constant growth, to satisfy the demand. At that point the rat race becomes not simply morally objectionable but self-defeating.

Finally there is the question of affirmative action. The demands of minorities and women for public assistance in redressing injustices that have been reinforced, and even instituted, by public policy is unassailable. But given the failure of the welfare state's economic managers to come up with an effective response to stagflation, this has led to struggles between minorities (which is more important, affirmative action against racism or against sexism? for blacks or for Hispanics?) or between minorities and ethnic groups only a few rungs above them on the social-class ladder. Obviously the solution is not to abandon affirmative action but to create an economic environment in which it can be much more effective than it is now, but to do it one must resolve the crisis of the welfare state and that is not a simple matter.

The case of affirmative action, moreover, bears very much on the reactionary use that can be made of the theme of the new social complexity created by the welfare state. A report to the Trilateral Commission in 1975, written by Michael Crozier, Samuel Huntington, and Joki Watanuki and entitled *The Crisis of Democracy,* and Ken Auletta's book *The Streets Were Paved with*

Gold (New York: Random House, 1978) are cases in point.

The Crisis of Democracy develops a number of the ideas just discussed. It found:

> the social democratic consensus [in Western Europe] is breaking down while the relationships between groups have become so complex and erratic that citizens are more and more frustrated. . . .
>
> *Citizens* [the authors write] make incompatible claims. Because they press for more action to meet the problems they have to face, they require more social control. At the same time they resist any kind of social control that is associated with the hierarchical values they have learned to discard and reject. [Emphasis added.]

The last comment is, in scholarly language, the substance of a criticism often directed at those of us who favor affirmative action. All of this culminates in a survey of "the dysfunctions of democracy." It is democracy—too much participation, egalitarianism, and responsiveness to group claims—which has brought us to this pass.

In *The Streets Were Paved with Gold* Auletta develops this concept in a journalistic analysis of the New York crisis (which has some value but only if its basic premises are carefully ignored). All the groups in New York—the bankers, the unions, the poor, the consumers of public services—were greedy. All of them looked out for their particular interest; none was concerned with the common good. What Auletta and the Trilateralists offer as a theory is vulgar pluralism. The impoverished black or Hispanic family who wanted their children to go to the City University, *and* the accountant who fought through his or her union to get a salary approaching a modest but adequate budget, *and* the people in Queens who wanted snow-removal service, *and* the banks that speculated in municipal papers at a profit—they all hid their knowledge of the crisis and then not only refused to help when judgment day came but also demanded that free tuition be abolished at City University, that municipal employees take a real wage cut, and claimed that people who talked about services were *all* greedy. In reality only the greed of the people at the top is both real and satisfied—while that of everyone else in this example is imposed on them because they do not have enough to make ends meet and it stays, in any case, frustrated.

Moreover, massive structures operating according to corporate priorities were, to stay with the New York case, financing the exodus of jobs and tax monies as well as the immigration of poor, and often desperate, people. The corporations were thus not one "interest group" among many but the dominant class whose very special greed is the mainspring of the entire system. Indeed a generalization made by Richard Titmus applies here: more often than not the welfare state is an inadequate response to the *dis*welfare state. After a corporate-dominated system destroys the economic basis of a minimally decent life in the South Bronx, the victims are given a few dollars in welfare and food stamps and excoriated for not achieving a minimally decent life on their own. But—and this is the terrible catch—those who are a rung or two above them on that ladder, unionized workers for instance, then perceive those welfare recipients as their enemy.

Much of the problem arises from the fact that there is a capitalist economy that "normally" leaves 25 percent of the people poor, and these then have to be propped up by a welfare-state apparatus that is nominally noncapitalist but actually operates on corporate priorities. But even though the welfare state thus discriminates in favor of the corporate rich in a way that is profoundly antisocial, the main beneficiaries of all this are as surly as anyone else.

In *Politics and Markets* Charles E. Lindblom (New York: Basic Books, 1977) discusses this point brilliantly. In Britain, Lindblom writes,

> Some observers hold union demands . . . to be the root cause of the "English sickness"—the decline of British productivity and economic stagnation. [And yet, when one looks at the reality in that country,] . . . for all their demands, union members have not won any great alteration in distribution of income or wealth, or in participation in management, or in recent decades any substantial equalization of educational opportunity for their children. It is difficult to reconcile these timidities or defeats with the hypothesis that unions have either disproportionately large political influence or the more modest hypothesis that they have influence equal to that of businessmen.

Lindblom's conclusion:

> A market-oriented system may require for its success so great a disproportion of business influence, both through the privileged position of business and through business disproportion in electoral and interest-group activity, that even modest challenges to it are disruptive to economic stability and growth.

Obviously two very different lessons could be drawn from this analysis: therefore one must retreat back to Herbert Hoover; or, therefore one must proceed far beyond Franklin Roosevelt. Clearly I am for the latter option (as is Lindblom). It suggests, among other things, the relevance of a point made by Gunnar Myrdal some years ago.

Bureaucracy proliferates in the welfare state, Myrdal argued, because everything has to exist twice. There is the uncontrolled, profit-maximizing private sector with its bureaucracies; there is the supposedly controlling, but often controlled, welfare state with its bureaucracies. But what if the social principles were located within, rather than imposed on, the economy? What if there were a growing public-energy sector developing new technology rather than a government subsidizing and monitoring the corporations as they try to resolve a crisis they did so much to create? What if it becomes the custom for auto workers and environmentalists and consumer advocates to sit on the board of directors of the Chrysler Corporation? I do not want to suggest for a minute that there is some simple way to cut the Gordian bureaucratic knot of the welfare state. The idea that public property miraculously cures all economic ills is in tatters. And yet moving in that direction is, for the reasons suggested by Lindblom among many, basic to the solution.

To return to the point with which this section began: there are unintended consequences of the welfare state that impinge on class structure and consciousness, making the work of building progressive coalitions both more imperative and more difficult than ever before. This complexity is itself part of the crisis of this system since it makes any resolution of its problems, from the right or the left, that much harder to achieve. There is, however, a way out that is easier to define than organize but no less necessary for that fact: *to go beyond the welfare state.* This requires the emergence of a new social consciousness and raises some vexing, and speculative, questions about values and the political consequences of the death of God.

THERE is bewilderment among the economic policy-makers because stagflation subverts the conventional wisdom of the last, Keynesian half century. There is confusion among the politicians because the traditional party loyalties are decomposing and no new realignment is taking their place. There is, all the polls report, a cynicism among the people who lack confidence not simply in politicians, businessmen, labor leaders—but in all of them at the same time. Under such circumstances it is not surprising that people might retreat within themselves. But what happens if—in their flight to the inner sanctuary of transcendental values—that hallowed refuge turns out to be empty? What if the death of God becomes particularly apparent in a time of the failure of Man?

Christopher Lasch raises one aspect of this problem in *The Culture of Narcissism.* He writes of the "psychological man of our time"—

> . . . the new narcissist . . . superficially relaxed and tolerant . . . finds little use for dogmas or racial and ethnic purity but at the same time forfeits the security of group loyalties and regards everyone as a rival for the favors conferred by a paternalistic state. . . . Having overthrown feudalism and slavery and then outgrown its own personal and familial forms, capitalism has evolved a new political ideology, welfare liberalism, which absolves individuals of more responsibility and treats them as victims of social circumstances. It has evolved new modes of social control which deal with the deviant as a patient and substitute medical rehabilitation for punishment.

This line of thought, as Dennis Wrong showed in the Summer 1979 *Dissent,* can be taken up by reactionaries and even fascists dedicated to the traditional values of *Kinder, Küche, Kirche.* But if these themes are used carefully, I think they are quite important. The welfare state is the first agnostic society in Western history. So religion—"the logic of the world in popular form"—is less and less of a force in the society.* Millions are thus liberated from the old values. Those values, however, are not replaced, as the classic Marxists hoped, by a new, this-worldly solidarity without need of absolutes. Rather they decay in a time of manipulated and collectivized individualism in which consumption is defined as civic virtue. The result is a crisis of atheistic humanism as well as of religion—a devastation, as Nietzsche put it, of all values.

Clearly the welfare state cannot be praised—or blamed—for a religious crisis that began at least as far back as the scientific revolution of the seventeenth century. But the fact that the crisis became particularly acute precisely during the time of the welfare state is relevant to its troubles. That is why I want to speculate, very briefly, on just a few of the political, social, and economic consequences of the death of God. The narcissistic personality that Lasch evokes is indeed a social product. It is also a postreligious product.

A number of significant thinkers long ago suggested that the decline of Christianity in Western society would require the creation of a new, secular faith. Rousseau's discussion of civil religion is well known; so is Robespierre's Cult of Reason. Saint-Simon, that extraordinarily rich thinker—the last gentleman and first socialist of France, the guiding spirit of that country's most advanced workers and bankers, the inspiration of Stalinists, technocrats, and anarchists—is perhaps a less familiar case. His new church was going to have a Council of Newton under the presidency of the mathematician who received the highest vote.

There were also those in the Marxist movement who recognized this problem. Both Antonio Labriola and Max Adler, two of the most intellectually sophisticated thinkers of the first generation after Marx's death, doubted the master's teaching about the disappearance of religion. On a less profound level Lunacharsky and Gorki became "God builders" in the years of reaction after

---

*The revival of fundamentalist religion is a confirmation of this point. The only form in which faith can now survive among masses of people is as a will to believe in belief. The complexities of the modern world, including those found in biblical scholarship, have to be ignored. One can retire to such a godly vendée for a while—but eventually the Revolution triumphs.

the failure of the 1905 revolution and advocated a new and atheist religion. More recently the cults of Hitler and Stalin were explained as the herd response of rootless masses to the loneliness of their alienation and anomie.

In short the underlying idea suggested here—that the crisis of religion is also a crisis of society—is hardly novel. And even extending that insight to the welfare state is not new, as Lasch's example and others show. Still I want to at least circle around this theme, not to exhaust it or even outline it, but rather to evoke it as a significant element in the present situation. In the process I will once again borrow from Fred Hirsch.

Capitalism was able to function in part because precapitalist religion survived within it. This was the case even though this social economic formation was the first truly secular order in the Western world. Feudalism, and indeed every form of domination in our history, had been sanctified by God—and supported by the crowd. Capitalism, on the contrary, claimed rational assent, its holy grail was a contract of mutual benefit, its priests were lawyers. Providence was now the invisible hand of the market. But Adam Smith, who theorized many of these concepts more profoundly than anyone else, recognized that people do not live by production alone. In the *Theory of Moral Sentiments* he had insisted that a certain altruism, a pleasure in other people's happiness, was necessary to society (there is a "young Smith, old Smith" debate, much like the young Marx, old Marx dispute, which bears on this text, but it need only be noted here).

So if capitalism claimed to be ruthlessly individualistic, it had the good grace to contradict itself. People were often honest because they believed in honesty and not just because it was the best "policy." Ironically, however, as life became more social, more interdependent, not least of all in the welfare state, it became more atomized. In Robert Merton's famous example, the welfare bureaucracy replaced the political club. That was an advance, but it had its price: life was becoming less personal even if it was also just a bit more fair. More broadly, mass society dissolved communities, which had been the social substratum of the religious survivals. Once people had observed a moral code because they believed in it, or because their neighbors would see them violate it, or for both reasons. Now there were fewer and fewer neighbors. New York City, to cite a trivial but not insignificant case, had to pass a law requiring people to clean up after their dogs.

Then in the 1960s hedonism for the people became a public dogma. In the rather simplistic, tax-cut Keynesianism of that decade, economic growth was to be stimulated by individual, not social, consumption. The latter policy, which was advocated at the time by the labor movement, the minorities, and economists like Galbraith and Keyserling, seemed to be much too radical to Kennedy and Johnson. Both felt that political wisdom required much more private affluence than public investment. Thus the new collectivist management was permeated by the old individualistic values.

So economic growth was to be achieved by a civic hedonism. Children, in David Riesman's marvelous phrase, became "consumer trainees." It was precisely in the 1960s that the culmination of this trend, and the religious and cultural and moral shifts, became most striking. Pornography appeared in candy stores, marijuana became ubiquitous, the academic doctrine of *in loco parentis* was destroyed in a few brief years, and so on. I do not want to suggest for a moment that the passing of many taboos and superstitions was bad. What concerns me here is that they disappeared within a culture and society with very little that was substantial to offer in their place. Many years ago, in a book that disbarred him from teaching at City College in New York, Bertrand Russell, a theorist and practioner of the new morality, said he feared that the liberation he urged just might trivialize sexuality. It is the trivialization of the liberation, not the liberation, that is the focus here.

The "*Playboy* philosophy" might serve as a paradigm. It was elaborated in a series of articles in *Playboy* magazine. On the one hand it championed an absolutist civil libertarianism that was compelling, fighting against the censors and the archaic laws with regard to private sexuality. On the other hand it put that freedom to work in the service of a glossy, thing-ridden, sexist, and bourgeois hedonism. Left-wing values were summoned to defend a particularly shallow and superficial version of the status quo.

Then came the 1970s. From 1969 to the present moment, as we have seen, the economy was completely unable to deliver on the promises of the 1960s. Politicians, some of whom had been cheerleaders for the collectivist hedonism of the 1960s, began to talk of austerity. In California a young governor who dated a rock star but would not live in a mansion inaugurated his second term by coming out for both gay rights and a balanced budget. Social radicalism and economic conservatism, somewhat on the *Playboy* model, went hand-in-hand.

People had been told by the new Coués that every day things were getting better in every way. Suddenly it was obvious that they were not. The old morality had become attenuated, the *Playboy* philosophy had become a national consensus—and now this philosophy would no longer work because of stagflation. This psychological, social, and even religious reality is, I think, one of the reasons for the militant unhappiness of the society. So many of the traditional sources of individual and community resilience have been sapped, the substitutes were shallow at best, and for a decade these have not even functioned.

This does not mean, however, that a new spirituality can be willed into existence. Something like that seemed to be implied in President Carter's analysis of the "crisis of confidence." If, the president argued, we would only say something good about America every day, then confidence would be restored and the crisis would come to an end. But this is failing to understand that the spiritual crisis is part of a profoundly material process, reacting reciprocally with it. In a complex fashion, the economic and social changes brought about by the welfare state have reinforced the long-run crisis of religious faith, and the absence of religious faith has made the crisis of the welfare state all the more difficult. If God is no longer in His/Her heaven and the government is no longer in control of the economy; if both the this-world and the other-world have become problematic and for related reasons —what is there for people to believe in?

The United States then is not simply going through a crisis that is systemic, i.e., derives in considerable measure from its capitalist structures. It is also experiencing the crisis of a civilization or rather the most recent manifestation of that crisis. There is no hope of even beginning to confront that second challenge if the first is not met. Socialism, one should always remember, is not a secular salvation, a new religion on Saint-Simonian or any other lines. It is a political, economic, and social movement with specific proposals to make that can resolve the problems of the mature capitalist economy. Its success depends not simply on developing the "correct" anticorporate program to transform the structures that are at the core of stagflation, but also on the ability to mobilize a democratic movement of men and women motivated by a practical solidarity. If that can be done—and it is a gigantic task we set ourselves—then souls will not be saved, but there will be an environment in which perhaps men and women will be able to find their best selves, and culture can recover its depths.

Henry Pachter

Freedom, Authority, Participation

Motto: "Learn to read and to write so that you may be relieved of labor and become an official with honor. The scribe is a master. His writing pad distinguishes him from the humble oarsman."

—An Egyptian father to his son, about 1400 B.C.

Socialism: The Highest Stage of Individualism

SOCIALISM strives to abolish exploitation and inequality. It seeks a society where merit and character are the only marks of distinction; where economic resources are controlled by public agencies, themselves under public scrutiny; where production is geared to the human needs of all and the product is distributed equitably; a society, finally, where man is no longer utilized as a means for purposes alien to him.

In practice, however, socialism has usually come to be identified with "collectivism," and two of its best known features are public ownership of the means of production and a comprehensive "plan" of production and distribution.

These are indeed characteristic of states that now call themselves "socialist," but a moment's reflection will show that they are inadequate to define socialism. Nationalization is not socialization, and a plan must have a purpose: it may be designed to enhance the development of man's potentialities or it may be the instrument of national ambitions. The Inca state and Egypt of the Pharaohs featured both public ownership and a plan, but paired with servitude and exploitation. Spartan communism subjected all citizens to equal political oppression. Bismarck nationalized the railroads and the health service; Hitler's war machine was powered by a planned "command economy." Some modern states have adopted a rapid industrialization plan which—though praiseworthy in its intention—ruthlessly subordinates the desires of the citizens to the needs of the state. Others have abolished the market for political reasons without, however, freeing the production units from the tyranny of profit calculations that continue to keep the workers under the yoke of exploitation.

To call this "socialism" is to misuse a good word. Socialism is not a technocratic scheme designed to run the capitalist economy more efficiently, nor is it an economy that has merely been rid of capitalistic parasites. Socialists hope to emancipate people from serving goals that have been imposed on them either by arbitrary masters or by abstract laws of economic development. They aim to make people responsible for their own destiny and to give everybody a chance to fulfill his or her aspirations as a person. This dream has been expressed in the socialist literature of all times. I shall cite one source that, because it may not be guessed easily, is especially significant:

> In place of the old bourgeois society, with its classes and antagonisms, we shall have an association in which the free development of each is the condition for the free development of all.

In most anthologies this sentence is the conclusion of the *Communist Manifesto* for it is indeed the end of its theoretical exposition. It must be assumed that Marx and Engels worded this ending with special care, and it is therefore noteworthy that they said "association" instead of "state," and that they did not consider the development of the whole a condition for the development of each, but on the contrary *"the development of each the condition for the development of all."*

I do not consider Marx and Engels oracles, but it is significant that these alleged "collectivists" placed the individual ahead of the collective. True, they proposed to abolish "private property," but not to put state property in its place. Their "association" was supposed to abolish the relationship of property between capital and worker, between dead and living labor; it was to substitute a direct, human relationship of cooperation for the mediated, material relationship of property and profitability.

Socialism has inherited this emancipatory dream from a long tradition of democratic revolutionary thinkers; as is well known, their revolutions were side-tracked and ended in capitalism—with individualism frozen in the property relationship and opportunity confined to the class of owners. Socialism continues the movement of emancipation that was started in the eighteenth century, and it wants to spread individualism to all, removing the fetters that capitalism has clasped on the fulfillment of many human aspirations. Freedom is not a luxury to be enjoyed only by the members of a ruling elite, but a basic human aspiration that was brought to flower only in the unique development of Western civilization, and it is still waiting for full and generalized realization. Civil rights and human rights are still expanding, and their wider scope is on the agenda of socialism. *Far from subduing the individual, socialism is the highest stage of individualism—its fruition for all.*

As an association of people, the socialist society certainly must reflect the democratic structure and behavior of its origin—the socialist movement. Readers interested in political theory may have noticed that in the passage I cited Marx and Engels fell into the language of Rousseau, although on other occasions they were highly critical of theories that attribute the founding of the state to a "contract"; but when they wrote the *Manifesto* they still saw the socialist revolution as the direct outgrowth of the democratic spirit of that revolution, they saw "the association" as the means to mediate between the demands of society and the rights of the individual. They could not conceive of a society (much less a state) that would set itself goals other than those that the citizens themselves had made their own.

But socialism begins with the insight that the whole is more than the sum of its parts. The association can envisage goals that unassociated individuals might not even be able to conceive. This is an opportunity as well as a danger. In the following pages I shall discuss problems that have arisen for socialism out of the conflict between the will of the whole and the will of the parts: how much freedom may smaller associations (the shop, the region, the profession, the ethnic or religious fraternity) reserve vis-à-vis the big association (the nation, an international authority)? How much discipline or obedience can the larger community expect from the smaller and from the individual? When does the public ethos prevail over the private conscience?

The Distributive Economy: A Political Economy

The socialist economy is designed to meet human needs; its production is for use, not for the creation of value. But it cannot claim, realistically, that it will do away with drudgery, will not demand exertions and sacrifices, and will be able to satisfy all demands. It can only promise that burdens and benefits will be shared as evenly as possible. It seeks equality in three areas:

—equality of opportunity for the self-fulfillment of all;
—equality of citizen's sacrifices and services;
—equality for each citizen of basic rewards (the national dividend).

This does not exclude differences of talent, achievement, and ambition; but it is assumed that some rewards of excellence will be sought in the shape of nonmaterial satisfactions, such as honors and responsible functions, and that material rewards will be held to a token level or taxed so that private accumulation of wealth is confined to tolerable limits.

Private enterprise, such as small businesses and family farms, are not incompatible with an economy whose big industries, utilities, and financial services are nationalized, and which also encourages cooperative enterprise. What matters is that big investment decisions and overall industry targets are controlled by public boards. In the light of experience it can be said that the extent and speed of the early nationalizations in Soviet Russia and those in Eastern Europe after World War II were politically motivated and economically unwise, and that some reprivatization has paid off in Eastern Europe without endangering the regimes.

At a certain level of technological development, the minimum that is guaranteed to all citizens can be large enough to reduce inequality to marginal amounts (to name an arbitrary proportion —the permissible maximum income could be twice as large as the median and four times as large as the minimum). Since basic needs are guaranteed to all, it will be the choice of each individual whether he or she wishes to work longer, acquire special skills, develop new lines of personal fulfillment. The border between work and play should become blurred. In a socialist society nobody should be called a parasite because he chooses to write poetry rather than advertising copy. Each citizen should have the free choice of occupation after he has delivered the minimum service that all are required to supply.

Unfortunately Marx called this requirement "labor service," and Hitler gave the same name to his preliminary training corps. It goes without saying that we, by contrast, have in mind those unpopular but necessary jobs that cannot be filled by special incentives in an economy of abundance (say, street cleaning, digging ditches, mining), and which could not be made a required stage in career training (as working as nurse's aid could be for medical students). This public service could be limited to, say, two years but it should be obligatory for all able-bodied citizens. There might be a choice of the age at which one fulfills this obligation, and also a choice between kinds of service. But it should be admitted that these will be jobs that must be filled after the reservoir of generous, public-spirited volunteers has been exhausted.

Conscription of labor can be held to a minimum if a system of incentives is available to those who engage in a career. At some point the government may have to choose between increasing the incentives, lowering the minimum sustenance, and increasing the years of required service. Obviously abundance is always relative, and no utopia can elude unforeseen problems. Marx did not know about erosion and pollution, and he took the threatening exhaustion of natural resources all too lightly. The neo-Malthusian Club of Rome builds its utopia on the premise of scarcity, or even impending famine. Against this kind of panic reaction, Marx's prediction was correct for one hundred years: population movement and the rate of inventions did adjust to the capabilities of a given economic system. But from now on we must husband and plan our resources so that the threat of scarcity may no longer be used as an excuse for inequality. "Relative abundance" means that we now have the technical means to control the factors that used to produce relative scarcity: we can control the growth of population; we can speed and plan the development of resources; we can direct investment in new technology so as to meet the true requirements; we can reduce the enormous waste of resources that occurs under capitalism.

Contrary to widespread misconceptions, socialism may not open up a period of unrivaled development. It may broaden consumption but provide no incentives to produce bigger cars and more sophisticated household equipment. A planned economy may postpone the use of an invention that might be marginally useful but would require excessive resources and unwarranted social costs. By contrast, it might develop industries that are not profitable today but would provide intangible benefits to the community. (This is, of course, not utopian; states and municipalities have always built parks, sewers, harbors, waterways, roads, etc.—certainly to help business but also to make the environment more livable for all; partial public planning has always been a necessary complement to "free" enterprise, which will not provide services deemed essential by the community.)

Competitive and unnecessary expansion and a run-away rate of growth are illusionary benefits. A rapid rate of investment reduces the resources available to consumers and strengthens the arguments of scarcity, that the rate of surplus value must be increased, management given more authority, and there is not enough to allow equal rations for all. A socialist economy is not subject to the whiplash of competition to expand production for the sake of profit, and it does not have to make work for the unemployed. It will distribute as much as possible of the national dividend and will allow improvements and innovations only where they benefit the consumers or save labor and resources. It will take into account environmental and social costs. It may spend more on safety measures and health protection, or on machines that do not save labor but reduce drudgery and discomfort. (Again to some extent this is achieved today through union activity: if a bulldozer operator is given an air-conditioned cabin the marginal decrease in his discomfort may not be matched by increased productivity.)

These conditions require a different notion of efficiency than exists today. (I should like to refer here to two earlier essays I wrote for *Dissent:* "The Right to be Lazy" and "Three Economic Models," now in the books *Voices of Dissent* and *The Radical Papers.*) The socialist plant manager need not strive for maximum profit, or seek the most "cost-effective" means. He may measure his performance—in a certain way similar to the old guild craftsman or the artist—by aesthetic criteria, sanitary standards, satisfaction of the workers with their work, environmental impact of his operations, but not necessarily by the quantity of output and the efficiency of his use of the equipment. He may not need to earn the amortization of invested capital; he may be able to reduce labor time instead of dismissing workers or seeking additional outlets.

Obviously I do not claim that a socialist economy will not make mistakes. The question is, what would be the consequences of these errors? Misinvestments in a capitalist economy lead to depression. A socialist economy can write off the losses and shift production; it can localize mistakes and smooth out fluctuations. Technological shifts, population movements, even fashion changes can produce problems very similar to those that occur in capitalist economies, but a socialist government need not take these catastrophes as God-given laws of nature against which man is powerless. It is equipped to deal with social change, and the structure of the socialist economy is so designed that it will absorb unforeseen irregularities.

To Control the Controllers

Some hints must be given on the structure of the socialist economy. Underdeveloped countries will rely largely on a central plan to develop their industries, but it should be kept in mind that in so doing they also depend on the population's ability to produce needed articles in their family, or to do without them. Even more advanced countries such as the Soviet Union have had crash programs rather than an integrated plan; they merely called "plan" the speedy development of certain key industries while they failed to provide satisfaction to their consumers. In Eastern Europe planning has usually meant the development of heavy industry, at great cost to workers' well-being and utter chaos in regard to consumer satisfaction. These models, which have given a bad name to socialism, are not the poorly managed samples of a basically sound structure, but are monstrosities in their very conception.

A socialist economy must be so designed that its functioning depends not on the vigilance of a government department but on self-adjusting mechanisms, steady feedback, and corrective action. Modern socialist theory has found that a certain freedom of the consumer markets and the price mechanism is an aid to flexible responses while an authoritatively imposed plan may lead to gross disregard of consumer needs. In the Soviet Union managers frequently have no incentive to follow demand, and hence merely fulfill the quantitative "plan target"—with the consequence that for a month people can buy only gloves of one size. Under "market socialism" consumers would have a choice of goods.

In a capitalist society cartels, on the other hand, may serve as a tool to organize a market, or the government may act as buyer of last resort to set prices and production goals. A socialist government can use similar mechanisms for different purposes: not to maintain high prices but to regulate production in accordance with needs. The techniques of guiding the markets have been worked out by the corporate economy and the relevant government departments, regulatory agencies, and international authorities (European Coal and Steel Community, Common Market Farm Program, etc.); we need not discuss them here, because new techniques that a socialist government might add to these will not make a substantial difference. But the purpose of these controls should be different.

I see the following possibilities:

• *control is largely in the hands of corporate managers who are in close contact with the regulatory bureaucracy;*
• *control is imposed by the bureaucracy that dominates the*

*industrial managers by political means, for instance, a strong
dictatorship;*
  • *control is exercised by democratic institutions through a bureaucracy (an unstable setup that may easily be transformed into
either of the preceding types);*
  • *control is exercised through democratic movements directly at
every level of production and distribution.*

The problem is to institutionalize democratic types of control
and organization in such a way that the new institutions cannot set
themselves up as governing elites or merge with them. And this
problem is compounded by the need to adjudicate the conflicts
that are likely to arise among industries, regions, control agencies,
and between workers and management, planners and consumers,
surplus producers and subsidized areas, etc. The complex apparatus of a modern industrialized economy cannot be ruled by
administrative fiat, and the courts are unable to resolve conflicts
that arise out of social change.

Inevitably, therefore, economic questions will have to be
thrashed out in the political arena, and this can only be done in a
democratic way. A dictatorship may surpass conflicts for some
time, but will experience undesirable reactions (black markets
forcing the state to become more tyrannical, economic deformities
creating pressures in other areas, etc.). A better way would be to
let conflicts come out into the open and to stress the associative
features of the socialist-democratic processes: by developing cooperation and codetermination, letting the governed participate in
decision-making, allowing a proliferation of committees and representative bodies. Such a multiplication of participatory bodies
may have its negative and even unpleasant or dangerous aspects. I
shall deal with them later. At this point I should like to emphasize
that the only other alternative is some form of corporate, bureaucratic, or state capitalism. Liberal capitalism was characterized by
the total separation of the state from the economy; twentieth-
century economy, by whatever name, is characterized by its
thorough politicization, and under democratic socialism economic
decisions would be political too.

Democracy: A Prerequisite of Socialism

Widest participation of the governed in the processes of decision-making is desirable not only on all levels of economic activity but also in schools, municipal affairs, all organizations of public interest. According to David Spitz democracy has "two ingredients . . . the free play of opinions [and] the constitutional responsibility of the rulers to the ruled," and Robert MacIver calls it "a way to determine who shall govern and, broadly, to what ends." These seem to be merely *formal* determinations that say nothing about the economic system and which class is to rule. Yet as democracy increasingly becomes majority rule, it will tend to pervade more and more areas of public life; it will develop a policy on education, family life, and health protection, on workers' rights, and above all on overall economic policies. The purely "formal" or procedural features of the democratic process are converted into substantive measures, and democratic government comes to be defined (by Aristotle, who hated it for that very reason) as a government that serves the interest of the majority. It still is hated for the same reasons: it will impose minimum wages and maximum hours, health protection and medical insurance, social security, the dole, death taxes, regulations of business, environmental protection, codetermination and grievance procedures, as well as civil rights and integration. None of these measures is socialist in itself. Together they not only impose elements of a distributive economy on an acquisitive system; they are also launching pads for further demands, and they support the movement for a more comprehensive change of the system. This is why socialists of the last century embraced democracy so fervently. They were confident that a majority of the people would act as a government for the people, breaking down the formal separation of the state from the social life of the country. In contrast to the liberal-republican state, the democratic state is not a limited state; it is porous to the influences that come from the community, and it is allied with socialism by unbreakable ties.

This is certainly true as long as socialism had not been totally victorious, and even during this period socialists will not rely exclusively on parliamentary institutions but have to pursue their goals through active, ever-renewed movements to counter the capitalistic-oligarchic influences on the liberal-representative state. (It is a mistake, of course, to reject those institutions because they give access to the levers of power all too impartially to the rich and to the poor. The answer is to find means of making the system work for the majority, for all alternative systems are worse.)

Quite a different problem arises when socialists obtain a majority and come into a position to impose their own system, i.e., create irreversible changes that might infringe on the rights of minorities. From Plato to Hegel and his latter-day disciples political theorists have maintained that the state should represent not the interest of the majority but that of the whole, or "the general will." In defense of democracy Rousseau put forward the sophistry that the elector does not vote his interest but what he thinks the majority will guess to be the general will. Khrushchev, when asked why there were no free elections in the Soviet Union, snapped back: "What if the people vote wrong?" The argument hinges on the assumption that someone (the philosopher, the dictator, the party) knows what is the interest of the whole. Most parties also claim that what they represent is not really a particular interest but "the best interests of all" or everybody's interest "if rightly understood." This presumably entitles them to disregard the minority, or even to prevent it from ever becoming a majority again. To state the argument in this form is almost tantamount to destroying it. Some writers influenced by the Frankfurt School have given it an even sharper, I mean to say more ludicrous, form. It seems to them that under socialism people will undergo a fundamental change of character: not being alienated, they will have neither different interests nor different opinions, but will gladly cooperate in any reasonable assignment that the government decides on. The government, *a fortiori,* would be possessed of infinite goodwill and wisdom, and therefore the people would have no need for democratic organs of control.

No one has the right to make such assumptions. Under socialism governments will continue to blunder and people will continue to want to control them and commit their own blunders. As Rosa Luxemburg was fond of saying, "The wisdom of the wisest Central

Committee cannot be a substitute for the experience people gain by making their own mistakes." I find it strange that socialist philosophers should expect a total psychological change and then not trust the "new man" to take part in decision-making. If socialism is to develop a social dynamism, it will need all the collaboration and self-criticism, all the participation in the selection of leaders and in the formulations of programs it can get. In the long run the health of the socialist system will depend on the amount of "self-activation" or "self-movement"—words Marx and Luxemburg repeated again and again. This means free discussion, free expression, free access to the means of criticism and to the media, the right to question yesterday's truth and correct yesterday's mistakes, the freedom to assemble, organize, and petition, the right to choose representatives and to form parties —even the right to refuse cooperation (to strike).

Fortunately we don't have to choose between welfare and freedom, democracy and socialism. But if I did have to choose, I would accept inequality under a democratic government rather than a despotic government offering equality. For under democracy I could fight for more equality, while despotism would inevitably bring back inequality. The leader who claims to represent the general will is most dangerous: he carries aggression abroad and oppression at home. For socialists it is better to claim that they represent nothing more than the will of the majority (if they do), and democracy means to carry out that will.

This leaves me with the question I slurred over a moment ago—what justification does the majority have when it passes over the will of the minority to impose structural changes? The problem has been put most succinctly by John Stuart Mill, in *On Liberty:*

> The "people" who exercise the power are not the same people over whom it is exercised; the self-government spoken of is not the government of each by himself but of each by all the rest.

We have a number of conventions by which we abide because they are practical and their observance does not impinge on either our individual rights or the system we have accepted. But consider abortion: if the right to have an abortion implies the right to have it in a public clinic (as I believe it does)—by what right do I campaign for a law that would force Catholics to contribute, through their tax payments, to acts their religion forbids? As F. A. Hayek has pointed out, the notion of law has moved in recent times from rules of conduct, mostly restrictive, to substantive commands, mostly counterdiscriminatory. To create equal opportunity for all indeed means to write laws that affect different groups differently. Advocates of affirmative action have hammered this lesson home, and there is no reason to believe that a socialist community may not discover problems requiring similarly discriminatory laws, be it that the majority becomes persuaded of a need for remedial action or that minorities form log-rolling coalitions. But whatever the mechanics of forming a majority, there is no virtue in blinking at the fact that its will overrides the will of the minority.

A gracious or guilt-ridden majority might grant certain dissenters conscientious objector status. I could, for instance, be persuaded to give Catholics a tax remission for services, such as school and abortion, which they do not require. Conflicts of this sort can be resolved by appropriate accommodations within the prevailing system, and I shall adopt for this type of conflict the name Mao Tse-tung has given them—nonantagonistic or within-system conflict. The other type of conflict, obviously, is of a nature that cannot be resolved within the system. (By "system" I mean an interconnected set of institutions, each functioning to permit all others to function properly.) To introduce a socialist economy means to create institutions that would be difficult to repeal. It means to create a situation where those advocating repeal cannot easily be accommodated. To impose majority will in order to introduce sweeping measures of socialization therefore places considerable responsibility on that majority. To appreciate this we have to examine more closely what is meant by revolution.

Political and Social Revolutions

Revolution is usually thought of as a single political act accomplished in a relatively short time, sharply separating two different systems or epochs. Thus for most people capitalism in Russia ended in November 1917 and socialism began shortly thereafter. Even those who would see a period of transition might be surprised to learn that as late as in 1921 Lenin wrote: "We have elements of a capitalist economy, of state capitalism, of socialism, and of a cooperative economy in our country." Likewise 1789 is seen as a watershed, even though Tocqueville showed how much of the ancien régime survived and how much of the new age it had anticipated.

The need to dramatize, to symbolize and periodicize is satisfied when a new age is proclaimed, and the proclamation helps people feel that indeed they owe allegiance to the new age. This stabilizes the revolutionary regime and relieves it of the need to justify itself again and again. Thus the dismantling of the soviets after Kronstadt and the NEP, Stalin's crimes and the pact with Hitler, the imperialist policies since World War II—all this is seen not as so many steps away from socialism, but as means to fortify its power in the U.S.S.R. *L'esprit de système* prevents the cool analysis of each action on its merits; one gives the system the benefit of every doubt and does not ask whether perhaps its behavior indicates a change in its nature.

Revolution is a powerful symbol: it reassures the revolutionary government that it can be dislodged only by counterrevolution; that it can dismiss unsympathetic teachers, officers, civil servants, judges who may have tenure; that it can swiftly create new offices and institutions to supersede the old; that it can take emergency measures to paralyze its enemies; that it may stay in power for more than one election period. Even if a socialist government did emerge nonviolently from ordinary election processes, it must fear a coup or foreign intervention; after the Kapp Putsch in Germany nearly overthrew the Republic, the Austrian Socialists adopted a program envisaging a defensive dictatorship against reactionary plotters. We also have seen that hostile powers are able to create conditions similar to civil war, which eventually seem to justify intervention by the armed forces against a lawfully elected government (Spain in 1936, Chile in 1973). The 1978 threat of a Socialist-Communist government in France paralyzed the capital market, and graver consequences might have ensued in case of that coalition's victory. For all these reasons it is necessary to make the following distinctions:

As long as socialists are a minority or only a weak majority they can press for reforms, may join governments committed to reforms, but are not in a position to introduce fundamental changes in the social-economic system.

Even where socialists and their allies may have won slight majorities, they must try to avoid the impression of revolutionary inroads but should quietly strengthen their positions in all democratic institutions, increase the pressure of mass organizations, and then, having proved that they can govern, ask for a clear mandate for major structural changes.

If socialists and their allies have reason to foresee a substantial majority for a program of large-scale structural reforms, their campaign may assume the symbolism of revolution. It is vital to tell the voters the truth, for introducing socialism behind their backs would only entail a prolonged dictatorship. (I think it is now time for socialists to speak frankly about Allende's mistakes; though he remains a martyr, he need not be a model. Allende came to power without a clear mandate, either in numbers or by force of his program; he allowed supporters whom he could not contain to carry the revolution into the countryside before he could obtain its consent, thus uniting his enemies. While recognition of such mistakes will in no way excuse the counterrevolutionary, fascist repression that followed, it must be asked whether the bloody coup would have been possible if the Chilean socialists had refrained from "revolutionary" gestures. After all, this happened in a country that had enjoyed democratic government for forty years and had the experience of the antisocialist coup of 1932.)

Where there is no tradition of democratic government and socialists come to power in the wake of civil war against a dictatorial or colonial regime, the chances for immediate transition to a left-wing dictatorship are greater, but a heavy price has to be paid. (Castro has done much that is admirable in Cuba, but he is dependent on Soviet aid, had to allow massive emigration, keeps up to 30,000 dissidents in prisonlike institutions, has not dared to face an election, and has been unable to create a socialist political structure.)

If a revolution is to legitimate a socialist government, it must respond to the deeply felt desire of the population; no idea, be it ever so pure and convincing, can be a substitute for the democratic expression of consent that makes it unnecessary for the revolution to suppress dissenters. We come here to a fundamental distinction that used to be taken for granted in the older socialist literature but became blurred in the minds of our contemporaries because of the brilliant imagery of the political revolutions in Russia in 1917, China in 1949, and Cuba in 1959, all based more or less explicitly on the model of the Great French Revolution of 1789. The alternative to this Jacobin-Bolshevist scenario was spelled out by Karl Kautsky in his 1902 pamphlet *The Social Revolution.* Kautsky distinguished the social from the *political* revolution, which in his time meant the establishment of majority rule. This, he explained, was half the battle; after it there would follow a period of intensified class struggles, in the course of which the working class would expand its power in all areas: press, business, politics, the judiciary, the school, the theater, etc. Foreseeing fascism, he warned that reactionary gangs would try to turn the clock back by force. To meet them the working class would need state power, but that would be only one episode in a long-drawn-out process.

Today we may amplify these insights by our better knowledge of the process of revolution. Even in the Great French Revolution the political events did not reflect the deep social upheaval that shook French society. But the classes that were most active in pushing the revolution on to its consummation were not the ones that finally substituted themselves for the ancien régime. We call it the "bourgeois revolution" because of its outcome, but "the third estate" was much larger than the bourgeoisie, and even at the height of the Terror the masses were not in power. Likewise in the Russian revolution the seizure of power by a Marxist party was not tantamount to a proletarian revolution. Lenin had foreseen only a bourgeois-democratic revolution under the "hegemony" of workers and peasants. But under the pressure of circumstances—the unique opportunity of the physical disappearance of the ruling class and the total collapse of the economy—the political revolution ran far ahead of the possibilities for a socialist revolution in Russia. The Bolsheviks had to retreat from War Communism when the radical impetus of 1917 was exhausted and was followed by a period of stabilization. Trotsky later wondered "whether we did not introduce Thermidor ourselves."

The Russian revolution led to the nationalization of most enterprises, and this model has been followed throughout Eastern Europe. In the West nationalizations have been more selective, and some are still on the agenda. The Russian and East European revolutions have also made the society of these countries more egalitarian and have given the workers security and welfare from the cradle to the grave. But they did not abolish exploitation, did not promote self-administration, did not increase productivity beyond the rate that was to be expected through technological advances, and have left the working population woefully behind their Western colleagues with respect to both income and supply, not to speak of freedom and happiness.

If the social revolution was to improve the living conditions of working families, the slow, undramatic advances in the West have added up to more than the leap in the East. The price Western workers have paid for their greater freedom is the seesaw battle of class war, the pressure to succeed, the lack of security. The democratic process has resulted in permanent improvements and institutions, confirmed (and often expanded) even by right-wing governments that had originally opposed them. But the system is enormously wasteful and frustrating; its redeeming feature is that the defects are clearly seen and openly discussed.

Comparing the two systems, one feels entitled to ask: Was it necessary to go through the painful process of revolution and to submit to bloody dictatorships only to end with a working class lagging behind those that had not made a proletarian revolution? Is it necessary to mobilize the symbolism of revolution in order to give the working classes of the West the assurance that the system works for them? To the first question Robert Heilbroner has answered: What about the suffering that is prevented by a revolution (the unborn children, or simply what Marx describes in the first volume of *Das Kapital*)? It seems to me more fruitful to deal with historical questions as history: in some countries, we have seen, the social revolution was accelerated by a political revolution that also established a certain type of state, the dictatorship of the Bolshevik party. Because of this accident of history the socialist revolution has come to be identified with such a seizure of political power.

Marx coined the phrase "dictatorship of the proletariat," but he always meant it in a sociological sense, and he envisaged it for only a brief period. Moreover it was to be the dictatorship not of a party but of the organs of socialist democracy opposed to the old state apparatus. Originally Lenin and Trotsky also thought of the Soviet dictatorship as an organ of popular democracy. Only later, when this was narrowed down to the dictatorship of the Politbureau, was the myth of the salvationist dictatorship created. Instead of seeing the need for dictatorship as a misfortune, Bolshevik propaganda had to insist that it was a virtue. This historical accident had grave ideological consequences. The dictatorship now was passed off as the model for all other revolutions; the vision of the social revolution became confused with the myth of the seizure of power.

Dictatorship and Progress

Where underdeveloped countries have not produced an enterprising middle class, the task of modernization depends on the new elites: army officers, urban intellectuals, civil servants, and classless students trained abroad. None of these classes has economic power of its own, but they all hope to use state power as the vehicle of their aspirations: to develop the country's resources and to prepare it for the race with other countries. For both purposes they offer elite leadership, for progress can no longer be left to the spontaneous processes of undirected growth.

Where no tradition of democracy exists, technocrats and bureaucrats are seen as pioneers of progress. The great prerevolutionary historian Vasili Klyuchevsky thought that in Russia the state had always been ahead of society in promoting development;

in fact only the West has been modernized by spontaneous social forces rather than by the will of the princes.

The state elites are more acutely aware of the dynamics of power than of the human desires of the awakening nation. The more urgent the need for speedy development and the more compelling the thrust for national power, the less will the leaders feel inclined to develop democracy. Nationalism is their justification, with socialism added on as an ideology, and both identified with their own usurpation of power.

Modernizing nationalism in some countries goes by the name of "socialism," but in others, as in Taiwan now and in Japan before World War II, under the name of a corporate economy. Historical parallels are also relevant here: despotic governments helped the development of capitalism; kings gave commercial privileges to their courtiers, established royal manufactures, sent the poor to workhouses, and drove the peasants off their meager holdings —under pretext of making them more efficient, in the name of national power, and for the sake of higher economic rationality. This system was called mercantilism, and its greatest contemporary representative is the shah of Iran.

Some friends of the Third World have argued that underdeveloped countries cannot hope to make adequate progress while remaining democratic. This was the ideology of Indira Gandhi; she was brought down by antimodernizing forces. This is no reason to acclaim every dictatorship as progressive or to accept its claim of being "socialist." So far dictatorships have not raised the living standards in their countries, and when the time comes that technological and financial infusions achieve an expansion of their national product, then it will also be time for vigorous democratic and labor organizations to fight for a share in decision-making and its results.

In a milder form the argument for dictatorship points to the huge and powerful bureaucracy that is needed to cope with all the tasks of a socialist economy. Usually one hears this argument from the enemies of socialism, and socialists tend to minimize its seriousness. Nevertheless there are two sides to this problem.

Bureaucracy as a Tool of Socialism

Socialism has two uses for bureaucracy. In the age of welfare reforms, government agencies are set up to control the anarchy of the markets, shield the environment and protect people from exploitation, and curb the rapacity of business. No wonder bureaucracy has a bad press in capitalist countries. Only recently the rejection by Congress of the proposed Consumer Agency was greeted as "a blow against overweening bureaucracy."

Second, bureaucracy may accomplish what private enterprise fails to provide or may provide it better (how wonderful are European railroads); it also is a necessary agent of public services.

In addition bureaucracy may develop programs and points of view that grow out of its assigned routine but point toward new possibilities—projects that may lead beyond the welfare purposes, or even critical views of existing policies and institutions. It is well known that Marx used British government reports in writing *Das Kapital,* and to this day practically all information on capitalistic malfunctions is based on official surveys, reports, investigations —it could not be different. In the West, moreover, the close association of academic, corporate, and government research keeps the society "open," and agencies of the establishment (e.g., the CIA in the Vietnam War) sometimes oppose adventurous policies that the government and the public have embraced. More important, their job may lead them to look beyond the present system and to project policies requiring a more rational economy. Any public official who has to think about the future of energy supply must become impatient with the influence of the oil companies.

Fear of *1984,* of *The Bureaucratization of the World,* of the "technocentric society" is based on the perception that these technocrats, who see the need for a centrally directed economy, may also want to use their strategic position—society's need of their skills in commanding functions—to seize power and make themselves the dominant class. However, the men with ideas usually are not the doers, and the so-called power elite is divided into at least three different strata:

—*the experts: scientists, technologists, officers, professionals;*
—*the bureaucrats: administrators, corporate directors, civil servants;*
—*the politicians: the party or military junta, the parliamentary parties.*

A complicating factor is that members of the elite groups may be employed by the government, the academy, private industry, and that, as C. Wright Mills has claimed, these elites tend to merge into what Eisenhower has called the industrial-military (and I would add: -academic) complex. But for our purpose it is preferable to divide the new class into two large groups:

—*the political avant-garde, the movers in government and business;*
—*the bureaucracy proper, the civil service and corporate managers.*

Whereas the first is flexible and dynamic, and derives its legitimation from the claim that it represents the people, the second has the "civil service mentality" of honesty, obedience, predictability, and sluggishness. These are ideal types, and one must be careful not to compare the vices of one group with the virtues of the other. Usually business claims the dynamism for itself and blames dullness on "the bureaucrats," but there are as many bureaucrats working in business as in government, and for all the talk of oppressive, immovable bureaucracy, the loudest complaints are heard when a dynamic bureaucracy tries to move an inflexible business corporation. An excess of bureaucratic virtues may be harmful, even oppressive, and if decision-making is left to the bureaucracy the system may become self-serving and unresponsive to the needs of the community. But let us not forget that part of the clumsiness of bureaucratic procedures is due to the safeguards against abuse. The danger that the administrative and technical bureaucracy will set itself up as the new masters is comparatively small—to do that the bureaucrats would need the leadership of a political elite. (After the death of Stalin, Beria found out that a modern country like Russia cannot be governed by the police, and Malenkov that it cannot be governed by the economic and administrative bureaucracy. It took a politician like Khrushchev to organize power, and when he turned against the party, he was ousted too.) The bureaucracy will usually serve the system in which it works, but it does not create a system. It does not produce a political will, but is the organ of a will. The Great Wall of China was not built because labor became available but because the tyrannical will of Shih Huang-ti made it available. The computer does not produce solutions for problems that have not been fed into it.

This analysis disagrees with the theories of Saint-Simon, Bell, Djilas, Orwell, Burnham, Wittfogel, Brzezinski, and Birnbaum, who all assume that somehow a managerial bureaucracy, a "technocentric structure" or "new class" emerges from the pores of our society—as the capitalist class developed in the interstices of the ancien régime. The antisocialists among them then will push the analogy further: just as the popular revolution of 1789 ended by bringing that capitalist class to power, so the socialist revolution of our time will end, or has ended in some countries where it was tried, by bringing the technocrats and bureaucrats to power. But Stalin was not merely the "top bureaucrat," and the Communist bureaucrats are not an exploitative class in the same sense as were capitalists and feudal lords. In the nonrevolutionary advances of Western socialism, by contrast, each wave of social legislation leaves, like a sediment, a bureaucracy that implements and institutionalizes it.

These bureaucracies tend to stabilize and perpetuate the new social relations. Their very mulishness will prevent reactionary forces from reversing the trend, and socialists depend very much on the self-preserving instincts of bureaucracy to protect social progress from political attacks. Harold Laski was merely witty but not profound when he said that experts should be on tap, not on top; in practice the technocentric structure is as much an ally of the labor movement as an impediment to stronger dynamism. Also, as Orlando Patterson remarks in his outstanding *Ethnic Chauvinism,* "a big impersonal state may be a better guardian of libertarian values than a small unit with its cronyism."

Although the various strata of the ruling class interchange

functions and recruitment, they also have rivals. Dutch sociologists have invented the term *verzoiling* (roughly: column-building) for the process of splitting society into professional camps: the corporate structure, the administrative structure, the military structure, the medical structure, the academic structure, the judiciary, the political structure, each with its top layer of a dominating elite. I find this model not only more persuasive than the myth of the technostructure, but also more practical. Rather than call upon the whole of society against "big brother," democrats could suggest two remedies against his domination: encouraging mobility within each column and rivalry between the columns. In each of the "columns" we find politicians who articulate the technical plans that come from their respective bureaucracies. The latter determine only feasibility, maybe desirability. It is for the political leaders to choose, to bargain among different interests, to hammer out a balance that can then be presented as the "general will."

Pluralism

Socialists attempt to expand the jurisdiction of public bodies and to institutionalize their material achievements. Eventually a point is reached where the haphazard, historical gains must be consolidated and systematized—if only to prevent them from getting into each other's bailiwicks. Then a grave decision will have to be approached: a new economic constitution must be codified, and it will tend either toward state capitalism and eventually fascism, or toward democratic socialism. The latter presupposes strong independent mass organizations and established traditions of constitutional government. Strongly centralized, overarching organs of decision-making will favor state capitalism; fragmentation of power will serve the interests of democracy. This includes the customary division of power among executive, legislative, and judiciary, between federal and regional, but also between planning agencies and claimant groups, between economic and political authorities, employing agencies and producers, etc.

The term "totalitarian" suggests the monolithic identity of the various elites and conceals the fact that oppression is first of all political. Stalin called on the "people" to help purge the bureaucrats and especially those who had developed some appreciation of the limitations of their power or maybe even a certain affection for the people under their jurisdiction. So did Mussolini; so did Hitler. Generals whose advice was professional had to go. As long as only bureaucrats rule they will be "corrupt," i.e., responsive to the parameters of their jobs. What is dictatorial and tyrannical is the General Will. Bureaucracy is a check on it, and the more so the less it is itself a monolith. It must be fragmented to reflect the plurality of interests and functions in a modern society —differences of class, region, race, philosophy, profession. Anchored in its various "columns" it cannot become an autonomous machinery of oppression. The divergent groups and antagonisms can act on the system.

This hope of rivalry has been translated into a political theory called "pluralism." It does not mean direct participation of the governed in the process of government, but it gives the representatives of interest groups access to the levers of decision-making. It guarantees a certain diversity of impulses that are brought to bear on the decision-making process, and to that extent is a safeguard against arbitrary government. How well this device will work obviously depends on the vigor and number of independent articulate forces in the society. Once again it becomes clear how merely "formal" requirements can be translated into substantive measures.

Self-Government and Participation

Self-government means actual participation of the governed in the process of decision-making and in the design of measures to carry out those decisions. It can be realized only if the governed have access to all levels of government. For this purpose a number of devices and designs rival for attention. I can here only give a brief run-down, and refer to other articles for details.

The councils: *A revolutionary organization that became an executive organ in the Russian revolution, and then also the model for movements in Europe. It was prominent in the Hungarian revolution of 1956 and in the German revolution of 1918. It means direct participation on the lower echelons but indirect participation through delegates on the higher levels.*

The syndicalist system: *Shops are run cooperatively by the trade unions and are free to compete, though investment decisions may be made centrally. This system was used in the Spanish Civil War and in parts of Israel. A combination of the council and the syndicalist systems has been used in Yugoslavia.*

Codetermination: *The system remains capitalist or state capitalist, but workers' representatives are elected to sit on the board of directors. The system, operative in Germany, and partly in France and other areas of the Common Market, involves shop stewards and trade unions in questions of management, gives them access to the books and a strong voice in personnel questions and, where public officials also sit on the board, the chance to form majorities.*

Sweden's "Meidner Plan," *under which control of each company would gradually pass into the employees' hands.*

Capitalistic variations of the codetermination scheme, *for instance the VW model where the workers own shares in small denominations, or the Sears Roebuck plan, where the employees' pension fund owns the shares.*

The public corporation model, *preferred in England, where control is in the hands of an authority or public board. (I leave out "capitalism without capitalists"—such national enterprises as Amtrak.)*

Characteristic of all codetermination schemes and also the Yugoslav form of the council scheme is participation on the lowest, most direct level, the shop. It also leaves the plan bureaucrats in control of the industry and fails to reflect other concerns of the masses—as consumers, as members of a church, etc.; it gives them little access to the formulation of policy on the national level. The large figures of "participation" that are often cited for Yugoslavia thus reflect only a rather truncated democracy. Moreover these councils are split locally. A real workers' representation requires an independent national union. Real professional and industry representation requires national chambers of the various professions, farm associations, etc. In Yugoslavia these have neither political nor economic power. The Weimar Constitution foresaw a National Economic Chamber, which however never acquired real power.

I reluctantly conclude that the councils are more likely to become the instruments of a strong political leadership, transmission belts between the national government and the shop, rather than true organs of democratic control. They could be that only if they were to develop their own political organ that would feed information to independent parties and trade unions. There is no substitute, no gimmick, organization, or scheme of participation that can or should take the place of political parties.

It must also be admitted that the democratic system of economic self-administration that exists in Yugoslavia has not diminished the dictatorship of the party, nor has it prevented the growth of a sprawling bureaucracy on the county, regional, and national levels, whose in-fighting is a burden to the country. Moreover the syndicalist and participatory schemes offer little protection against parochialism, industry egoism, and communal rivalry. (Nor should we be oblivious of recent examples in the U.S. where even Paul Goodman, our most ardent advocate of local self-government, called on the central New York school board to assert its authority.)

The most serious enemy of self-government, however, is apathy and indifference; it not only strikes all theories of spontaneity and participation with paralysis, but it also makes participatory schemes the playground of sectarians and fanatics. The fatigue of drawn-out committee meetings or disgust with factionalism all too easily leave the field to a determined group which takes over and makes a mockery out of the best schemes. Nor should this problem be shrugged off with assertions that under socialism people will be different. Dedication and spontaneity come in bursts, or at best waves, and there is no guarantee that only the capable and well-intentioned will constitute themselves as the permanent avant-garde.

Participatory experience on the local and factory level, therefore, is welcome as a recruiting school for the trade union and party activities; it is a contributing factor to decentralizations, but it should not be used as a pretext for withholding the essential political and ideological freedom.

The Continued Relevance of Class War

My conception of democratic socialism is as far from revisionism as from utopian visions of a world without problems and conflict. I do not recommend any specific set of institutions, organization schemes, or election procedures. I am concerned with the involvement of the greatest number of people in the management of their destiny on all levels of economic, cultural, and political decision-making. Whether they do this in the form of a council movement, in the form of trade unions or cooperatives, or in parliamentary forms, success will always depend on the amount of interest and action they put into the organ of self-administration. No government or party can place self-administration on a platter and hand it to the people by decree; they must develop it by their own efforts and ingenuity. Not only that, they must continue to develop them even after they have been institutionalized. For every human institution can become obsolete, rigid, perverted, alienated from its original intentions.

The East European examples, which seem to contradict the possibility of democratic socialism, should not deter us; they are based on the experience of countries that never or rarely had enjoyed democratic institutions and citizens' rights. In the Western nations we have a long tradition of independent judges, an independent press, the freedom of the universities, or undiminished rights of assembly and of parliamentary representation. The continued presence of opposition parties, of alternatives, and of constitutional guarantees will assure that no matter under which social-economic system, the further evolution toward greater freedom will not be permanently abridged.

Democracy is movement of people, constant struggle to enlarge their rights and to bring more of them into the peer group. This will not be achieved without their own participation and without pressures, even fighting. The aim of socialism of course is to make further frictions as tolerable as possible, to achieve a consensus that is not imposed from above but agreed to by the interested parties. But if the society is not stagnant, new claimant groups might appear or new problems of adjustment might be discovered. The mere fact that material worries have been removed may bring psychological and family troubles to the fore. Recent experience even indicates that such problems may lead to asocial, antagonistic behavior. Precisely because I don't expect paradise to break out I must be prepared to allow conflict, movement, evolution, even revolution. Not all conflict may be susceptible to litigation. Political outlets must be available for those who, rightly or wrongly, do not feel that their aspirations can be fulfilled within the existing institutions.

In all the so-called socialist countries revolutionary or quasi-revolutionary action may be required to overthrow the oppressive political dictatorship. This revolution will be supported by a large part of the technical intelligentsia, which sees both the material possibilities and its own ambitions curbed by the dictatorship. In the underdeveloped countries popular revolutions are less likely to succeed: they may topple one kind of dictatorship only to fall prey to another. Or else they may have to pay for freedom by readmitting alien capitalism (which may be good for development but is not tolerated gladly in the present climate of opinion).

In most of the Western countries we now have a system that combines representative government and civic freedom with welfare-state institutions—partly nationalized industries, guidance and manipulation or direct controls, public services, redistribution of income through taxation and services, but on the whole still criteria of profitability for economic activity. Trade unions and consumer organizations confront corporate power; civil-rights claimants, farmers, and church groups fight for influence. Reformist action by labor parties and governments has reached limits where further major progress can be made only by measures that seem to "go beyond the welfare state," notably: overall planning of social welfare, distribution of a national dividend, preponderance of public enterprises whose rationale is not profitability. Further reforms would be "structural," i.e., instead of alleviating the condition of individuals they would change the way the system operates.

What prevents the adoption of these measures is not political

oppression but their inherent risk, the absence of organizations
that have a clear and popular plan and are ready to fight for it.
New ventures are introduced piecemeal, and often without the
clear awareness that their full benefits could become visible only in
a totally different context.

Here we come once more to the problems of "system": socialism today does not confront the capitalist model with a utopian
model. It is not a predesigned plan that can only be accepted or
rejected in toto. On the contrary it is an open development of the
economy based on an equally open movement for the betterment
of living conditions. It is a movement, more and more, of all the
people and not only the laboring classes. The new possibilities of
the welfare state have brought to the fore problems that previously
had been hidden by the need for fighting first for material
satisfactions. Socialism has become (again, as in Marx's own time)
a cultural movement striving not only for the improvement of
material conditions but for the emancipation of the individual
personality. It certainly is not a movement of technocrats for a
more efficient organization of society. It is a movement of people,
and its idea cannot be divorced from their eternal yearning for
freedom.

Robert A. Dahl

On Removing Certain Impediments to Democracy in the United States

WHAT this nation can become will be influenced, though not fully determined, by the ways in which we think about ourselves as people. With a people as with a person it is a sign of wisdom and maturity to understand and accept limits that are imposed by nature's laws and the scarcity of resources, whether physical, human, or political. In this sense we Americans may at last be entering into our maturity. But to accept as real the limits that are imposed only by our own minds is not wisdom but self-inflicted blindness.

Out of our past we have inherited ways of thinking about ourselves that condemn us to try too much and accomplish too little. We fail not so much because our aspirations are too high but because they conflict; and within ourselves too we are conflicted in ways we do not fully recognize. In this sense our consciousness, both individual and collective, distorts our understanding of ourselves and our possibilities.

This article is reprinted with permission from *Political Science Quarterly*, Spring 1977, vol. 92, no. 1, pp. 1-20, and is drawn from my lecture, "Liberal Democracy in the United States," delivered at the University of Texas, February 25, 1976, and published in *The Prospects for Liberal Democracy*, edited by William Livingston (University of Texas Press, 1979).

An important part of this distortion comes out of a series of historical commitments this country has made. It might free our consciousness for greater political creativity if we were to see those commitments more clearly, to understand better how they conflict with one another, and to choose self-consciously rather than blindly among our possible futures.

The expression "historical commitment" may carry misleading connotations. A historical commitment in the context of this essay is nothing neat, tidy, wholly self-conscious, broadly understood, much less agreed to by all, nor a well-shaped historical drama with a clear beginning, a middle, and an end. Rather it pertains to periods in our history in which some alternative possibilities seemed open to the principal historical actors who, however, were in conflict over the relative desirability of the alternatives they perceived. The conflict among them became overt, bitter, sometimes prolonged, and in one way or another finally came to involve a substantial number of citizens. In time, however, one set of advocates won out. Thereafter the issues so fiercely contested ceased to be salient in American political life. What had recently been a sharply contested possibility thus came to be accepted as pretty much an undebatable aspect of the status quo by the major parties, political leaders, writers and publicists, and (so far as these things can be discerned) the voters themselves. If dissenters continued to fight rearguard actions, they were few in number and on the margins of American politics, public attention, and political acceptability. Thus the historic commitments soon came to possess all the extraordinary advantages of things as they are and, after a generation or so, as they seem always to have been. This essay will focus on five historical commitments this country has made to goals that are in some respects incompatible and will condemn us to a confused sense of national purpose unless and until we recognize these conflicts and decide on our priorities.

Five American Commitments

1. The first commitment was the one this country made to a liberal political and constitutional order that gave primacy to the

protection of certain political and civil rights among its citizens. Although the whole colonial period was crucial to the development of sentiment favoring that commitment, the most active stage might be conveniently if rather arbitrarily placed somewhere between 1776 and 1800 or thereabouts. Sometime not long after 1800 conflict over the validity of the existing Constitution pretty much recedes and soon hardly an American voice is heard in opposition to it. So profound is its acceptance in fact that the great constitutional quarrels to follow were not so much over the validity of the Constitution as over its meaning, assuming its unquestioned validity.

2. The second historical commitment, consolidated somewhere between 1800 and 1836 or thereabouts, was to the belief that the only proper constitutional and political system for Americans is a democracy. Although democracy mainly meant adhering to democratic procedures in the operation of the government, it also carried with it notions of a larger society within which social and economic conditions would favor the high degree of political, social, and economic equality necessary to democracy. By extraordinary luck such a social order already existed in the United States. This was an agrarian society where, in an economy predominantly of family farms, the adult white male citizens lived with fewer social, economic, and political inequalities than any large number of persons in history that had existed up to this time, and very likely since. Tocqueville was not the first observer nor would he be the last, though he may have been the most gifted, to see how marvelously the agrarian society fostered a condition of equality among the citizens, or rather among the white males.

Yet that agrarian order was not only a historical rarity, but it had no future. During the harsh struggles over the new socioeconomic order that was to replace it, Americans who wished to retain the old order were the most numerous, persistent, and politically successful opponents of the new. But even with the whole weight of tradition on their side, they and their occasional allies were unable to prevent the displacement of the old agrarian order by a new order based on commercial and industrial capitalism, in which the ideal engine of economic production and growth was no longer to be the privately owned family farm but the privately owned

commercial, financial, or industrial corporation. The contest that
eventuated in the triumph of the new order over the old dominated American political life through the last three decades of the
nineteenth century. During this time a number of alternatives to
the new order—agrarianism, anarchism, socialism, individually
owned consumers' and producers' cooperatives, selective government ownership and operation, economic regulation, limits on
corporate size, monetary schemes, enforced competition, and
many others—were thrust forward, debated, and finally pretty
much defeated. The election of 1896 might be taken as the turning
point in the victory of the new order over its rivals.

3. Thereafter the national commitment to the socioeconomic
order of corporate capitalism swelled into a current so powerful
that opponents could make no headway against it and were swept
out of the mainstream of American life. Even socialists, who in
Britain and Europe gained greater support as industrial capitalism
expanded, remained a small and largely uninfluential minority in
the United States.

If by 1900 or so this country was committed to corporate
capitalism, aspects of the new order nonetheless remained at issue.
Widespread hardships were engendered by an economy with as
little public control as the dominant political coalition demanded.
These hardships were real enough to ensure a following for a
politician who advocated reform—at any rate so long as he did not
attack the basic commitment to private ownership, whereupon his
following would shrink into the futilities of minor party politics.
Thus if socialism was unpopular, reform was not. As a result, from
time to time regulatory laws won out in particular states and
occasionally, as with Wilson's New Freedom, even in the federal
government. But the country's commitment to only a modest
interference by government in the conduct of corporate capitalism
was more accurately reflected by the administrations of McKinley,
Taft, Harding, Coolidge, and Hoover, and by Theodore Roosevelt's bombastic style and ineffectual policies—speak loudly.but
carry a small stick—than by the brief interlude of reform during
Wilson's first term. As we all know, it took the trauma of the
Great Depression finally to convert a hitherto oppositional minority into a majority coalition.

4. The product of this coalition was the fourth historic commitment, which was of course to the idea and institutions of a welfare state. The prior commitment to private ownership and control of economic enterprises, and thus to corporate capitalism, was mainly upheld. Yet some of the most acute hardships and injustices generated in the socioeconomic order were to be removed or alleviated by government actions—mainly by the federal government. Orthodox as this commitment now seems, one who did not live through that period may find it difficult to recapture how intense, bitter, and at times violent was the conflict over the inauguration of a welfare state by Franklin Roosevelt and the New Deal. However, as with the preceding commitments, the main elements of this one soon gained such wide acceptability that opposition to the commitment itself, as distinguished from criticism of specific means, came to be an exercise in political futility.

5. Even before the main battles of the New Deal were finished, conflict had begun over what was to be the fifth historic commitment. This was the commitment to play an international role as a world power. Again it may be hard to recapture how bitterly divided Americans were over this issue in the late 1930s. Yet the advocates of an American role as an active world power were riding an overpowering current of events that swept along most of their opponents and swamped the rest or left the few survivors stranded far behind the main body of American opinion.

All five of these historic commitments remain strong. Even after the shame and disaster of Vietnam, there is not really much likelihood of our renouncing our position as a world power, though the way we use our position and power cannot possibly be to everyone's liking or, alas, to everyone's benefit, and could easily be as harmful to ourselves and others once again as it has been in the recent past. Within limits, the strength of each of the five commitments seems to wax and wane; one is eroded here and another grows firmer there. But the commitments still dominate the way we think about ourselves and our future. And that is a source of difficulty, for the commitments are in some ways incompatible.

Impediments to Democracy

Certain impediments to the realization of democracy in the
United States have resulted from the other historic commitments.
We can begin with the Constitution itself, the political system it
helped to form, and the political ideas and beliefs embedded in
and strengthened by the constitutional and political system. As we
have seen, this country's commitment to democracy came after
and not before the formation and adoption of the Constitution.
Even as late as the Constitutional Convention the desirability of a
representative democracy was a debatable issue. Consequently the
framers could not and did not agree to establish a representative
democracy. They could and did agree to establish a representative
republic with a framework of government that would, as they
believed, rest on popular consent and yet ensure as best they knew
how the preservation of certain basic rights to life, liberty, and
property that they held to be morally inalienable. In this sense the
framers were liberals and republicans though they were not
democrats; they intended to establish a liberal framework of
government, though it could be, and later was, democratized to a
degree that for a time would astonish the world.

The political system the framers helped bring into existence was
in at least two major respects defective by democratic criteria.
First, in spite of the eloquent universality of the language used in
the Declaration of Independence and common at the time, in
actuality the framers gave much narrower scope to the principles
of consent and political equality. Without seriously qualifying,
much less abandoning their universal norms, they nonetheless
created a government that would demand obedience to its laws
from a majority of adults—women, nonwhites, and some white
males—who were excluded from active participation in making
those laws, whether directly or through their elected representatives. The majority of adults were thus provided with as little
opportunity to give their active consent to the laws that they were
bound to obey as their colonial predecessors had enjoyed under
laws enacted by the English Parliament.

Second, in order to achieve their goal of preserving a set of
inalienable rights superior to the majority principle—a goal many

of us would surely share—the framers deliberately created a framework of government that was carefully designed to impede and even prevent the operation of majority rule. Thus when the country committed itself to their framework of government, two different arguments became confounded in the national consciousness, and they remain confounded to this day. There is the liberal argument that certain rights are so fundamental to the attainment of human goals, needs, interests, and fulfillment that governments must never be allowed to derogate from them. But in addition there is the American constitutional argument that the highly specific, indeed unique, set of political arrangements embodied in our constitutional and political practices is necessary to preserve these rights. While I accept the liberal argument, the American constitutional argument seems to me seriously defective.

Now the matter of what ought to constitute inalienable rights beyond the reach of any government and the proper relationship between such rights and democratic procedures are questions far too complex to examine here. Certainly the solutions are not easy to come by, either theoretically or practically. Moreover we might agree on the need to preserve fundamental rights against government without necessarily agreeing on what these rights should be. The point is, however, that the elaborate system of checks and balances, separation of powers, constitutional federalism, and other institutional arrangements influenced by these structures and the constitutional views they reflect are both adverse to the majority principle, and in that sense to democracy, and yet arbitrary and unfair in the protection they give to rights. However laudable their ends, in their means the framers were guilty of overkill. As only one example, the presidential veto has generally been used for purposes no loftier than simply to prevent the adoption of policies disliked by the president and the political coalition whose interests he seeks to advance. It is not as if a president uses the veto only when a majority coalition threatens the inalienable rights of a minority. What is typically at stake is purely a disagreement about policy. Insofar as all policies have costs and gains and thus influence the distribution of advantages and disadvantages, the policies of a majority (like those of a minority) are likely to be adverse to the interests of some persons;

but we can hardly say—nor can the framers have intended to say—that every privilege that happens to exist does so by inalienable right.

Yet there is this strong bias against majorities in the political system the framers helped to create. Because they succeeded in designing a system that makes it easier for privileged minorities to prevent changes they dislike than for majorities to bring about the changes they want, it is strongly tilted in favor of the status quo and against reform. In their effort to protect basic rights, what the framers did in effect was to hand out extra chips in the game of politics to people who are already advantaged, while they handicapped the disadvantaged who would like to change the status quo. From a moral perspective the consequences seem arbitrary and quite lacking in a principled justification.

We ought to be able to design a way of preserving fundamental rights that is not so biased in favor of existing privilege and against reform. A number of other countries that place fewer barriers in the way of majority rule than exist under our political system manage to preserve at least as high a standard of political liberty, with less procedural unfairness. But of course to bring about such changes meets precisely the obstacle to change just mentioned, the antimajoritarian bias of the constitutional and political system.

This brings us to another consequence of the framers' antimajoritarian design that is unsatisfactory both as a protection for morally inalienable rights and as a device for procedural democracy. It may not be going too far to say that although the framers were unable to prevent the democratization of the constitutional system, they created a potentially lethal instrument for that democratization in the presidency. When the democratic commitment referred to earlier was undertaken, the antimajoritarian constitutional design was not merely preserved but identified with democratic government itself, a confusion that remains all but universal among Americans, as visitors from other democratic countries and teachers of political science to American undergraduates repeatedly discover. However, democratizing the Constitution required a transformation that some of the framers had feared and had sought to prevent. The claim was now made that the president was the sole authentic spokesman for and representative of national majorities. Indeed the constitutional framework hardly provided any other possibility. Given the nature of the Senate and even of the House, the claim on behalf of the presidency was plausible, and one that the defenders of Congress found hard to rebut. In the long run, as we know, Congress failed to uphold its claim, and the claims made on behalf of the presidency pretty much won out. Endowed with legitimacy deriving both from constitutional interpretation and democratic ideology, the presidency became the institutional center from which a majority coalition, if there was to be one at all, would be mobilized, organized, and given voice. Thus one consequence of the framers' institutional design was to channel the process of democratizing the Constitution into transforming the presidency, a process that was not to end, if it has yet ended, before that office became what lately has been variously called an elective monarchy, an imperial presidency, a plebiscitary chief executive, and other epithets still harsher.

The irony is then that the first and second historic commitments taken in their entirety endow us with a political system in which any majority coalition supporting changes adverse to existing privileges is likely to succeed only if the presidency has access to a concentration of political resources great enough to make the office a standing danger to majority rule and procedural democracy itself. Thus the justifiable effort to strengthen the majority principle in a constitutional system that was designed to impede it has led not to democratization of the Constitution but rather to the pseudodemocratization of the presidency.

Under the agrarian economic order the pseudodemocratization of the presidency did not matter very much nor would it have gone very far. The white males who comprised the demos enjoyed an astounding degree of autonomy in relation to one another and to all governments. Their political resources, and the opportunities and incentives for using them should the need arise, were vast in comparison with the weak coercive means available to any of the American governments. Hence the potentiality of widespread governmental coercion of the demos or any substantial part of it was perhaps as minimal as it had ever been anywhere among a numerous body of people. As for the members of the excluded majority, their very exclusion from political rights meant that they could not successfully appeal to the government to prevent private or public coercion, unless they happened to have the support of a majority of white males, and not necessarily even then if a substantial minority in the demos opposed the change sought by or in behalf of the disfranchised. In practice, then, the excluded groups had little protection against oppression.

The third historic commitment was to change the distribution of resources so favorable to the demos. An agrarian order that historically speaking was extraordinarily congenial to democracy was now displaced by a new socioeconomic order of corporate capitalism that was much less compatible. The basis of the new order was a fundamentally different kind of economic enterprise. The small family-owned and -operated farm that was modal if not universal in the agrarian order was now displaced by one of the most radical innovations that mankind has ever invented for economic organization, control, and growth. This was the privately owned and operated business corporation. Through a highly successful case of ideological transfer, the Lockean defense of private property, which in the agrarian order made good sense morally and politically, was shifted over intact to corporate enterprise. This ideological triumph successfully warded off attacks not only from nascent socialist movements opposed to private property in the means of production but also from the historical rear guard defending the old agrarian order, which had at hand no convincing way of distinguishing private ownership and control of one kind of enterprise, the farm, from private ownership and control of a radically different kind, the business corporation. Thus by an extraordinary ideological sleight of hand the corporation took on the legitimacy of the farmer's home, tools, and land, and what he produced out of his land, labor, ingenuity, anguish, planning, forbearance, sacrifice, risk, and hope. The upshot was that the quite exceptional degree of autonomy the farmer members of the demos had enjoyed under the old order, an autonomy vis-à-vis both government and one another, was now granted to the corporation.

Two consequences of this new order were particularly adverse to democracy. First, the new order generated much greater differences than the old in political resources, skills, and incentives within the demos itself. The degree of social and economic differentiation that had already been foreshadowed in the cities of the Eastern Seaboard was no longer marginal, as it had been when the socioeconomic order was overwhelmingly agrarian, but central to the new order. Great differences in wealth, income, social esteem, education, occupational skills, and ethnic status now differentiated wage-earners and pieceworkers in industry, ship, mine, and forest—a rising proportion of whom were immigrants —from the middling strata of white-collar and professional people, who for some time to come were predominantly Anglo-American in origins, and these in turn from the opulent few. Because differences like these are readily convertible into political resources, the wide if by no means perfectly equal dispersion of political resources among the demos in the agrarian order was now considerably more concentrated. Inequalities in political resources added further to the handicaps of any majority coalition that sought changes in the allocation of privileges and disadvantages.

Second, because the internal government of the corporation was not itself democratic but hierarchical and often despotic, the rapid expansion of this revolutionary form of economic enterprise meant that an increasing proportion of the demos would live out their working lives, and most of their daily existence, not within a democratic system but instead within a hierarchical structure of subordination. To this extent democracy was necessarily marginal to the actual political system in which the members of the demos lived their daily lives. Thus the transfer of the Lockean view to the corporation was a double triumph. By making ownership the only, or at least primary, source of legitimate control over corporate decisions, the new order not only excluded democratic controls in the internal government of the enterprise but placed powerful ideological barriers against the imposition of external controls by a government that, for all its deficiencies, was much more democratic than were the governments of business firms.

The fourth and fifth commitments extended the domain of hierarchy even further. To be sure, from the New Deal onward the commitment to a welfare state helped to reduce the autonomy of economic enterprises. By protecting the rights of workers to join unions and bargain collectively with employers the New Deal helped to democratize some aspect of some enterprises for some employees. By regulatory devices of various kinds it also reduced the autonomy and thus the arbitrary and sometimes despotic power of the rulers of economic enterprises. However, if the commitment to a welfare state has altered, it has not profoundly reduced the two adverse consequences of the corporate capitalist order mentioned a moment ago. The evidence seems to show that what appear to be great changes in levels of taxation and transfer payments have not much reduced the inequalities in the distribution of wealth and income and thus the relative political advantage or disadvantage associated, at least loosely, with access to these resources. And except for the limited effects of trade unions among a minority segment of the labor force, the American commitment to a welfare state has not done much to alter the hierarchical structures of corporate government under which so many Americans live.

The commitment to a welfare state in fact has added even more burdens to democracy. For one thing the reforms undertaken in behalf of the commitment could not be carried through without the leadership of an energetic president, who could increase, organize, and exploit all the political resources of the office. If we want to find the recent rather than the Jacksonian origins of the imperial presidency, as good a place as anywhere to begin is the presidency of Franklin Roosevelt. Among other things what his presidency did was to disarm most intellectuals and academics, not least political scientists who, being mostly in favor of reform, enthusiastically came forward with whatever was needed in the way of a justification for enhanced presidential power. Moreover in order to achieve its gains the welfare state needed extensive governmental bureaucracies. Even if these are never fully controlled by official hierarchies or for that matter by anyone else, they do provide an ambitious president with very considerable political resources—far beyond anything the framers ·ever dreamed of—for persuasion, inducement, manipulation, and coercion. By now this proposition needs no documentation beyond what Watergate has furnished us. Finally, like the governments of corporate enterprise, the bureaucracies in the government of the state are also hierarchical in structure. Far from diminishing hierarchy, therefore, even in the course of regulating economic enterprise the welfare state has multiplied the number, domain, and scope of hierarchies in American life.

The fifth commitment, of course, compounded these consequences adverse to democracy. As an active world power the country had need—at first quite suddenly—of a large military establishment, thus still another hierarchy, even more rigidly hierarchical than the rest, one perhaps even more difficult to control, yet available to the president for executing foreign and military policies that could be, as events were to show, the arbitrary and personal expressions of a chief executive whose decisions on these matters were for all practical purposes beyond the control of Congress, the courts, or the demos. In a further irony constitutional language and interpretation had left a substantial gap in the framers' imposing array of checks and balances. Successive presidents plunged through and widened this gap. By action and inaction, the Congress, the courts, and the demos —cheered on, it has to be said, by political scientists, historians, lawyers, and other intellectual spokesmen who should have known better—all gave their blessing to the emerging imperial presidency. It took national shame, disaster, scandal, and prolonged investigation to make us realize what sort of institution the presidency had become.

To understand these changes in the presidency it is important to keep in mind that for the better part of two generations this country was involved in war, near-war, war crisis, or cold war. Three decades of war would be enough, one might think, to undermine a weaker republic. Perhaps we should consider ourselves lucky that our first two commitments held as well as they did. Even so, as a world power things were done and widely thought to be justified that surely would have been condemned as unjustifiable in less paranoid circumstances. An obsession with national security and loyalty fostered secrecy in government, the enormous expansion of domestic spying, the harassment of radicals, and other excrescences. And even if some important reforms were carried out, mainly with respect to civil rights, these decades were on the whole unfavorable to reform, and certainly to any changes that might seem to question the validity of our historic commitments.

The Doctrine of Procedural Democracy

If we were now to search for a perspective on our potentialities as a people that would not be distorted either by self-glorification or self-hatred, that recognized our capacities for great evil, great good, and plain mediocrity, and discerned in the conflicting commitments of our past that weigh heavily on our present some criteria of excellence against which to measure our achievements in the future, where would we begin?

We might begin near the beginning, with our first two commitments. Ignoring for a moment the contradictions described earlier, these may be interpreted as an aspiration toward a society with a political system in which liberty, equality, and justice would jointly prosper, a society therefore requiring also a socioeconomic system that would foster these ends by supporting the kind of polity necessary to them. Thus interpreted, these two commitments would give priority to political ends over economic ends, to liberty, equality, and justice over efficiency, prosperity, and growth, a priority that the commitment to corporate capitalism reversed both in ideology and in practice, and that has remained reversed down to our own day.

The guiding criteria against which to measure political performance implied by this interpretation are, in my view, the criteria of procedural democracy, which, together with their most crucial assumptions, constitute what one might call the doctrine of procedural democracy. What follows is a very brief and incomplete account of that doctrine.

To become fully operative with respect to any association the doctrine of procedural democracy presupposes a judgment that at least two conditions exist among some set of persons who constitute or intend to constitute an association.

First, there is a *need for collective decisions* that are binding on the members of the association. This set of persons is confronted by a matter that would be disadvantageous to leave entirely to individual action or to choices made exclusively through a market, and comparatively advantageous to make collectively and enforce on the members.

Second, among the persons obligated to abide by collective decisions on this matter, there is a subset, the *demos*, whose members are *roughly equally qualified, taken all around*. That is, no member of this qualified subset, or demos, believes that any other member of the association or any subset of persons different from the demos is significantly more qualified than the demos to arrive at a correct choice with respect to matters requiring collective decisions. Under the *maximal* interpretation, the members believe that the demos includes all qualified members of the association and all members of the demos are in all relevant characteristics equally qualified with respect to matters requiring collective decisions. Under the *minimal* interpretation, no members of the association are in any relevant characteristic so clearly more qualified as to justify their making the decision for all the others on the matter at hand.

A government of any association in which these conditions are judged to exist is, on these matters, a *putatively democratic government in relation to its demos*. Thus a judgment that these conditions exist implies a rejection of claims that might be advanced on behalf of a government over the demos on these matters by a putative aristocracy, meritocracy, or governing elite.

The doctrine of procedural democracy holds that for any putatively democratic government, collective decision-making by the demos should satisfy at least three criteria:

1. The criterion of political equality. *The decision rule for determining outcomes must equally take into account the preferences of each member of the demos as to the outcome. To reject this criterion is to deny the condition of roughly equal qualification, taken all around. This criterion implies that the procedures and performance of any putatively democratic government ought to be evaluated according to the extent to which the preferences of every member of the demos are given weight in collective decisions, particularly on matters members think are important to them.*

2. The criterion of effective participation. *In order for the preferences of each member of the demos to be equally taken into*

account, every member must have equal opportunities for express-
ing preferences, and the grounds for them, throughout the process
of collective decision-making. This criterion implies, then, that any
putatively democratic government ought to be evaluated according
to the opportunities it provides for, or the costs it imposes on,
expression and participation by the demos.

3. The criterion of enlightened understanding. *In order to*
express preferences accurately, each member of the demos ought to
have adequate and equal opportunities for discovering and validat-
ing, in the time available, what his or her preferences are on the
matter to be decided. This criterion thus implies that any putatively
democratic government ought to be evaluated according to the
opportunities it furnishes for the acquisition of knowledge of ends
and means, of oneself and other selves, by the demos.

Any government that satisfies these criteria, and only such a
government, is *procedurally democratic in relation to its demos*.

As the doctrine is interpreted here, the demos defines itself.
This is one of the trickiest and most difficult aspects of democratic
theory and practice. Because the demos defines itself it need not
include all the members of the association who are obliged to obey
its rules. Whenever this is so some members of the association,
who are excluded from the demos, will also be excluded from the
rights, opportunities, and protections of procedural democracy.
Probably no association that has ever attempted to constitute a
government for a state has admitted children into the demos. Now
if children are excluded from the demos because they are judged to
be unqualified, and yet are subject to the laws, then of course they
are governed without their consent. Yet few of us would argue that
the interests of children, inadequately as they are often protected,
would be served better if they were made full voting members of
the demos. To protect the rights, needs, and interests of children
we must rely not on procedural democracy but on the strength of
adult feelings toward children of love, nurturance, pity, joy,
compassion, and hope, and on laws and practices that these
feelings may foster.

It is a very different matter with adults, among whom these
feelings are ordinarily much too weak to ensure adequate protec-

tion for those who may be excluded from the demos. Consequently we need to make explicit in the doctrine a proposition that has often been omitted or obscured. To do so requires a fourth criterion, that of *inclusiveness*: the demos ought to include all adults who are obliged to obey the rules of the association. Because the demos is inclusive, the criteria of procedural democracy apply to all the adults. Any government that satisfies all four criteria might be called a *full procedural democracy*.

One further point: Probably no one who believes that full procedural democracy is a relevant aspiration thinks that it must hold for all matters, including judgments on highly technical, judicial, and administrative matters of every kind. Rhetorical assertions that seem to make procedural democracy the only proper method of making decisions have again and again been shown to be illusory and self-defeating. Yet as with the problem of inclusion, there is an exceptionally tricky problem here, one that can be dealt with only summarily in this essay by stipulating a fifth criterion, that of *final control by the demos* ("popular sovereignty"). That is, the scope, domain, and procedures for making decisions other than by full procedural democracy are subject to decisions made by full procedural democracy. An association that satisfies all five criteria might thus be called a *fully democratic association in the procedural sense*.

Before turning to the implications of this doctrine for the United States, let us consider several objections. It is often said that procedural justice, and thus procedural democracy, will not guarantee substantive justice. This is true. It is said further, however, that as a consequence substantive justice should take priority over procedural justice and therefore over procedural democracy. This is partly right but mainly wrong. It is partly right because procedures should be judged by the ends they serve. Procedures that do not tend toward good ends cannot be judged good procedures. But the criticism is mainly wrong in implying that other solutions, particularly solutions that accept the claims of a putative governing elite, are more likely to lead to substantive justice. This is rarely a better short-run solution and practically always worse in the longer run. Finally, it is said that procedural democracy is in any case too anemic in its standards to compel us toward the robust aspirations of our nobler selves, for it speaks only to process and thus says nothing about the content of a good society. This criticism is only partly right in its premise and thoroughly wrong in its conclusion. It is obvious that all societies, including our own, fall very far short of satisfying the criteria of procedural democracy. If we in this country are to reduce the gap between criteria and performance in a large way, we shall have to make changes of great moment. What is more, these changes will have the effect of satisfying many of the claims for substantive justice as well. Such claims as could remain would constitute the very essence of healthy controversy—controversies that are properly adjudicated by means of procedural democracy and not by yielding to the claims of a putative governing elite or allowing a minority to impose its views on a majority.

Needs and Prospects

Suppose we were to interpret our first two historic commitments, taken together and after eliminating the inconsistencies, as a commitment to procedural democracy. Suppose further that we were to test our commitments against the requirements of this doctrine. Suppose, finally, that we resolved to move toward procedural democracy by reducing obstacles to it, at any rate up to some limit at which the trade-offs in other values became excessive. Given these suppositions, what changes would we make? Of course not everyone accepts these suppositions; and even if they did, we might disagree about the answers. We might disagree both because the location of the limit at which trade-offs become excessive cannot be satisfactorily described in a precise way, and also because different persons will evaluate the trade-offs differently and thus reach different judgments about the location of the limit.

Nonetheless it is possible to specify some directions in which changes are needed. At the outset these require changes in the way we think about ourselves and our institutions.

Consider the liberal thrust of the first historic commitment, to the preservation of morally inalienable rights. Such rights are assumed to be beyond the reach of government, and superior to any claims to other rights that conflict with them. But it has never been clear what rights are to be understood as inalienable or primary, and what rights are secondary and alienable and hence must yield when they conflict with primary rights. The difficulty is that the grounds are not at all clear on which the distinction between primary and secondary, or inalienable and alienable rights, is to be made and justified.

Yet the conditions and criteria contained in the doctrine of procedural democracy are very rich in their implications for rights. For example, any judgment that the conditions for a putatively democratic government exist among some set of persons asserts a right to a government that satisfies the criteria of procedural democracy. Obviously an assertion never establishes the validity of a claim. As with other rights there is no automatic, self-enforcing determination of the validity of a claim. Judgments have to be made, and among a large number of people such judgments will rarely be unanimous. Claims may be rejected, justly or unjustly. Rights asserted usually have to be fought for.

Consider claims advanced on behalf of adults excluded from the demos that they are qualified to participate in American political life. The whole burden of American experience demonstrates not only that any group of adults excluded from the demos will be lethally weakened in its own defense, but also that those who govern will fail to protect the rights, needs, and interests of the excluded group. There is no convincing evidence in American history for the existence of one group of adults qualified to rule over adults who are excluded from full citizenship in the demos.

Yet for two hundred years after the lovely universalistic phrases of the Declaration, the wellsprings of American national life were poisoned by the denial of claims to full citizenship, and by the injustice and oppression this denial entailed. To reject these claims, as American policy and practice did, was in effect to deny that full procedural democracy ought to exist in the United States. If we are now on, or past, the threshold at which claims are finally accepted as valid, then we are also obliged to accept the criteria of procedural democracy as valid measures of our national performance.

These criteria imply the existence of a body of primary rights, the rights necessary, though not sufficient, if a people is to govern itself. It could be readily shown that this body of primary rights must include most, though not all, of the rights and liberties the Supreme Court has held to be protected by the Constitution. As long as the primary rights necessary to procedural democracy exist, then all political rights exist that are necessary if a people is to govern itself. Surely no narrower definition of inalienable rights ought to be acceptable to us. At the same time, however, any broader definition that includes rights inconsistent with these primary rights ought not to be acceptable to us. For to claim a right inconsistent with the primary rights necessary to procedural democracy is to deny the validity of procedural democracy and thus the capacity and right of a people to govern itself. If doctrine and practice were to treat these primary rights as inalienable, then all claims by rights inconsistent with these primary rights would be subject to final determination by the ordinary processes of collective decision-making, and thus by voters, representatives, and legislators. To hold otherwise would be to deny that, taken all around, citizens are roughly equally qualified to make judgments on matters involving secondary rights. But since practically any public policy will infringe on someone's existing privileges and thus give rise to a claim that a right has been diminished, if citizens are held to be incompetent on all matters involving secondary rights, what matters are they qualified to decide?

Viewed in this light, the commitment to corporate capitalism needs to be reconsidered. Earlier, when the framers had discussed their fears about majorities that might invade the rights of minorities, more often than not they mentioned rights to property. Their reasoned justification of a right to property, if they held one, would no doubt have been Lockean. Yet the Lockean justification of property makes no sense, it was suggested earlier, when it is applied to the large modern business corporation. It is absurd to regard as inalienable one's right to buy and thereafter own shares in ITT, and it approaches the ridiculous to argue that because one owns shares in ITT one possesses an inalienable and exclusive, if in practice quite useless, right to choose the directors of the firm, and that the primary legal obligation of the directors and management is, by a legal extension of the original doctrine, to protect the interests of owners above those of any other claimants.

If we abandon the absurdities in extending Locke on private property to ownership or control of the modern business corporation, then the rights of owners must be seen as secondary in relation to the primary rights that are necessary to self-government.

If ownership and control of corporate enterprise are matters of secondary not primary right, then the mere assertion of a right to private property does not provide a rational justification for private ownership of a large economic enterprise. If privately owned enterprise can be justified at all, it must be on the grounds of comparative social effectiveness: that is, of all the possible alternatives, this form provides the greatest social advantage with least social disadvantage. The only question we need to ask, then, is whether a privately owned corporation is more effective in achieving our social purposes, including procedural democracy, than all the possible alternatives to it.

In this perspective, any large economic enterprise is in principle a public enterprise. It exists not by private right but only to meet social goals. Questions about these social goals, and the comparative advantages and disadvantages of different forms, are properly in the public domain, matters for public discussion, choice, and decision, to be determined collectively by processes that satisfy the criteria of procedural democracy.

To be sure, none of this implies a direct answer to the question of how a large enterprise should be organized, controlled, or owned. To arrive at a correct answer depends as much on technical as on philosophical or ideological judgments, and perhaps a good deal more. Although this assertion contradicts a nearly universal dogma held on all sides, it is readily demonstrable by even the briefest consideration of the range of alternatives. If we were to take into account only the most obvious possibilities with respect to the internal government of enterprises, external controls, markets, prices, and the locus of ownership together with the rights and obligations of owners, we would quickly arrive at a very large array of theoretically possible combinations. Few of these can be dismissed a priori as unsuitable. Probably none can be shown to be superior to all others in all circumstances. Consequently what has already become standard practice in advanced countries in this century will, one hopes, be taken for granted by citizens in advanced societies in the twenty-first century: a complex society cannot protect the rights, needs, and interests of its people with one single, prevailing form of economic organization but requires instead a network of enterprises organized in many different combinations of internal government, external controls, and ownership.

In choosing among the large number of possible combinations available in any particular instance, however, citizens of a country committed to procedural democracy would obviously want to avoid consequences adverse to procedural democracy. I suggested earlier that this country's commitment to corporate capitalism resulted in at least two such adverse consequences. As to those resulting from the unequal distribution of political resources, a country committed to procedural democracy must either place effective limits on the extent to which economic resources can be converted into political resources, or else ensure that economic resources are much more equally distributed than they are in the United States at present. So far we have tried only the first; that approach has largely failed. Perhaps it may prove possible by regulation to reduce the direct and indirect impact on political equality, effective participation, and political understanding of vast differences in income and wealth, but the record so far is dispiriting. It is time—long past time—to consider the other approach. Moreover, considerations of substantive distributive justice would seem to require a considerable reduction in inequalities in wealth and incomes. At the very least the question of distribution of wealth and income ought to be high on the agenda of a national politics.

As to the second of the adverse consequences of corporate capitalism, the enormous expansion of hierarchical systems of control, we need to be open to new ideas about governing economic enterprises and to a rapidly growing body of experience and experiments in this country and abroad. I believe that the requisites of procedural democracy hold for the people who work in economic enterprises, and that the criteria of procedural democracy ought therefore to be applied to the government of firms. But a reasonable claim can be made for each of many other possibilities. Moreover it seems obvious, though often ignored, that forms of control are not fully determined by forms of ownership. Government ownership is as consistent as private ownership with despotic control of enterprises. The form of control should be treated as a problem that is prior to the question of the form of ownership. What is a desirable form of ownership ought to be viewed, at least in part, as subordinate to and dependent on a judgment as to what is a desirable form of control. In any case the range of alternatives this country ought to consider and experiment with is really quite broad and needs a great deal of systematic study.

Let us now turn back to the fourth and fifth historic commitments of the United States mentioned earlier. It is not an excessively harsh judgment to say that over three decades the presidency was transformed into a kind of plebiscitary principate with despotic tendencies toward arbitrary, ruthless, and self-aggrandizing exploitation of power. What is more, the other major political actors, including the Congress, the Supreme Court, the parties, the electorate, and the most active and attentive political strata all collaborated in that transformation. Only with the utmost reluctance and in the final hour was the Congress compelled to rediscover in the impeachment process a constitutional means for firing a president guilty of criminal acts. Now that that process has been used successfully and shown to be effective and salubrious, it is not too much to hope that the machinery will be kept oiled and ready for use. No president should ever again forget that he or she is anything other than the chief executive officer of a democratic republic.

If one part of the Constitution has proved to be workable, the fact that there was a need for impeachment proved how badly the constitutional system had been working. Yet nothing has changed in the fundamental institutional structure itself to reduce the pressures toward the pseudodemocratization of the presidency. For it still remains true that without a strong concentration of political resources in the presidential office, the policies preferred by a majority of citizens and their elected representatives stand a good chance of defeat by a well-entrenched opposition. Not only is this arrangement inconsistent with procedural democracy but it is arbitrary and unfair in its substantive results. Moreover taken over any considerable period of time the evidence does not show that these minority vetoes constitute a defense of primary rights; rather they tend to ensure the triumph of secondary rights or privileges over primary rights.

Taking all these problems into account, political scientists need to begin a serious and systematic reexamination of the constitutional system much beyond anything done up to now. They need to give serious and systematic attention to possibilities that may initially seem unrealistic, such as abolishing the presidential veto; creating a collegial chief executive; institutionalizing adversary processes in policy decisions; establishing an office of advocacy to represent interests not otherwise adequately represented in or before Congress and the administrative agencies, including future generations; creating randomly selected citizen assemblies parallel with the major standing committees of the Congress to analyze policy and make recommendations; creating a unicameral Congress; inaugurating proportional representation and a multiparty system in congressional elections; and many other possibilities. Unfortunately designing a constitution is very far from an exact science. It is questionable whether the best political scientists, or for that matter citizens drawn from any source, have the knowledge and skills to exceed the performance of the framers. Probably we do not even know how best to proceed toward the cultivation of the knowledge and skills of constitution-making that we or our successors may one day be expected to provide.

The difficulty of arriving at knowledge of this kind points directly to the most challenging of the criteria of procedural democracy, the criterion of enlightened understanding. The criteria of political equality and effective participation are intended to ensure that citizens have a final say as to the goals that effectively determine the ends of public policy, and whenever they wish a final say as to the means as well. But if a people were to meet these criteria perfectly and yet meet the criterion of enlightened understanding badly, the democratic process would be irrelevant to their preferences, needs, and interests. For if people regularly choose means that impede rather than facilitate attaining their goals, or if they invariably choose goals that damage their deeper needs, then of how much value is the process?

The criterion of enlightened understanding is not only the most difficult to meet but the most resistant to precise statement. Every key word in the criterion as it was presented earlier is ambiguous, and the concepts the words are intended to signify are difficult and complex. However, even if it might well be impossible to define the criterion so rigorously as to specify quite precisely what we would regard as a condition of satisfactory fulfillment, it is a much less difficult task to judge when the criterion is *not* satisfactorily met and what some of the obstacles are. Surely it is far from being satisfactorily attained in this country and elsewhere.

In a loose and general way it is obvious that if people are to know their preferences, they need knowledge both of means and ends. Adequate knowledge of means and ends requires an understanding not only of the external world but also of the inner world of the self.

It seems obvious too that if citizens are to understand the external world they must have access to experts. It may have been realistic for Rousseau or Jefferson or the framers but it would be profoundly unrealistic today to expect citizens, even highly educated ones, to have enough technical knowledge. Think of the complexities of current policy decisions: breeder reactor, B-1, Trident, Middle East, catalytic converter, inflation/unemployment trade-offs, rate of increase in the money supply, costs and administrative problems of alternative health-care arrangements, SST, Amtrak, limitations on artificial losses, outer continental shelf. . . . Most of the time all of us are ordinary citizens without a great deal of technical knowledge about such matters. Consequently whatever may have been the situation in previous centuries, in our own, and surely in the next, it is foolish to think that the demos can achieve its purposes without experts.

Yet even in the best of circumstances experts are hard to control. Decisions as to means can also determine ends. Democracy only for general ends and meritocracy for means will soon become meritocracy for both means *and* ends. Thus if the demos is to retain final control over ends, citizens will also need responsible and responsive intermediaries—quasi-experts—to help them hold experts accountable, and to gain an adequate understanding of their own basic rights, needs, and interests, and of the policies best designed to satisfy these needs. Even if all our elected officials were to perform this intermediary role well—and many do not—they would not be enough. We need quasi-expert intermediaries spread among the whole body of citizens, so that every citizen has ready access to technical understanding. While it is surely asking too much to expect that most citizens can be experts on many of the issues of national politics, it is not foolish to hope that one day almost every citizen might be sufficiently informed about some of the issues so that a less informed citizen could readily turn to a more informed fellow citizen, a quasi-expert, for a responsible clarification of the matter at hand.

When we turn toward the inner self and ask what we need in order to understand the needs and interests of the self, including those crucial aspects of oneself that are inextricably bound up with and require a sympathetic understanding of other selves, we confront a question to which the answer is inescapably open-ended. The answer must be open-ended because at any given moment human consciousness is necessarily limited by itself, that is, by its own condition. It seems not wildly unrealistic to hope that in the epoch ahead human consciousness will change profoundly, and that what we might now consider as enlightened understanding, and the best ways to reach it, will be seen by our successors in a vastly different perspective. If mankind is spared as much time as separates us from Socrates, or even as brief an interval as separates us from the historical situation that necessarily limited the understanding of Mill, Lincoln, Freud, and Marx, we cannot say what vast transformations human consciousness may undergo. The criterion of enlightened understanding beckons us forward but it cannot tell us what we shall discover.

It goes without saying, of course, that the world is full of the most acute dangers to human progress and even to human survival. More perhaps than at any time in some millions of years the prospects of humankind depend on the outcome of a perilous race in which the growth of an enlightened understanding of ourselves and our universe is pitted against the consequences of actions taken out of ignorance or misunderstanding of our most fundamental needs and interests.

No matter what it does, this country alone cannot ensure a successful outcome to that race, though we can by our own unaided mistakes cause a fatal outcome. Some Americans may be tempted to conclude that in a world so hazardous, our salvation and that of the world require us to bring the rest of humanity rapidly around to our way of thinking. But experience suggests that when Americans, or anyone else for that matter, begin to talk about a national mission to save the world, it is time for everyone to run for cover. Instead one might propose a very different approach. If we want to move a bit closer toward the best standards to which we are already committed by our national experience, a good way to start is not so much by trying to change others as by changing ourselves.

Philip Green

What Is Political Equality? A Reply to Dahl

WHAT is political equality? Any simple definition of such a vague concept is unlikely to be more than a slogan. We must begin somewhere though, and Robert Dahl's essay "On Removing Certain Impediments to Democracy in the United States" offers an excellent starting point, for which we should all be grateful.

Professor Dahl is the leading theorist of modern American liberalism, and in his most recent work he has tried mightily to escape from the inhibiting confines of that philosophical stance. As we shall see, the escape is finally unsuccessful. Dahl's conventionally liberal understanding of "political equality" prevents him from breaking decisively with the kind of polity, marked by polarities of domination and subordination, inclusion and exclusion—all in the name of "representative government" —which he rightfully styles "pseudodemocracy." Yet it is helpful to engage in a critique of his effort, not because he is so far from a useful solution to the problem of achieving democratic equality but rather because he comes so close to it. His failure has its roots in two aspects of modern liberalism (or its philosophical twin, social democracy): its atomistic individualism, and its concomitant concentration on distribution as the key variable in the search for alternative social formations.

The criterion of "political equality," Dahl writes, is that the "decision rule for determining outcomes must equally take into account the preference of each member of the demos as to the outcome. To reject this criterion is to deny the condition of roughly equal qualification, taken all around." To this criterion Dahl adds two further criteria that would satisfy what he calls "the doctrines of procedural democracy." These are the criterion of "effective participation," by which he means that "every member [of the demos] must have equal opportunities for expressing preferences," and the criterion of "enlightened understandings," which requires that "each member of the demos ought to have adequate and equal opportunities for discovering and validating, in the time available, what his or her preferences are on the matter to be decided." And in a general discussion of what these criteria might imply about the social order, he writes:

> If privately owned enterprise can be justified at all, it must be on the grounds of comparative social effectiveness: that is, of all the possible alternatives, this form provided the greatest social advantage with least social disadvantage. The only question we need to ask, then, is whether a privately owned corporation is more effective in achieving our social purposes, *including procedural democracy*, than all the possible alternatives to it. . . . To be sure, none of this implies a direct answer to the question of how a large enterprise should be organized, controlled, or owned. To arrive at a correct answer depends as much on *technical* as on philosophical or ideological judgments, *and perhaps a good deal more.* . . . If we were to take into account only the most obvious possibilities with respect to the internal government of enterprises, external controls, markets, prices, and the locus of ownership together with the rights and obligations of owners, we would quickly arrive at a very large array of theoretically possible combinations. Few of these can be dismissed a priori as unsuitable. . . .
>
> In choosing among the large number of possible combinations available in any particular instance, however, citizens of a country committed to procedural democracy would obviously want to avoid consequences adverse to procedural democracy . . . [a] country committed to procedural democracy must either place effective limits on the extent to which economic resources can be converted into political resources, or else ensure that economic resources are much more equally distributed than they are in the United States at present. . . . At the very least, the question of distribution of wealth and income ought to be high on the agenda of a national politics. . . .
>
> Government ownership is as consistent as private ownership with despotic control of enterprises. The form of control should be treated

as a problem that is prior to the question of the form of ownership.
. . . [Emphasis added throughout.]

If we begin where Dahl begins, we must certainly agree that the
"condition of roughly equal qualification" is, as Bentham long ago
asserted, the *sine qua non* of political equality. But it cannot be
political equality, any more than the right to hold a job "is"
economic equality. It is in the pursuit of this distinction that we
discover that a "procedural" definition of political democracy is
unsatisfactory, and that whatever the "technical" advantages of
the privately owned or controlled corporation might turn out to
be, the latter can only be the enemy of political equality, not its
potential handmaiden.

The right to a job is not economic equality because, by virtue of
circumstances most of which are out of our individual control,
some of us have financial or physical investment capital, others
have realizable skills, and still others only salable labor power.
Each of these quite different types of "human capital" provides,
on the average, a quantitatively and qualitatively different return.
It is important to note the qualitative aspect of class differentiation. Those with capital have greater access to the wellsprings of
economic and social life—power over the determination of its
contours, in sum—than do those with mere skills, and the latter in
turn have more economic power than do wage-laborers.

In this respect "political man" is analogous to "economic man,"
and the maldistributions of political as well as economic power are
therefore secondary to the existence of social classes that set
boundaries to one's political existence. In failing to discuss class
rather than distribution Dahl has missed the most crucial point.
This failure, a commonplace of liberal theory, renders his definition of "political equality" otiose.

In the political realm, capital exists in the form of built-in access
to decision-makers. That excess is not uniquely available to
members of the capitalist class, but they are its chief possessors. A
good many more of us possess realizable political skills: the trained
capacity to do research, argue effectively, work with compilations
of esoteric materials, write well, etc. But by far the greatest
number possess only *voting power*—the "right" of "equal partici-

pation." To be fair, Dahl obviously considers a much broader range of factors than mere suffrage as elements of equal citizenship, but in the end his conception of civil rights extends only to those aspects of citizenship that make possible the kind of "participation" we have learned to expect from representative government: being heard, or unheard, as an individual.

Yet individual voting power (or the power to engage in any similar form of "participation") is strikingly different from the control of social capital or the possession of an individual skill. The former especially, but the latter also, gives a direct return to the person who has them. By virtue of his ownership or control of capital the capitalist is sure to have either his individual interests, or his version of society's general interests, attended to with great particularity. By virtue of their ownership of a politically useful skill the members of the professional or paraprofessional political class also have access to decision-makers, though usually only insofar as their ideas and skills are useful to those with more power than they have themselves. Besides, skilled persons also hold the bulk of political jobs; they fill secondary positions of authority merely by virtue of their skills, and thus develop some degree of political power on that basis.

In sum for both those classes, though clearly for one much more than the other, the factor-shares model of neoclassical economics works well in the political realm (with hardly any metaphorical component at all). The capitalist gets political profit, the possessor of skill gets the political version of economic rent (as the skills are fairly widespread, the rent is minor by comparison with the profit of the much rarer capitalist). But the factor-shares model works for the average voter, as for the average worker, in a different way.

By far the greatest number of voters possess neither capital nor a particular skill but only their voting power. This power, unlike capital or skill but much like labor power, creates "products" that pass out of our grasp as soon as we have made them. These products are not commodities but rather are office-holders, and as Rousseau argued two centuries ago, the moment we install them is the very moment in which we lose whatever power we had over them. From being a real individual at the moment of voting I become part of a hypothetical mass, relevant as a mass to the office-holder's desire for reelection—no more. Nothing about me as a person enters into what might be called the calculus of reelectability (indeed if I knew the office-holder as a candidate but on a merely personal basis, then the act of election depersonalizes that very relationship); nothing about me as a person enters into the office-holder's decision-making calculus. Yet it was my personal act that helped create the office-holder. Rather than belonging to me (to us, the whole class of merely individual voters) and becoming a potential extension of our joint human powers, the office-holder—the voters' "commodity"—is installed by us in a realm that is apart from and even potentially opposed to us.

The vote, of course, can hardly be deemed worthless, for otherwise the struggles to possess it would not be so prolonged and bloody. But the concrete marginal return from that vote diminishes sharply with each additional group. And when all groups finally share in the game of representation they benefit, on the whole, only to the extent of their social positions rather than, as liberal mythology would have it, because of their actual number. To return to the level of metaphor, those who possess nothing but the vote are political wage-earners, and their labor-power does not earn a return equivalent to a capitalist's political investment: yet why should it, since to vote, or even to write a letter to one's "representative," is to "do" virtually nothing by comparison to what the possessors of capital or even of skill can do. The voter's "product" is alienated precisely because voters are not able to engage in the kind of political work necessary to make it their own; and thus, as producers, voters are devalued by those who truly govern.

YET, this alienation of the voter's commodity from the voter is perfectly compatible with Dahl's seemingly egalitarian decision rule of "procedural democracy." There are two reasons for the inadequacy of Dahl's procedurally individualist, value-neutral approach to political equality, and the two are closely linked. The first often has been noted by critics of Dahl: there is a class of people who set the authoritative agenda of politics that is different from the class of those who merely "prefer" or "participate." Not that there is a hidden conspiracy of the wealthy to place some issues "on the agenda" rather than others, nor is it even that some people find access to decision-makers more difficult to obtain than do others. Surely the latter condition always does hold in "pseudodemocracies," and so often also does the former. But in both cases Dahl could plausibly argue that some individuals (*Homo politicus*) simply maintain a higher level of interest than will the mass of the electorate (*Homo civicus*)—who can, however, insert themselves into the democratic process whenever they really desire to get together and do so.

Dahl did in fact argue exactly this point in his well-known book *Who Governs?* Indeed there he seemed tacitly to endorse the crude formulation of his ex-student Nelson Polsby that if, say, poor people fail to vote in large numbers it must be because they think they have something better to do on election day. He now seems to realize that there is a difficulty in his earlier reasoning, but he still has not perceived the necessity for a structural account of why some people voluntarily become *Homo politicus* and others do not. (What corporate leader ever turned down an invitation to a meeting at the White House because he had something better to do that day?) Trying now to be an egalitarian, he proposes the provision of an opportunity for "enlightened understanding" to everyone (for realizing that it is time to become *Homo politicus*), almost as though enlightenment were a freely available consumer good. But now, too, he fails to perceive a second and even deeper pitfall of liberal individualist theory.

The problem is that information-gathering entails costs that most people usually do not wish to incur. Two centuries ago Bentham and Hume made the point unarguably: if knowledge of their self-interests is what most people pursue, they will never be able to play an "equal" part in the definition and pursuit of general interests.

If governance must wait on the acquisition of an enlightened understanding of their own interests and of the general interest by all, it will never take place. If political institutions can be democratized only by equal and "enlightened" participation through voting—which is what taking into account the preference of each member of the demos must surely mean—then we are left with the unavoidable conclusion that democracy disappears every time mass voting does not govern decisions directly, or every time unenlightened mass voting does, or every time large numbers of people don't bother to vote. That is to say, we are left with the unavoidable conclusion that all of Dahl's definitional egalitarianism is beside the point, for egalitarian democracy cannot exist.

Dahl himself is really aware of this tendency in his argument, and this becomes plain when we compare this latest work to his earliest theoretical statement about democracy, *A Preface to Democratic Theory*. In this work he offered eight characteristics, or conditions, of what he called polyarchal (liberal and pluralist) democracy. These conditions, he said, must exist "in a relatively high degree" for a system to be called polyarchal. Among them are the following:

> 4. Any member who perceives a set of alternatives, at least one of which he regards as preferable to any of the alternatives presently scheduled, can insert his preferred alternative(s) among those scheduled for voting.
> 5. All individuals possess identical information about the alternatives.
> 6. Alternatives (leaders or policies) with the greatest number of votes displace any alternatives (leaders or policies) with fewer votes.
> 7. The orders of elected officials are executed.

"Polyarchal democracy" indeed is a strange conception. If mass voting is the ultimate act of sovereignty then none of these "characteristics" can possibly characterize the polity (except to some extent no. 6). Dahl himself asserted that the condition he describes in no. 4 exists "in no organization of which I have any knowledge," and that "much the same remarks apply to the fifth condition."

Having said as much, Dahl went on to present polyarchal democracy as a model to be approximated "as closely as possible." He then offered as examples of democratic polyarchies

> certain aspects of the governments of nation-states such as the United States, Great Britain, the Dominions (South Africa possibly excepted), the Scandinavian countries, Mexico, Italy, and France; states and provinces, such as the states of this country and the provinces of Canada; numerous cities and towns. . . . [The] number

of polyarchies is large [he added, but the] number of egalitarian polyarchies is probably relatively small or perhaps none exist at all.

But these rules for egalitarian polyarchy are equivalent to the criteria of "political equality" and "effective participation." To say that the former do not and probably cannot exist is to say the same of the latter.

Dahl's problem—the problem of liberal theory in general—is that an individualistic approach to political equality contradicts the egalitarian ends. If Dahl's earlier statement of the conditions of political equality were to be consistent with the realities of liberal individualism, it would have to be rewritten as follows (and these are of course my own rough formulations). In a polyarchy:

4. Only a relatively few powerful members of the society can insert their preferred alternatives among those scheduled for voting—otherwise voters, being a mass, would overload the voting system with their individual preferences. Those men and women who are either far from the institutional heart of the system, or lack access to the media of mass communication, can hardly ever affect the choice of alternatives that are to be presented to them.

5. Individuals possess unequal information about alternatives: those for whom voting is the only or chief act of commitment to politics cannot possibly have adequate information about the range of policies, and about the precise options realistically available in each policy area, that are going to be acted on by political leaders. Conversely, those close to the institutions of governance must have superior information about available policy choices.

6. Alternative leaders with the greatest number of votes displace any alternative leaders with lesser numbers of votes. But since they were voted on only as potential leaders, and are the executors of a myriad of policies about which the electorate cannot possibly be closely informed, there is no reason to believe that the detailed policy preferences of the electorate, if one could know what those actually were, will govern their actions.

7. The orders of elected officials are sometimes executed. But rarely are they executed when those officials, whose only mandate is a loosely expressed popular vote, come into conflict with other

officials or citizens who have a high stake in a specific policy and the resources to back up their preferences.

In other words, in striving to equate the impact of *individual* acts of political preference, we really *eschew rather than approach* political equality—to produce precisely "pseudodemocracy."

All the above reformulations, in the end, are only an updated version of Gaetano Mosca's insight that an unorganized mass can never control a cohesive elite. We do not need to accept Mosca's further assertion that any society must always be divided into a mass and an elite. But it would be absurd to deny that—where the political structures of a society incorporate a voting mass on the one hand, and a relatively separated elite of decision-makers and those persons with whom they directly interact on the other hand—Mosca's denial of the possibility of democratic equality must hold good. Polyarchy as a system of competing elites with slightly different preferences on certain issues can and does exist; polyarchy that approaches the realization of Dahl's conditions "in a relatively high degree" is a contradiction in terms.

To repeat, if institutions can be democratized only by the vote, they cannot be democratized inasmuch as preferences can never enter the decision-making system through the mechanism of voting. The extreme Rousseauian individualism of Dahl's formulation about political equality, which makes it so attractive at first glance, is precisely its irremediable flaw. In any social unit larger than the commune, to prescribe that "the decision rule for determining outcomes must equally take into account the preference of each member" is to prescribe total chaos. A decision-making system based on that rule can only work if the rule itself is not really observed—if the system is pseudodemocratic rather than democratic. Dahl's critique of pseudodemocracy is certainly one of the most trenchant ever produced from within the liberal tradition—but by setting up impossible standards the critique turns on itself and ends in an implicit denial of the possibility of real political equality, even if that is not what Dahl intends.

THE approach to political equality via conventional liberalism— an approach that by its nature, as it turns out, can only fail to attain its object—leaves us with a critical insight: whatever political equality is, it cannot be something that is obtained by maximizing individual choices. The equality referred to must exist among groups, or communities, to which people belong by virtue of their work, or place of residence, or any other fundamental way in which they define their lives. Above all else then, prescriptions for political equality must be aimed not at minimizing inequalities among individuals but at minimizing inequalities among *classes*. Only then might the inhabitants of such communities have truly common interests that can be represented to the outside world without every single individual necessarily possessing an equally "enlightened understanding" of those interests; and only then might communities be represented by persons who do not have fundamentally divergent interests from theirs.

Here too Dahl's formulation is finally unsatisfactory. It is certainly a long and useful step from the traditional recommendations of liberalism to his endorsement of some aspects of democratic socialism: yet a lingering value-neutrality with respect to economic organization ("few of these can be dismissed a priori as unsuitable") and an unrealistic concentration on "redistribution" undercut its potential impact. To begin with, when we think about democratic political economy with class relations rather than distribution in mind, we see that one "theoretically possible combination" with respect to the governance of enterprises can and indeed must be ruled out *tout court*—despite the "technical" advantages it might occasionally demonstrate. *The existence of any large-scale productive enterprise supplying social necessities,* which is operated according to rules formulated independently of the people who work in it, live around it, or otherwise rely on it in any decisive way, is incompatible with political equality.

The multiple qualifications in the italicized phrase are essential, not incidental. The philosophy of political equality is not a philosophy requiring absolute equality in the realm of income, or the abolition of money or of the division of labor in the workplace. It does require the abolition of particular kinds of class division, but only insofar as they have political implications. A brief review of some inequalities that do *not* have political implications will highlight the areas in which drastic change is necessary, and those areas in which it is not necessary, in order to achieve political equality.

First, the small, owner-operated firm (or retail establishment), which employs casual local labor, does not create cumulative inequalities unless such firms form part of a more complex system of dual labor markets. Under corporate capitalism the dual labor market is a restrictive device. Collusion between job- and income-protective labor unions and profit- or stability-maximizing managements tends to exclude those who are defined as "nonproductive" workers from both the organized core industries and the skilled trades, which on the average offer both much greater long-term job stability and much greater pecuniary reward to labor than does the less articulated, more chaotic secondary market.

In the secondary market some workers make a temporary and genuinely voluntary commitment: college students, would-be artists, etc. But many others are locked into a less rewarding and more isolating job structure through no choice of their own. Except for some bleak Soviet anti-Utopia of gigantic GUM department stores with endless lines of would-be consumers, there will always be a peripheral sector and a secondary labor market —not merely because of consumer pressure but because there will always be workers and entrepreneurs who prefer the more independent and casual style of the small parochial enterprise. But if they are in the secondary sector involuntarily, then political equality has been denied them, for they are frozen by no choice of their own into a way of life that precludes effective organization and economic pressure (except for small-enterprise owners at the small-town level).

The critical condition that alone could make the existence of a dual labor market compatible with the demands of political equality, then, is that the primary labor market be open to anyone who prefers instead a life of organized work in large-scale, high-paying productive enterprises with established democratic relations among workers and managers. Put most simply, small private firms at the periphery of the economy, employing labor according to the hierarchical principles, do not interfere with the search for political equality as long as job provision, for all who want it, takes precedence over "marginal productivity" at the democratically controlled core.

The same considerations hold, it seems to me, for organizations that are less directly "productive," such as those that provide services. If the public schools of a nation are run in such a way that teachers have no say in their operation, then something like a political class division is created. Society at large must deal solely with a stratum of principals, school superintendents, etc., who have the kind of social power that we associate with ownership or control of the means of production: they control a vital resource. On the other hand if there are only a handful of preparatory schools run by autocratic headmasters who manage to attract, on a voluntary basis, like-minded (or submissive) staff, no harm is done to the polity at large.

Second, the existence even of quite large firms under strictly private control is compatible with political equality if those firms supply society with luxuries rather than necessities. If, for example, we now imagine the present lifestyle of Americans transposed to a realm of political equality, we might surely be able to say that the existence of a supply of small power-boats at a price low enough to be afforded by the average skilled worker might be a part of the way we then would live, make our lives more enjoyable, and would be intimately and naturally related to the existence of an immense number of glacial lakes and rivers on the North American continent. Luxurious ocean-going yachts, however, will never be a mass-consumer product, and neither their availability nor their nonavailability has the slightest effect on an estimation of the pleasures that are a part of the way we live now. Monopoly in the production of such yachts, therefore, would be completely trivial, and the monopolist who escaped from the strictures of public control would harm no one. Moreover since this product would be socially irrelevant, he could not possibly accrue any political power (except in a community of the wealthy, and if any such existed we would surely not worry about the democratization of their public lives). In other words—just as the theory of political equality is indifferent to the quality of truly voluntary relationships among workers and owners, so is it indifferent to the quality of truly voluntary relationships among suppliers and consumers.

Third, the notion of political equality is also indifferent to the existence of (relative) individual wealth based neither on exploitation of workers nor on extortion from consumers. The Emersonian injunction to reward the builders of better mousetraps appears as a historical accompaniment to the birth of American capitalism, but it does not have to be linked to that kind of inegalitarian social formation. If a people decides, upon serious reflection, that the price of a desired amount of technological advance is the provision of an economic incentive to inventors, it cannot reward them with sole control over the development of "their" technique without also giving them an excess of political power. But if inventors, instead of being rewarded with an exclusive property right that translates into personal or corporate political influence, indeed are rewarded with a lump-sum payment enabling them to retire on the spot to the Riviera, no political harm is done. Moralists of all kinds, and especially socialists who insist on wearing a Puritan's hairshirt, might raise objections. But it cannot be said that society is allowing a separate class to develop in its midst, for consumption differences do not cut people off from each other the way classes related to productive work do. The lifestyles of consumption classes are more or less like each other, but they are not essentially incompatible.

The same considerations apply, obviously, to those who make their fortune by marketing their personalities or entertainment skills to the public at large. Again only a (perhaps) defensible, but politically pointless, moralism objects to the special reward that such persons can gain in capitalist society (or even in contemporary Communist society, though less of that reward takes a monetary form). Certainly there can be no objection that they are "unproductive": so was the get-rich-quick inventor of the hula hoop, and he probably provided less pleasure to American society than did Willie Mays. As an aesthetic matter the existence of riches in the midst of poverty must always be offensive (except to those who are tone-deaf to all considerations of decency). But whereas wealth made in manufactures and resource development or in the provision of such necessities as housing is directly related to, and in some senses causative of, the existence of mass poverty, the wealth of the beautiful individual lies mostly outside the causal nexus of "poverty amid plenty."

THIS discussion of exceptions, then, suggests a rule for any definition of political equality. If people attain their most effective relationship to political life not as "individuals" but rather as the members of communities, then the communities that make up a society must themselves be of roughly equal effectiveness. If that is to be the case, the membership of any *economically* differentiated community must be voluntary, in the sense that the difference is desired by the members of the community rather than imposed on them willy-nilly.

Of course there will always be inequality among communities of people, especially to the extent that communities define themselves geographically, for different geographical communities are based on different physical resources, some much more valuable to the world at large than others. To say this is no more than to say that "the state," that is, some locus for the resolution of conflict, cannot wither away. There will always be accommodations to be reached between the controllers of different resources, and to imagine that accommodations will be reached by means of the formulation of a set of bargaining rules to be observed by all—rather than by an endless series of ad-hoc fights—is to imagine the existence of public political institutions.

The existence of such a "state" is perfectly compatible with political equality, as long as we understand that political equality does not, cannot, and need not ensure absolutely equal outcomes from all social bargains. After all, the classical theorists were correct in arguing that, under ideal conditions, "free trade" will secure the real exchange of equivalents among communities with different resource bases. Although the usefulness of this metaphor, within or among self-defined national communities, is presently limited by the existence of deforming, and man-made, regional imbalances ("uneven development"), it is only in extreme cases of imbalance that the relations among regions would "naturally" be those of dominance and subordination rather than merely quantitative advantages or disadvantages (and a community so resource-poor that even in an egalitarian society it could not strike a decent bargain for itself would simply be deserted). In that sense, indeed, "life is unfair": but it is not necessarily oppressive.

Yet the existence of the kind of state with which we are presently familiar (and of which Marx spoke in his few utterances on the subject) is *not at all* compatible with political equality. For our state exists chiefly as a locus for the resolution of conflicts between and within the social classes generated by the institutional structure of capitalism—and those social classes by their nature, as we have seen, provide political dominance for some and political exclusion for many others. More: Social classes under capitalism are neither regional nor sectional. Each (except for that of the totally excluded) has interests that lead it to aim at dominance. The corporate capitalist class penetrates and dominates the state in order to protect the productive relations of capitalism, and the resultant distribution of power, from attack; the middle class and the working class seek to penetrate the state in turn, in order to protect themselves against corporate capitalism (and sometimes against each other too). As a result the capitalist state *is* necessarily oppressive, since not accommodation but dominance is the purpose of controlling it.

Moreover the capitalist state is also necessarily undemocratic in a fundamental sense. Except under unusual conditions of social cohesion and primary resource abundance (as in Sweden and Norway), governors who are constrained by the legal relations of capitalism cannot really engage in the planning required to wipe out regional and other disparities caused by uneven capitalist development. Those relations require of the "owner" merely that he make a competitive profit, and if a different kind of behavior would maintain or improve present rates of profit, it would already have been undertaken.

Again, of course, one group of capitalists can make mistakes and be less productive than possible, and other capitalists can help them use the state to improve or relocate their operations—that kind of "planning" (on the French model) is always possible under capitalism. Ultimately, too, simply outrageous behavior in the pursuit of profit, even when the latter is legitimized by all the laws and customs of a society, will cause a dangerous backlash, so that profit-seekers are occasionally disciplined, or warned off before they can go "too far." But in both these respects the voting mass again operates simply as an amorphous, abstract threat, possessing only reactive political power by virtue of its mass existence but hardly any initiatory power at all. The authoritative owners of capital, by contrast, hold society to ransom without ever lifting a finger.

In sum, liberal fury at Charles Wilson for his injudicious remark that "What's good for General Motors is good for the country" has always had a good deal of self-deception in it, since the injudiciousness of Wilson's remark is precisely that he was speaking the truth. It is not even conceptually possible to discuss a hypothetical "bankruptcy" of General Motors, for that would be a consequence, not a cause, of the "bankruptcy" of the United States. The U.S. government must pay attention to any claim made by General Motors' management about the viability of their industry. For in the government's view nothing can be allowed to harm the competitive position of the American auto industry, its ability to provide both mass employment and mass consumption, to enable the government to fend off further balance-of-payment disasters, etc. After serious scrutiny state officials might find that the corporate managers' claims were actually wrong (that is, not factual), but this would demonstrate merely that the latter had been mistaken, not in what is "good for the country," but in what is "good for General Motors." A different vision of "the corporate good" would be substituted for that of GM's managers, but it would emanate from the same interests: and this is what it really means for a class to have "political" power.

General Motors, furthermore, is defined by the financial and productive capital it commands, and by its organization for producing and distributing—not by the bulk of the human beings who actually work for it. Unlike all but the worst-off regional communities, the members of the economic working class —which, politically, also is a great part of the voting mass—have little to bargain with in the struggle for political power (and the class of truly marginal persons cast aside in the pursuit of individual economic betterment has nothing to bargain with at all, except their bodies and lives). They are largely interchangeable and dispensable. They can threaten to strike, but that is a greater threat to themselves than to the polity at large, and is thus credible only when restricted to a predefined set of situations involving only limited demands.

The main resource of the powerful, by contrast, is that, given capitalist relations of production, they have legal command of "large-scale productive enterprises supplying social necessities," and that the law not only permits them to "operate independently of the people who work for them, live around them, or otherwise rely on them in any decisive way," but actually supports that independence against attempts to penetrate it with the armed might of the state. Therefore a class of people who, as Marx said, contribute nothing to actual production (except to satisfy the legal requirement that there be a private owner) but have formal control of all the proceeds from it *must* dominate the capitalist state regardless of whether the people who man political offices are from Harvard, Georgia Tech, the local commercial college, or even the executive offices of a labor federation. As long as the production of autos and associated goods is legally under the control of private "owners," nothing can be done about its organization that does not meet with the owners' final approval —else they will take their products or their profits or even their actual plants elsewhere.

Whereas the great historical general strikes of labor have usually been disasters for the working class, the general strike of owners of capital is constantly in the wings, and in some nations, such as Great Britain, government is permanently constituted by the necessity of preventing the export of capital, no matter what political party is in power. To overcome the advantages of entrenched class positions through the mechanisms of either industrial militancy or the vote—through mass mobilization—is, though possible, both painful and time-consuming; and thus a society in which class conveys the advantages of entrenchment to a few is not and cannot be politically egalitarian.

THUS when Dahl calls for a redistribution of wealth and income ("economic resources"), and then adds that "the form of control should be treated as a problem that is prior to the question of the form of ownership," he still, it seems to me, has not grasped the real problem. Neither redistribution nor "industrial democracy" will take place to any significant extent as long as the present legal relations of corporate capitalism persist. For those legal relations, which legitimize the private ownership and deployment of capital, entail the economic and political division of labor by classes. In an individualist society the point of corporate ownership and control is to have power, both over the workplace and over the nation. Take away the reward and no one will want to do the job—who would be a "private" or even "public" manager of capital if the only substantial reward were to be hounded by works committees, citizens groups, and so forth? No doubt the political power of those who control the lifeblood of a nation's economy can never be eliminated. The crucial question is whether control is in the hands of the few, a separate and ultimately independent class, or is shared among various publics operating when practically necessary through delegates but retaining the legal powers of ownership.

It is of course historically quite true, as Dahl says, that "government ownership is as consistent as private ownership with despotic control of enterprises," but this is not nearly as true of community or cooperative ownership. In any event the road to political equality can only lead through some form of democratic public control of the core economy, and that requires the abolition of private ownership at the core. Socialization, of course, would only be the first of many tortuous steps necessary to make sure that the kind of "pseudodemocratic" representation we are presently familiar with in the political sphere does not simply replicate itself in the corporate sphere (as has happened, notoriously, in Great Britain, France, and Italy).

But how essential the first step is we can best see by way of an apparent paradox. In no sphere are the dangers of public control of capital more obvious than with respect to the media—such as television and the press—which provide information on a mass basis. Here more than anywhere traditional liberalism would properly have us guard against the tyranny of a centralized bureaucracy. Yet, plainly, the monopolistic control of the provision of that information by a handful of rich men makes political equality impossible. The democrat may agonize about *how* to take control of these agglomerations—but not *whether*.

FINALLY, we must emphasize one other element in our search for a usable definition of political equality. We have seen that communities of choice, rather than idealized but actually powerless individuals, are the only possible building blocks of genuine political equality. We have seen also that any hope of achieving roughly equal bargaining and exchange among such communities requires the abolition of the social class known as "owners of the means of production" (they being defined as those persons who have effective legal control over the core sectors of national or local economies), for owners divert the sources of communal strength to their own class uses, thus favoring some communities, despoiling others, and reducing everywhere the political role of nonowners to a secondary or even nonexistent status.

But there remains yet another class division that Dahl does not discuss at all and that is highlighted by this emphasis on communities. In their interchanges all communities must be represented —be they great or small, watershed areas or city blocks, giant factories or collections of craftspeople—just as *within* such communities individual members will often require representation in dealing with each other. Whatever methods we devise for delegation and rotation in office, the permanent requirement of representation in some manner or other defines the social class division between experts and their clients (which includes the division between representatives and constituents). This is the politicized form of what Marx called the division between mental and physical labor, which obviously carries with it a tremendous potential for freezing in place another form of political inequality. This potential exists when we speak of an elected works manager or a local civil servant as much as it does when we speak of an independent, self-employed professional or a "faceless bureaucrat."

What distinguishes all members of this class from the traditional working class is that the latter has no means other than the self-denying weapon of the strike of imposing its will on either employers or employers' customers. The professional salariat, by contrast, makes rules that the rest of us must obey, and quite independently of whether it is overworked or underpaid by some general social standard. Moreover, however "democratic" our intentions there is nothing even in small-scale human relationships that necessarily conduces to client control over experts, or community control over elected representatives where the representation is itself based on expertise; and there is much that militates against it. As Nicos Poulantzas has remarked about the "neo-technocratic talk of a State which . . . is administered by left experts and controlled simply through the mechanisms of direct democracy," the picture conjured up is one of technocrats

> flanked by [self-management commissars]—a prospect which hardly frightens the various specialists, who are even manifesting a sudden passion for self-management because they know that, at the end of the day, the masses will propose and the State will decide.

Obviously the problem is an immense one (much more troubling in fact than the problem allegedly posed by the class division between "owners" and "workers," which is based on an entirely artificial distinction). It is a problem not susceptible to solution by formula. Still, the previous discussion suggests a possible argument. If political equality is realized through membership in communities, and if the expert-amateur distinction is (often, if not always) real, then experts must be of and by rather than merely "for" communities. All our notions of the training of experts must be turned around. An understanding of the notions of service and representation has to replace the acquisition of technique as the first skill demanded of the professional; and the opportunity for training must be something both desired by individuals and given to them by communities that wish to be represented, rather than being the product of nothing but the drive to advance private interests.

So we come full circle in our escape from the constricting individualism of the liberal version of political equality: abolish the primary social-class division and we can begin to attain the equality of communities. Thus communities can begin to regain control of the ways in which their needs are met and participate equally in attenuating the force of the secondary social-class division. None of this requires the utopian achievement of an end to the division of labor, or the abolition of careers or professions or (unequal) incomes. But political equality does require that a citizenry find democratic ways of training "experts," installing them in office, overseeing their performance, and removing them; and that it not think of political, professional, or managerial life merely as a series of individual incentives and rewards.

If we are truly locked into the way of life of individualism we will not, of course, give it up in response to moralizing appeals. If we come to see, however, that this way of life is not compatible with real political equality, which is also an ultimate good for millions of people in all the liberal societies, then we will at least be able to confront a basic choice with an understanding of the issues that does not effectively preclude one resolution altogether.

Meanwhile, democrats should not concentrate their efforts (which are bound to be chimerical), on finding ways to increase individual participation or enlightenment in Dahl's sense. Rather we should encourage and if possible participate in the kinds of spontaneous community or workplace organizations, with their demands for direct representation in decision-making, that have been bourgeoning all over the world in the past dozen years; and we should support as well public attacks and inroads on corporate power wherever they appear.

Robert A. Dahl

In Rebuttal

I APPRECIATE the opportunity to clarify some of the questions raised by my essay and Philip Green's comments.

I am not surprised that Professor Green has misunderstood my description of the democratic process, for the account given in the article is highly condensed and incomplete. In one crucial detail it is potentially misleading. If a reader as deeply informed on these matters as Professor Green has misunderstood my argument, others may also. I want therefore to add a few words that may help to clarify my account.

My purpose was to provide a description of the democratic process at the limit of possibility. The criteria I offered may be thought of as ideal standards against which to evaluate the performance of an existing process, institution, or regime, and possible alternatives to them. From certain assumptions not set out there, I derived five criteria that a democratic process ought to satisfy:

1. *Equality in Voting:* The rule for determining outcomes at the decisive stage should take into account, and take equally into account, the expressed preferences—the vote—of each citizen.

2. *Effective Participation:* Throughout the process of making binding decisions, each citizen should have an adequate opportunity, and an equal opportunity, to express his or her preferences as to the final outcome, including an opportunity to place questions on the agenda.

3. *Enlightened Understanding:* In order to express one's prefer-

ences accurately, each citizen ought to have adequate and equal opportunities for discovering and validating, in the time permitted by the need for a decision, what one's preferences are on the matter to be decided.

4. *Final Control of the Agenda by the Citizens:* The citizens ought to have the exclusive opportunity to decide what matters are to be, or are not to be, decided by means of the democratic process.

5. *Inclusiveness:* The citizen body (the demos) ought to include all adults subject to the laws, except transients.

A process satisfying these five criteria would be, in my view, fully democratic. I do not see how anything less could be judged fully democratic, and I do not see how any process could be more democratic. Whether any large group of persons could govern themselves by a process that was *fully* democratic seems to me rather doubtful. Nonetheless we may judge processes and regimes as relatively more democratic, or less, according to these criteria. If the democratic process were our sole standard (which I doubt), we could judge a process or regime as better or worse to the extent that it satisfied, or failed to satisfy, the criteria.

Of course we live in a world of unsatisfactory processes, institutions, and regimes. In my view some are considerably worse than others. Moreover we can conceive of very much better processes, institutions, and regimes that may be within our capacities to attain.

Regimes in various countries that we tend to call democratic are, by these criteria, really not very democratic. Yet I do not believe that all regimes are equally undemocratic, nor, I imagine, does Professor Green. Regimes with certain institutional guarantees that provide considerable freedom of expression, fair and frequent elections, a plurality of political parties, toleration of organized oppositions, and so on, seem to me more democratic according to the criteria than regimes that lack these institutional guarantees; they are, to that extent, better. I prefer to call regimes of this kind *polyarchies*. There is a view on the left, represented most clearly by orthodox Leninism, that the political institutions of polyarchies—"bourgeois democracies"—are a contemptible sham, in practice no different in nature or value from openly authoritarian regimes. In my view this has been a tragic misconception. Polyarchies *are* more democratic than authoritarian regimes, and to that extent they are better.

Yet polyarchies are not sufficiently democratic. They all fall far short of the criteria for a democratic process. They ought to be democratized further. How they can be democratized further is a problem to which both Professor Green and I seek solutions.

THE misleading detail in the account given in my essay* has to do with the label I attached to criterion 1. Though I defined it in the same way, instead of "equality in voting" I called it "political equality." One problem in discussing political ideas, and certainly in any discussion of democracy, is that a very large number of key terms are jampacked with meanings, ambiguities, and emotions. Political equality is surely one, and I should have foreseen that the term would produce misunderstanding.**

However, the essential point is not the label, after all, but the meaning it is given. The meaning is clear enough: a process ought not to be called democratic unless the vote of each citizen is counted as equal with that of any other citizen. The requirement is hardly original with me. Nevertheless it appears that Professor Green considered the label rather than the definition, and understood me to mean that equality in the voting is the whole substance of "political equality" in the much broader (and more ambiguous) sense. The matter seems clear enough to me, but if Professor Green was misled then no doubt other readers were also.

Let me now try to erase the last shadow of ambiguity. If I understand Professor Green rightly, he does not believe that individual equality in voting is a necessary condition for

---

*For those who might be interested, a fuller version has since become available. "Procedural Democracy," in James Fishkin and Peter Laslett, eds., *Philosophy, Politics, and Society,* Fifth Series (1979). Even in this more complete account, however, I excluded several crucial problems that I hope to deal with in the larger work of which it is only a part.

**Unfortunately I continued it in the later article, where, however, the fuller account may help to prevent misreading its meaning.

democracy—or for "political equality" in the broader sense. I shall come back to his own solution later. Meanwhile let me state unambiguously that I do indeed believe that individual equality in voting is a *necessary* condition for democracy. But it ought to be perfectly obvious that it cannot be a *sufficient* condition. For many additional conditions are required, including, I believe, the other four criteria for the democratic process.

I am not sure how much of Professor Green's criticism arises from his supposing that I meant to define equality in voting as not merely necessary but sufficient for democracy and for political equality in the broad sense. Evidently that confusion is the source of a good deal of his concern. To that extent his criticism is misconceived.

AMONG the many conditions necessary to the democratic process it is obvious that the socioeconomic order must be of crucial importance. Moreover the question of the best socioeconomic order lays a claim on our concerns to some extent independent of the question of the democratic process. The universe of important values does not consist only of the values of the democratic process. However, in my article my intentions were limited to the narrower problem: If Americans were to take the values of the democratic process seriously, what obstacles would we need to remove and what alternative arrangements would be better?

Here I think Professor Green misunderstands the argument of the essay, as I think he misunderstands what I have written elsewhere. I do not believe that democracy requires capitalism, and never have. Where I may differ from Professor Green is in thinking that the relation between democracy and the socioeconomic order, far from being as clear as orthodox socialists and antisocialists seem to believe, is highly problematical.

For its time, a form of agrarian capitalism based on rather widespread ownership of farms was relatively favorable to democracy in the United States, as it was also in a few other countries such as Norway. But that kind of agrarian capitalism was uncommon. In any case it was historically ephemeral. The system of corporate capitalism that replaced it is much less favorable to the democratic process, not least because it generates greater inequalities in political resources.

In my view in a modern economic order that would be more congenial to democracy the economy would have to be seen as essentially public or social, not private. Enterprises would be understood to be social, not private. The economic "surplus" above survival needs that is available for increased consumption, investment, public goods, and savings would be viewed as a social product jointly created by a multiplicity of social factors—not merely entrepreneurial or managerial inputs, or for that matter only labor inputs. In such a society people would take it for granted that economic activity was a matter not of private concern and private control but of public concern and public control.

This view may not be too different from Professor Green's. However, to say that the economy ought to be viewed as public, not private, is not a solution; it is only a beginning. Where Professor Green and I disagree, I expect, is regarding the nature of a desirable solution. For one thing I believe it has been simplistic and unproductive for advocates of capitalism and socialism to focus so much attention on ownership rather than on control. Unless one is quite clear about questions of control—how decisions are to be made that govern particular enterprises and the larger coordinating functions of the economy—the consequences are likely to be disastrous, not only theoretically but, what is more important, in practice. In considering alternative economic systems one needs to give high priority to two central questions about control over the economy: *Who* should control decisions about inputs, outputs, prices, allocations, investment, locations, and so on? And *how* can this control actually be exercised? We are unlikely to discover satisfactory answers in the ideologies of the nineteenth century. At this late stage in the twentieth there is too much concrete experience available to allow ourselves the vague generalities that once might have been acceptable.

To be sure, within the limits of his comments it would be unfair to expect that Professor Green would describe his solution in much detail. It is not unfair, however, to suggest that he should have openly confronted a difficulty with his solution that many readers will find profoundly troublesome and some may regard as lethal to his proposal.

LET me now turn to that problem, and to a point on which we flatly disagree. In more than one place Professor Green rejects the value of political equality among individuals, which he seems to regard as a lamentable legacy of obsolete liberal ideas. His own solution, if I grasp it correctly, is to provide equality not among individual persons but among communities:

> Communities of choice [he writes], rather than idealized but actually powerless individuals, are the *only possible* building blocks of *genuine* political equality. [It is therefore only by abolishing] the social class known as "owners of the means of production" [that we have] any hope of achieving *roughly equal* bargaining and exchange among such communities.

Now there happens to be a fundamental dilemma of political life of which Professor Green does not warn us. Without being precise about the exact nature of the relation, we can all readily agree that political equality must be a relation of equality among units of some kind. Suppose we were to define that relation of equality without specifying the units: the units might be individuals or they might be collectivities. Unless it should happen that the collectivities are all equal in the number of persons they contain, the following is obviously true: it is impossible that political equality exists simultaneously among individuals and among communities (or other collectivities). One *necessarily* excludes the other. The reason is self-evident. If Community A consists of 100 citizens and Community B of 1000; if the two communities are to be politically equal; if their equality includes something like equal power in voting and bargaining; and if their equality in voting and bargaining produces something like equality in exchange or allocations, then at the individual level each citizen in A counts for much more than each citizen in B, and presumably gains more from their transactions.

Hidden in this conception of collective rather than of individual equality is a curious, rather corporatist notion of justice. In effect

Professor Green tells us that justice does not require equality or equal bargaining power among collectivities. To put it in another way, equality among collectivities is given priority over equality among individual persons.

As a general principle this is open to so many objections and difficulties that it finally verges on absurdity. To begin with, the fundamental conception of justice that it violates is more than simply liberal. I think that virtually all important views about justice have held that the good of each human being ought to be considered of equal value, and no human being ought to be considered as *intrinsically* more valuable than another. If Professor Green proposes to replace the good of individual human beings in moral reasoning with the good of collectivities, I hope he is prepared to take on quite explicitly the task of showing us why we should accept his principle of justice and reject that of almost all moral reasoning. As it stands his principle seems to be simply arbitrary.

But aside from this philosophical problem, his principle encounters a host of practical difficulties. For one thing it provides no solution to the problem of the relations that ought to prevail *within* each of his communities. I imagine that he would recoil from the *reductio ad absurdum* of his argument. Would he insist that *within* each political community the "only possible building blocks of political equality" are still smaller communities? Sooner or later we shall have to reach "communities" of one person.

If we try to apply his solution *within* a community, then it looks to be self-contradictory or vacuous. Surely a process for making binding decisions within one of his communities, if it were to be democratic, would have to satisfy my criteria, not his. And must these criteria not include, among other things, equality in voting?

Again, Professor Green's voluntary communities evidently could vary indefinitely in size. The size of a community would be quite arbitrary. But if the size of the community were arbitrary, would this not make allocations and distributions arbitrary also? If resources are bargained over, and communities are roughly equal in their bargaining and exchange, as he says, then individuals in the smaller communities would, as we have seen, acquire more resources than individuals in the larger—concretely, I suppose, more per capita for education, medical care, housing, and so on. Is this not a strange principle of distributive justice?

Let me mention one more defect. If the size of a community were not fixed, then the unhappy consequence I just mentioned would tend to produce another. There would be very strong incentives for larger communities to split endlessly into smaller communities. In fact it is hard to see how the process could ever stabilize or where it would end. It is possible that Professor Green believes that the unseen hand of competition among communities would somehow yield a rational and desirable outcome, but if so he ought to explain how this would come about.

ALTHOUGH he is in my view quite wrong in proposing that *as a general principle* political equality among communities ought to override political equality among individuals, he is quite right in saying that democratic ideas and practices are bound to be unsatisfactory unless they provide for communities—to which I would add other kinds of groups and associations as well. (Let me simply use the term associations as a label for these smaller groups within the larger polity—communities, collectivities, subsystems, organizations.)

Since my account of the democratic process did not speak to the question of associations, it is to that extent incomplete, and what is more, defective. To complete the account in a satisfactory way is a task far beyond the limits of an essay, and far more complex than may be commonly supposed—as I am only too painfully aware, since it is a task in which I am engaged. Even so, a word or two may help to clarify the main points of agreement and disagreement between Professor Green and myself.

It is a serious defect of democratic ideas that from the Greeks to Rousseau, for the most part they did not allow sufficiently for the presence of associations within the state. In its philosophical origins democratic theory tended to be strongly monistic: there were individuals and the state but (other than the family) not associations. We have not yet learned theoretically, or in practice, how to deal with the presence of associations, that is, with pluralism. Once one concludes that democracy must allow for associations, then formidable questions arise, as Rousseau clearly understood in his attack on associations. As Rousseau also understood, associations are a natural part of human existence and would be inevitable in a democratic polity larger than a very small city-state, perhaps no bigger than a village. Whenever an attempt is made to institute democratic process on a scale larger than, say, a village, then a variety of associations will exist, each partly autonomous in relation to the others and to the state. If I understand his argument rightly, Professor Green's communities are intended to reflect this assumption.

The trouble is that any polity containing a number of somewhat autonomous associations is prone to certain problems. There is the problem that Professor Green has in mind: inequalities may —probably will—develop among the associations; and there is the problem I had in mind: these inequalities in turn will produce morally unacceptable inequalities among individuals. In addition there is the problem exhibited every day in pluralist orders. To put the problem in classical terms, how are the particularistic ends sought by the associations and their members to be reconciled with the good of others and, finally, the good of all?

Now it is a common error of socialists to think that a socially owned and controlled economy would, somehow, miraculously solve such problems. I cannot say whether Professor Green believes this to be true, though he sometimes sounds as if he does. In any case it is a dangerous illusion. To be sure, as we all know an authoritarian regime could provide for "social" ownership and control of the economy, and deny autonomy to associations and organizations of all kinds, including economic enterprises, political parties, and local governments. Democratic socialists are inclined to deny that this would be socialism—and clearly it would not be democratic. But if autonomous associations and organizations *are* permitted to exist, then social ownership will not rescue a democratic socialist order from the problems of pluralism. One may of course simply stipulate that what one *means* by such an order is that these problems no longer exist, or that "socialist consciousness" would have eliminated them. But to solve problems by stipulation is not to solve them at all.

Such relevant experience as is now available confirms my

forecast. Although so far as I am aware no country exists that combines a socially owned economy with a democratic polity, the experiences in East European countries where liberalization and decentralization have gone furthest show pretty decisively that the problems of pluralism transcend economic orders.

This is not to say, certainly, that all solutions to the problems of pluralism are equally good or bad. Professor Green and I would agree, I think, that solutions requiring the suppression of all autonomous associations are very bad indeed. Certain changes in structures and in civic consciousness that democratic socialism might help to bring about could also make the problems of pluralism less virulent and intractable. Yet I think the problems will still be serious enough, for they are bound to arise in any attempt to apply democracy on a large scale, and therefore to allow a variety of autonomous associations and organizations to exist.

In clarifying his account of a society that is both socialist and democratic, as I hope he does, Professor Green is going to have to come to grips with these problems. Though he may not altogether appreciate my saying so, he will discover that at heart he is really a pluralist. And as a democrat he will have to confront the problems that are bound to exist in any system of democratic pluralism. I wish him luck.

Michael Walzer

Politics in the Welfare State: Concerning the Role of American Radicals

ONE day, not soon, the welfare state will extend its benefits to all those men and women who are at present its occasional victims, its nominal or partial members. That day will not be the end of political history. But it will represent the end of a particular history, and one in which socialists have been very much involved, if not always on our own terms.

It is worth reflecting on what that day will be like—what will we want *then?*—even while we fight to perfect the system of benefits and argue among ourselves about the best strategies. For we are not entering, we are not going to enter, the new world of state-administered prosperity all at once. It is in the nature of the welfare state, I think, that men break into it in groups, some sooner, some much later, some with only moderate difficulty, some after long and bloody struggles. Many of us are inside already, better served by machines and bureaucrats than men ever were by servants and slaves. What do we want *now?*

Liberal theorists of the welfare state have always claimed to know what we want. Their work rests on two assumptions: first, that politics ought to be the instrument of human desire; second, that the nature of human desire is obvious. People want pleasure, but such pleasure as cannot be shared, individual delight, egoistic satisfaction. The state cannot at the moment provide any sort of direct delight; perhaps one day it will simply administer the appropriate chemicals to its members. Today it can provide only the material prerequisites of individual delight, that is, first security, and then all those services conveniently grouped under the rubric of "welfare"—education, public health, economic controls, relief for the aged and the unemployed, and so on. These are vitally important services, and liberal theory is vindicated, at least in part, by the fact that they are in great demand. Every attempt to restrict them to selected groups of people has been, and will surely continue to be, resisted. The welfare state has grown through invasion—a clear tribute to its attractiveness.

In the heat of battle, goals have sometimes been suggested which elude or transcend the liberal definition of human desire. Wild hopes for equality and fraternity have been proclaimed. But each success has turned out to be a further triumph for what might best be called political utilitarianism. If we or our ancestors or our comrades in this or that struggle have sought the actuality of freedom and love, we have settled readily enough for the pursuit of private happiness—so readily, indeed, that it would be difficult to deny that private happiness is all we ever wanted.

The cumulative effects, the likely future effects, of these successive triumphs are now becoming visible, even though there are important victories yet to be won (and the last battles may be the hardest). What I propose in this essay is a theoretical examination of these effects, of the welfare state as our collective project, our common future. I want to argue that the success, or the likely success, of welfarism makes necessary (as it makes possible) a new and radical challenge to political utilitarianism. Whatever the nature of our past demands, what we want *next* is not on any of the liberal lists. But first I must try to suggest the enormous achievements and the special characteristics of welfare politics. For we cannot say what it is we want until we have understood what we have got and are getting.

FIRST of all, the development of the welfare state has generated a pervasive enlightenment about the functions of political organizations. For the first time in history masses of men know with absolute clarity that the state ought to be doing something for them. They are rationalists-of-everyday-life, each one demanding, "What has it done for me?" Prewelfare theorists have generally denied the validity of this simple question, insisting that the state always *is* more than it *does*. They have described it as a closely knit body, dense and opaque, whose members were involved emotionally as well as materially, mysteriously as well as rationally, in the fate of the whole. The members ought to be involved, it was said, not for the sake of concrete benefits of any sort, but simply for the sake of communion. Since loyalty was a gift for which there was to be no necessary return, it could not be predicated on anything so clear-cut as interest. It depended instead on all sorts of ideological and ceremonial mystification: anointed kings, oaths, rituals, divine laws, and so on.

The state still does depend on ideology and mystery, but to a far lesser degree than ever before. It has been the great triumph of liberal theorists and politicians to undermine every sort of political divinity, to shatter all forms of ritual obfuscation, and to turn the mysterious oath into a rational contract. The state itself they have made over from a "body-politic" into a machine, the instrument of its citizens (rather than their mythical common life), devoted to what Jeremy Bentham called "welfare-production." It is judged, as it ought to be, by the amounts of welfare it produces and by the justice and efficiency of its distributive system.

Political unreason survives, of course, and especially in the form of an extraordinary devotion to the modern nation-state and to its leaders, a collective zeal all too often unmitigated by individual interest or by any demand for functional transparency. But here too the direction of political utilitarianism is clearly marked out. Thus an eighteenth-century *philosophe:* "What is patriotism? It is an enlightened love of ourselves, which teaches us to love the government which protects us . . . the society which works for our happiness." This definition suggests that many of us are patriotic, if we are, for wrong or inadequate reasons. I will try to describe some of these reasons a little later on.

Second, the expansion of welfare production gives to the state a new and thoroughly rational legitimacy. The state is always immoral when viewed from the standpoint of its invisible and degraded men. Whatever the ideologies of which they are the primary victims, oppressed classes come eventually to regard the claims of their rulers with a deep-rooted skepticism and hostility.

But the claims of the liberals are of a different sort, not mysterious but hypocritical. Therefore the hostility of the oppressed takes a new form: not sullen and inarticulate disbelief, but a positive demand that the claims be realized. Do the middle classes claim to increase the general prosperity? Let them increase *our* prosperity. Do the police claim to defend public security? Let them defend *our* security. Do the rulers of the welfare state claim to maximize the happiness of the greatest number? Let them maximize *our* happiness.

Now insofar as the state becomes a general welfare state, excluding nobody, it meets these demands and so generates a legitimacy such as no previous political system has ever achieved. If no man is invisible, the state is not immoral. The recognition of its members as concrete individuals with needs and desires may seem a minimal requirement of any political system and hardly capable of producing significant moral attachments. In fact, however, such recognition, when it is finally achieved, will be the outcome of centuries of struggle; the right to be visible is always hard-won. And the liberal state which finally recognizes all men and grants them their humanity will inherit from those centuries an extraordinary moral power. The state will never again be so easy to challenge as it was in the days of mass invisibility.

Third, the development of the welfare state has gone hand-in-hand with a transformation in the scale of political organization. This is due not only to increases in the rates of infant and adult survival—the first benefit of the welfare state is life—but also to the progressive extension of political membership to previously invisible men. The tiny political public of an earlier period has been broken into by successive waves of lower-class invaders. It has expanded to absorb each wave; it will probably expand to absorb each future wave.

Liberal theorists and politicians have discovered that there are no necessary limits on the size of the public—so long as its members are conceived as individual recipients of benefits, so long as the problems of political communion, the sharing of a common life, are carefully avoided. Now that there really are concrete benefits to be divided, the first political problem is distribution. And the members of the state, precisely because they are recognized as needful persons, seen by the impersonal public eye and assisted by an impersonal administration, need no longer be able to recognize and assist one another. The size of the citizen body of a Greek polis, like that of an early modern aristocracy, was limited by the requirement that its members be known to each other and so distinguishable from the faceless mass. But once invisibility is banished, the need for political "friendship" is also banished. The members of the welfare state need not have even the most remote acquaintance with each other. And so the welfare state is potentially of infinite extent.

The fourth tendency of successful welfare production is to decrease the importance of politics itself and to turn the state from a political order into an administrative agency. This was always the goal of liberalism and it is the key reason for the liberal insistence on the transparent material purposes of the state. Beyond welfare the liberal state cannot go: the world of the mind, philosophy, art, literature, and religion; the world of the emotions, friendship, sex, and love—all these have been set outside its limits. They have been freed from politics, protected against heavy-handed and intolerant magistrates. Simultaneously, liberal politics has been freed from philosophy, art, literature, religion, friendship, sex, and love.

Politics is now concerned only with the provision of a plentiful and enjoyable external world and with the promotion of longevity so that this world can be enjoyed as long as possible. And it has been the assumption of liberal theorists ever since Hobbes and Locke that once security and welfare were assured, once the utilitarian purposes of politics were achieved, men would turn away from public to private life, to business and family, or to religion and self-cultivation. Indeed it was this turning away —which might be called legitimate apathy since it rests on the satisfaction of all recognized needs and desires—that would assure the stability of the liberal achievement. Conflict would disappear; the state would become a neutral agency for the administration of security and welfare. This was a liberal even before it was a

Marxian vision, as Marx himself suggested when he wrote that political emancipation, as practiced by the liberals, "was at the same time the emancipation of civil society from politics."

The state is an instrument and not an end in itself. Politics is an activity with a purpose and not itself an enjoyable activity. These are axioms of liberal enlightenment; the attack on the opacity of the traditional polity turns out to be an attack on the value of political life. Why should we be active in politics? asked Thomas Hobbes, and his sarcastic reply suggests the central animus of liberal theory:

> —to have our wisdom undervalued before our own faces; by an uncertain trial of a little vain-glory to undergo most certain enmities . . . to hate and be hated . . . to lay open our secret councils and advices to all, to no purpose and without any benefit; to neglect the affairs of our own families.

So long as the state establishes peace and—added later liberal writers—promotes welfare, public activity is a waste of time, positively dysfunctional in the economy of private life. Happiness begins and ends at home. One of the ways in which the welfare state promotes happiness is by encouraging men to stay home. Hence the crucial principles of welfare distribution are, first, that benefits ought to be distributed to individuals and second, that they ought to be designed to enhance private worlds. In the perfected welfare state, enjoyment will always be private; only administration will be public—the policeman and the welfare administrator will be the only public men.

Now obviously this is no description of our present experience. Never in human history has politics been so important to so many people, never have so many been active in politics, as in the past century and a half. Never before has the state stood at the center of so large a circle of conflict, agitation, and maneuver. Politics has been the crucial means of becoming visible, of winning recognition for mass needs and desires. Nor has it been only a means: political activity has also brought the first joyful sense of membership in a community. It has provided the positive pleasures of self-assertion and mutual recognition, of collective effort and achievement.

Unlike the welfare state itself, the struggle groups which have demanded and won the various benefits the state now provides —the unions, parties, and movements—have been shaped to a human scale: their members have also been colleagues; they have called one another brethren, citizens, comrades. For a brief moment in time they created a communion which was not mysterious or opaque precisely because it was a common creation.

As the organizations of the oppressed win their battles, however, they are gradually integrated into the system of welfare administration. Their purposes are not given up, or not wholly given up, but rather give rise, under new circumstances, to new organizational forms: the struggle groups become pressure groups. Public life ceases to engage the minds and emotions of their members; local activity drops off; popular participation declines sharply. The tenacious sense of detail peculiar to highly qualified bureaucrats replaces the enthusiasm of members: it is more useful, even to the members themselves.

The pleasures of political struggle cannot be sustained once victory has been won. And it is in the nature of the infinitely expandable welfare state that victories can in fact be won. Thus it happens that communion is replaced by distribution, generalized aspiration by concrete expectation. Erstwhile militants are isolated and immobilized by the sheer size of the state into which they have won admission, mollified by its apparent legitimacy, by the obvious sincerity of its administrators and the transparency of their purposes. The history of the welfare state begins with the coerced passivity of invisible and degraded men, mystified by ideology. And it ends, or will one day end, with the voluntary passivity of enlightened men, their human desires recognized and (in part) gratified by the public authorities. So, at any rate, we have been led to believe by liberal writers.

What more can we possibly ask?

ALL these developments—the growing rationality and legitimacy of the state, the vast increase in its size, and the decline of political life—are not only compatible with classical liberal theory but actually represent its fulfillment. But there is one further corollary of welfare production which raises the most serious problems for liberalism: the growth of state power.

There can be no question that the development of welfare programs has involved (or required) an extraordinary expansion of the machinery of everyday state administration and therefore an increase in the degree, intensity, and detail of social control. In part this increase stems directly from the progressive enlargement of bureaucratic systems and from improvements in the training and discipline of their personnel. But it is also closely related to the very nature of the utilitarian service state and to the character of the political struggles of the past century and a half.*

For all that time liberals (and socialists too) have been like that character of Gogol's who "wanted to bring government into everything, even into his daily quarrels with his wife"—though some of them would have stopped short at the seat of domestic bliss. Everywhere else the agents of government have been invited to roam. This was true even during the brief moment of *laissez-faire,* for the restrictions on commerce which were then overcome were largely local and corporate, and only the central government could overcome them.

Indeed the state has been an instrument absolutely necessary to reformers of every sort: it shatters the authority of local and traditional elites; it destroys the old corporations and regulates the new ones; it establishes minimal standards for masses of men whose own organizations, however powerful, cannot do so by themselves; it protects racial and religious minorities. It is, so to speak, the crucial licensing agency of modern society, increasingly the only one; it accords recognition, turning oppressed subjects into full-fledged members. And it absorbs the power of every defunct agency as it wins the support of every newly enfranchised member.

Nor is its usefulness at an end. Given the continued creation of new groups, the continued raising of the level of material desire, the perfection of welfare production may well be an asymptotic goal and the state an eternally progressive force. But this does not mean that the character of political struggle will remain unchanged

---

*The single greatest factor in the expansion of state power has, of course, been external war, and it is probably true that the greatest dangers posed by the modern liberal state are not those which its own citizens must face. But I have, perhaps arbitrarily, excluded foreign policy and war from this discussion.

as new groups and new desires replace the old. For from a certain point in time the new groups will almost certainly cease to have the same communal structure as the old. The deprivations of their members are more likely to be experienced by each man in his private, state-protected world, experienced simultaneously but not shared.

Thus the black is one kind of invisible man, bound to his fellows in a community of suffering and anger and therefore capable of collective action. The man who drives a dangerous car or breathes polluted air is another kind, largely unaware of the risks he shares with others, only marginally aware of the existence of others, and probably incapable of significant efforts on his own behalf. Precisely because of the privatizing results of the benefits he has already won (his automobile, for example), he now stands alone and helpless in the face of one or another sort of corporate power. He is dependent on the muckraking of freelance journalists and academic experts and, much more, on the benevolence of the state.

This benevolence has its price: the increased power of the benevolent administrators, the increasing control over the recipients of benefits. Perhaps the most impressive feature of modern welfare administration is the sheer variety of its coercive and deterrent instruments. Every newly recognized need, every service received, creates a new dependency and so a new social bond.

"A wife and a child are so many pledges a man gives to the world for his good behavior," wrote Jeremy Bentham. This is true only insofar as the world—economy and state—actually provides or promises a decent living to the wife and child. If it does, the pledge is serious indeed. And the better the living the world promises, the more good behavior it requires. Welfare politics thus has a dialectical pattern: pressure from below for more protection or benefits meets pressure from above for better (more disciplined, or orderly, or sociable) behavior. A balance is struck, breaks down, is struck again. Each new balance is achieved at a higher level of welfare production, includes more people, provides new reasons (and new sanctions) for good behavior.

Eventually every antisocial act is interpreted as a demand for increased benefits. So it is. And so welfare is the obvious and only antidote to delinquency and riot. For who would be unwilling, if actually given the chance, to pay the price of social discipline, orderly conduct, hard work, and public decency for the sake of the pursuit of happiness? Only much later does it turn out that the price and the purchase are very nearly the same thing. Happiness *is* good behavior, and this equation, fervently endorsed by the authorities, is the ultimate sanction.

Like the public recognition of needs, so the recognition of men—our hard-won visibility—becomes a source of intensified social control. Never have ordinary citizens been so well-known to the public authorities as in the welfare state. We are all counted, numbered, classified, catalogued, polled, interviewed, watched, and filed away. The IBM card is the very means of our visibility, the guarantee that we are not forgotten among so many millions —even as it is simultaneously a symbol of our bondage to the bureaucratic machine.

Invisible men are invisible first of all to the officials of the state (and that is a worse bondage). Precisely because they are not seen as citizens, they are exposed to arbitrary cruelty and neglect. Because they are not numbered, they are always treated *en masse*. Because they are never polled, they are thought to have no opinions. Even their crimes, so long as they injure only one another, are not recorded. When their country goes to war, they are impressed (that is, kidnapped), but not conscripted. Gradually, with the development of the welfare state, all this changes. An extraordinary traffic opens up between the visible and the previously invisible sections of society. Individuals and groups win public recognition, learn good behavior, and march out of the slums and ghettos. At the same time, policemen, census takers, recruiting officers, tax collectors, welfare workers, radical organizers, and sociologists (in roughly that historical order) march in.

In the long run the two parts of society will merge into one world of absolutely visible men (that does not mean a world of equals), known not to each other but to the specialists in such knowledge, not personally but statistically. The universal character of this new knowledge doubtless will protect individuals from magisterial whim and prejudice. That is one of its purposes. But it will also involve a new kind of exposure: to the developing administrative sciences of anticipation and prevention.

"It's the anarchy of poverty / Delights me . . ." wrote William Carlos Williams. He was too easily delighted, or rather his delight was that of an onlooker and not a participant in the "anarchic" culture of the poor. Few men who are actually poor would share it. But having said that, it is still worth adding: It's the regiment of the contented / That haunts me.

LIBERALS have not been unaware of the dangers of administrative tyranny. Wherever possible they have sought to avoid even benevolent regimentation by giving those whose welfare is at stake "sovereign" power, that is, by establishing governments representative of everyone who receives benefits. In the past that has generally meant of all property owners, for they have been the most important welfare recipients. It obviously means more today, though just how much more is unclear.

The expansion of the range of state benefits and the extension of the ballot to new social groups have been parallel and related processes. Suffrage is the first badge of membership; it is a means of winning benefits and also, presumably, of determining their character and the nature of their administration. In practice, however, it is something less than this. "Welfare without representation," Sargent Shriver has said, "is tyranny." That is certainly true. But it is not the case that the only alternative to tyranny is a full-scale democracy.

In theory, of course, the purpose of representative government is to make the mass of people all-powerful. Representatives are to be delegates, asserting popular desires, and then legislators, enacting the popular will. Administrators are to be nothing more than servants of the people, bound absolutely by legislative decree. The quality of security and welfare is thus popularly determined, at only one remove. The government of representatives cannot be made responsible to the people on a day-to-day basis, but its general responsibility can be maintained by periodic elections and, more important, by continuous political activity between elections. The ultimate defense against bureaucratic omnicompetence is the self-interested assertiveness of ordinary men.

If things have not worked out this way, and do not seem likely to, it is at least partly because liberals never developed a system of democratic activism sufficient to bind administrators to representatives and representatives to constituents. Political parties might have served this purpose, but in the U.S. at least, parties have not developed as membership organizations capable of stimulating commitment and action on the grass-roots level. Local politics has never been competitive with business and family. And it has been discovered that the enhancement of private life through public welfare really does not require any very rigorous and energetic self-government. It may well require a period of sustained struggle, but once that has been won, continued political participation (beyond occasional voting) seems unnecessary and even uneconomical.

Nor is it obvious that the closely articulated representative system that might make such activity worthwhile is really feasible, given the potentially infinite size and the extraordinary administrative complexity of the modern state. Administration has already outdistanced every other branch of government in the sheer accumulation of resources: competent staff, statistical knowledge, patronage, fiscal controls, regulatory powers, secrecy when that is required, publicity when it is not, and so on. Legislative activity has ceased in virtually every respect to be the central feature of the governmental process. It has been replaced in part by administration itself, in part by bargaining between state bureaucrats and the (nonelected) representatives of a great variety of social constituencies.

Thus a modern worker or farmer is far more usefully represented, his interests more successfully defended, by the Washington-based lobbyist of his union than by his locally based congressman. This is true even though his congressman is elected in a democratic fashion, while the officers of his union are probably coopted and the lobbyist appointed. It is virtually a law of political life that power be imitated, that those who seek benefits copy the organizational style of those who dispense benefits. Today it is palpably the executive rather than the legislative branch of government that is copied. At least it is copied by those secondary associations already within the welfare system; outside, other models are still possible. In any case the electoral process has gradually taken on the character of an outer limit, a form of ultimate popular defense rather than of popular self-government, while the day-to-day visibility of workers and farmers and the legitimacy of their government are both maintained by processes largely, though by no means entirely, independent of democratic elections. The modern welfare state is an example of limited government, but not yet of popular sovereignty.

THE failure of self-government reveals the fundamental difficulty of liberal utilitarianism. Its standard of utility is the welfare of an individual absolutely free to make his own choices and measure his own happiness. In fact, however, no such individual has ever existed.

Men live in groups and always find that they have limited choices and share, without having chosen, social measurements. If they are ever free to choose new limits and measurements, they must do so in some cooperative fashion, arguing among themselves, reaching a common decision. But to do this, to act collectively like the sovereign individual of the utilitarians, they must share political power. Government must be responsive to their concrete wills and not merely (as at present) to their conventionally defined desires. If they do not share power, they inevitably become the prisoners of the established social systems which they invade or into which they are admitted.

State recognition of new groups obviously affects the structure of social power and value, but there is very little evidence to suggest that it does so in fundamental ways. It clearly does not do so in the ways anticipated during the long struggles for recognition, that is, it does not open the way to social and economic equality. The welfare state has turned out to be perfectly compatible with inequality. Bureaucratic benevolence even bolsters inequality insofar as it neutralizes the struggle groups, decomposing and privatizing popular willfulness. Fundamental social change would require that the state embody this willfulness, inviting its new members to choose their own limits and measurements. This it does not, perhaps cannot, do.

Instead welfare administrators function, whether consciously or not, as double agents: serving the minimal material interests of the invaders and upholding at the same time the social system that is being invaded. That is why welfare administration, especially in its more direct forms (social work, for example), tends so generally toward paternalism. The administrators are committed in advance to the common limits and measurements, to the established modes of security and welfare. They are knowledgeable about these modes and patronizing toward anyone who is ignorant or uncommitted. But the invaders have burst into a world they never chose. They have to be helped, guided, educated in the acceptable forms of aspiration and action. They are, in a word, newly licensed to have needs, but not yet intentions or plans of their own.

The perfected welfare state will bring with it an end to the terrible oppressiveness of poverty and invisibility. Once all men are recognized as members (even if only by a distant and powerful government), the sheer magnitude of state terrorism and economic exploitation, and so of human misery, will be enormously reduced. At the same time it needs to be said that security and welfare are not open-ended categories whose final character will be determined by the freedmen of the liberal state. The pursuit of private happiness may be endless, but its direction, for most of us, is given. The newer welfare recipients are not and are not likely to become self-determining men; they remain subject to the determinations of others, not only in the state but in society and economy as well. Indeed the established forms of social and economic (that is, corporate) power are likely to be strengthened just as state power has been strengthened: by the general expansion in scale, by the increase in legitimacy that derives from the admission, however reluctant, of all outsiders, by the universal improvement in everyday social behavior, by the new forms of bureaucratic surveillance and record-keeping. For these same reasons the individual member is taken into account in a new way. When his rulers claim to serve him, the claim is not a lie; it is his political destiny to receive services. The reception of services brings freedom of a limited sort, but of a sort rare enough to be valuable. The citizen of the welfare state is free (and in many cases newly enabled) to pursue private happiness within the established social and economic system. He is not free to shape or reshape the system, for he has not seized and, except in minimal ways, he does not share political power.

THERE is no readily accessible meaning in the frequent assertion that socialism lies "beyond the welfare state." No evidence suggests that socialism represents the next stage of history, or that the full development of welfare production entails a socialist society. "Beyond," in that hopeful phrase, has neither a historical nor a logical sense.

Although socialist parties and movements have often been in the forefront of the struggle for welfare, and above all for equality in the distribution of benefits, it remains true that socialist theory belongs to a tradition of thought and aspiration not only different from, but also in perennial competition with liberal utilitarianism. Against the utilitarians, socialists have argued that mere private life, however enhanced by state action, cannot sustain a significant human culture; that the family does not provide an adequate arena for the human emotions; that man has both a mind and a passion for society; that he requires an active public life. Against the private man of liberal theory, socialists have defended the free citizen.*

This disagreement is in no sense adequately summed up in the words "individualism" and "collectivism." In both traditions the individual is recognized as the ultimate value; socialists and liberals unite in opposing any ideology which assigns to the state a

*Utilitarianism is not, of course, the only form of liberal politics; liberals have also been interested in local government and voluntary association; pluralism, before it became an ideological catchword, was as much a liberal as a socialist theory, and for both liberals and socialists it emphasized the values of political participation and communal life. But I do not think it is unfair to suggest that utilitarianism has been for some time the dominant form of liberalism and, more important, that it has been the central creed of liberals-in-power. I suppose utilitarianism has also been the central creed of socialists-in-power, but socialists, perhaps fortunately for socialism, have been in power less often.

moral being independent of the willfulness and rationality of its particular members. But to deny the claims of statist ideologies is not necessarily to assert a purely instrumentalist political theory.

Individual men can still recognize the pleasures of politics, can still choose political life as an end-in-itself. For politics is something more than welfare production. It is a vital and exciting world of work and struggle; of aspiration, initiative, intrigue, and argument; of collective effort, mutual recognition, and *amour social*; of organized hostility; of public venture and social achievement; of personal triumph and failure.

The welfare state offers no satisfactory substitute for any of these. Its theorists claim that all the intellectual and emotional energies of political men can be rechanneled into private life, and their creativity coopted by intelligent administrators. Neither of these claims is true. The welfare state requires the virtual withering away of political energy and the disappearance, at least from public life, of any very significant popular creativity. This requirement is first of all an extreme restriction on the pursuit of happiness—because political activity is or might be one of the forms that pursuit takes for many people. Even more important, it involves a surrender of everyone's say in the determination of further restrictions (or expansions), a surrender of any popular role in determining the shape and substance, the day-to-day quality, of our common life. This is the socialist indictment of liberal utilitarianism.

The terms of the indictment have not often been made clear in the recent past because so many of us who regard ourselves as socialists have found a kind of political fulfillment in the struggles for the welfare state. We have allied ourselves with the crowds of men battering at the gates of American society. Their cause has been our public passion. This will continue to be so for some time to come, probably for the foreseeable future.

Nevertheless as we campaign for this or that welfare measure, we are driven to ask ourselves John Stuart Mill's famous question: "Suppose that . . . all the changes in institutions and opinions which you [are] looking forward to could be completely effected at this very instant: would this be a joy and a happiness to you?" And as with Mill, so with us "an irrepressible self-consciousness distinctly answers, No!"

THE welfare state is not the name of our desire. And what is more, the achievement of the welfare state might well entail the end of that public activity which has until now been a joy and a happiness to us. When contemporary writers talk about the "end of ideology," the disappearance of generalized aspiration, they are describing just this closing down of the possibilities for public intellectual and emotional commitment. Though their announcements are at the very least premature, they linger in our minds as disturbing predictions.

But if we are right in thinking that there are human desires that the welfare state cannot fulfill, then surely these desires will continue to be expressed in the form of collective demands and claims. If men really do seek the common achievements and shared excitements of politics, then they will have them, in one form or another. And they will produce new ideologies to validate their new activities.

In a sense the welfare state makes these new activities possible, even though it decrees that they must be pursued without the goad of material need and even though its officials hope that they will not in fact be pursued. Political life, if it is to have any significance, must now be chosen for its own sake, and only now can be chosen for its own sake. I am going to assume that liberal ideologists' predictions of the "end of ideology" are wrong and that large numbers of people (not all people) are prone to make this choice. They demand or will demand some form of political participation, some share in political power. How shall their demand be met?

It might be met by the state itself. For there is no obvious reason why the officials of the welfare state, pressed by their constituents or by their own ambitions, should not move beyond the narrow limits of liberal utilitarianism. They will be, they are already, tempted to do so, for two not entirely consistent reasons: first, to avoid the great difficulties that will inevitably be encountered in the expansion of welfare production beyond its present limits; second, to avoid the boredom of success. In the long run the second is the more important: while the building of the welfare state will have its exciting and morally significant moments, its administration will not. Its administrators will rarely feel themselves buoyed up and sustained by the zeal of their clients. The pride they may well take in the material services they render will never be elevated by the inner conviction of a higher purpose.

But beyond welfare there are many areas in which such purposes might be sought: education, culture, communications, mental health, city planning (and most tempting and dangerous of all, though not within the range of this discussion, foreign policy). In all these areas the state can be active; in all of them political energies can be expended and emotional commitments made; in all of them common goods can be discovered, goods to be shared and not merely distributed.

Imagine then that the state moves into the field of "culture promotion." Won't the possibilities of cooperative choice and political self-determination be enhanced? Won't the citizens of such a state, the recipients not only of material but also of spiritual benefits, feel themselves to be members of a moral community, a world of rights and obligations?

Perhaps they will; our feelings are not always under our own control. Indeed we know they will, for the modern state always intrudes, in greater or lesser degree, into areas that lie beyond welfare, most often in the name of political socialization. Obviously it does so with considerable success. But all this has nothing to do with socialism or with a meaningful common life, for reasons which go to the very heart of the theory of citizenship and participation.

Unlike the defenders of the welfare state, theorists of citizenship have always been concerned with the problem of social scale. If human emotional and intellectual needs are to be partially fulfilled within political society, they have argued, then that society cannot be of any size or shape. It must be built on a human scale, accessible to our minds and feelings, responsive to our decisions.

Exactly what constitutes a human scale is and ought to be a subject of debate, but this is a debate likely to be carried on chiefly among radical democrats and socialists; it is not a debate in which liberal utilitarians take much interest. For it cannot be established that security and welfare are more efficiently administered to two million or fifty million or two hundred million people. In fact it is virtually certain that the quality of security and welfare need not change with the size of the population.

But this is probably not the case with regard to the fulfillment of nonmaterial desires. The quality and authenticity of emotional commitment, for example, does appear to vary with population size, though not absolutely or without reference to other factors: human emotions are more easily manipulated the wider their focus and the more they are cut away from immediate personal experience. Participation in cultural life probably varies the same way: the larger the audience, the more passive its members, the more stereotyped the products they consume. Once again the formula is too pat but surely contains an element of truth, and its significance may plausibly be extended to politics as well.

The increasing size of the state, the growing power of administration, the decline of political life: all these turn politics from a concrete activity into what Marx once called the fantasy of everyday life. The state becomes an arena in which men do not act but watch the action, and like other audiences, are acted upon. Patriotic communion is always a fraud when it is nothing more than the communion of an audience with its favorite actors, of passive subjects and heroes of the stage. Our emotions are merely tricked by parades and pageants, the rise and fall of political gladiators, the deaths of beloved chiefs, the somber or startling rites of a debased religion. It could be done to anyone, whereas patriotism ought to be the pride of a particular man, the enjoyment of particular activities.

When the modern state moves beyond welfare, it does not bring us the satisfactions of citizenship but only vicarious participation, the illusion of a common life. We find ourselves as if in a dream, living once again in a world which is morally dense and opaque, mystified by ideologies, dominated by leaders whose purposes are not obvious. We are oppressed in the name of a public interest, a national purpose, a solemn commitment, which is neither yours nor mine, nor ours, in any usual sense of those perfectly simple pronouns. It is difficult not to conclude, as the liberals do, that with the provision of individual material needs the state reaches or ought to reach its limits. That is the end of its history, the culmination of its legitimacy. There is no state beyond the welfare state.

THE struggle to control the modern state is a battle for the perfection of the welfare system. Any political leader who claims that it is more than this, who claims, for example, that citizens should do more for the state than the state does for them, is a dangerous man. He aims to avoid the problems of welfare production, or he seeks some sort of totalitarian "transcendence" (or he is preparing the nation for one or another kind of imperial adventure).

The fight over welfare is important enough. Given the most immediate desires of the poor themselves, given the sheer avariciousness of the rich and the powerful, the fight for some minimal standards of distributive justice takes on all the moral significance that has been attributed to it in the past century and a half. Nevertheless it is not the only fight—nor ought the state to be the only focus of contemporary political struggle.

Even if the welfare state were to be perfected under the best possible conditions and under socialist auspices, the dangers of bureaucratic omnicompetence and popular passivity would not be avoided. Nor would a socialist government create a socialist society. That requires a different kind of politics, not the kind to which we are all so well accustomed, aimed permanently at the state, but a politics of immediate self-government, a politics of (relatively) small groups.

Socialist writers have never had a great deal that was new or interesting to say about the state. Despite vague phrases about its withering away, they seem to presuppose, as they probably must, an efficient and benevolent bureaucracy, hovering, so to speak, in the background, its central offices as far away as possible. The chief concern of the best left-wing theorists has always been with that day-to-day cooperation in productive activity which occupies the foreground of social life. That means, with those "life-giving nuclei," as Simone Weil called them, within which the local, immediate character of work and culture is determined.

Such secondary associations exist, or can exist, *within* the welfare state, but insofar as they are of some human value they exist in permanent tension with the centralized administrative system necessary to welfare production. It is not the natural tendency even of liberal bureaucracy to encourage the formation of autonomous groups. This is so both because of the individualist bias of the welfare system and because of the perennial efforts of administrators to escape the system's utilitarian limits and meet the demand for meaningful citizenship in their own (fraudulent) fashion.

What socialism requires then is not that the welfare state be surpassed or transcended, whatever that would mean, but that it be held tightly to its own limits, drained of whatever superfluous moral content and unnecessary political power it has usurped, reduced so far as possible to a transparent administrative shell (overarching, protective, enabling) within which smaller groups can grow and prosper. The state is not going to wither away; it must be hollowed out.

What sorts of groups can fill the shell? Two are of special interest here. First, the great functional organizations, labor unions, professional associations, and so on: these are the crucial representative bodies of the present day. Their strength and inclusiveness is the best guarantee we can have of the benevolence of the welfare bureaucracy. Unorganized men are unrepresented and unprotected men, their claims unheard or but distantly heard at the centers of power. If they are benefited at all, they are subject to the most extreme paternalism.

The perfection of the welfare state will require the organization of all possible functional groups, even, or rather especially, the group of those who receive direct state assistance. In a society which still exploits masses of men, poverty itself is a function and no one so desperately requires representation as the man without an adequate income. But all these organizations, as I have argued, tend to become integrated into the welfare system: for them, success *is* integration. They are then trapped in more or less stable bargaining arrangements with governmental or corporate bureaucracies and forced to discipline their own members. They are simultaneously agents of distributive justice and social control. They are not, and probably cannot be expected to become, arenas of democratic decision-making (even though they will be the occasional focus of democratic revolts).

Second, all the local units of social life, work, education, and culture: cities and towns, factories, union locals, universities, churches, political clubs, neighborhood associations, theater groups, editorial boards, and so on. These might be conceived as overlapping circles of engagement and action, closed circles (though not closed in any coercive sense), whose members face inward at least some of the time, and within which resources are contained.

These are the most likely arenas of a genuinely democratic politics. The great danger of the perfected welfare state is that all or most of them would be broken open, so that resources leak away, independence is lost, and the members turn outward to face the powerful state, where all the action is, from which all good things come. To some extent this has already happened. But the process is by no means so far advanced as some of the more extreme versions of the theory of "mass society" suggest. Associations and neighborhoods continue to provide important social space for agitation and activity. Indeed it needs to be said that the advance of the liberal state often transforms traditionalist communities (like the old churches) into new political arenas.

At the same time, however, the same process cuts individuals loose, isolates them from communal ties, drives them into a material and then an emotional dependency on the central authorities. It is in response to the expectant faces of these "liberated" individuals that state administrators proclaim the mysteries of national purpose and decide that they must pursue "excellence" or promote culture (or defend freedom), rewarding their eager, needful, and bored constituents with inflated rhetoric and byzantine artifacts, and all too often eliciting from them an irrational and unreflective patriotism.

Now all such pursuits and promotions lie outside the competence of the state; they belong to a different sphere of activity; they require a smaller scale of organization. To make these points and to make them stick is the major purpose of socialist politics in the welfare state. It amounts to saying that what we want *next*, and what we want to share, are the pleasures of power. This demand for local self-determination, since it is made in the face of a state whose power is unprecedented in human history, is sometimes called by the melodramatic but useful name "insurgency."*

ANY member of the welfare state who is willful as well as desirous and who seeks some local space in which to act out his willfulness can be called insurgent. He insists on his intentions as well as his needs. He seeks to close the circle (not every circle) against bureaucratic intrusions. He reargues the old democratic proposition that decisions should be made by those who are most affected by them. He calls into question the omnicompetence of the service state and of all the organizations created in its image.

In schools, factories, and neighborhoods where social workers pursue their errands of decency, or union officials defend the interests of their members, or provosts and deans plan the educational experiences of the young, insurgency is likely to be a perennial phenomenon. It takes the form of wildcat strikes, welfare unions, student rebellions. Already a sense of professional *esprit* is growing up among those who know, or think they know, how to "handle" such outbursts. They believe that insurgency is a repudiation of services rendered, stupidly self-destructive since the services are so obviously helpful, even if they are often ineptly or impersonally delivered.

But insurgency is, or ought to be, very different from this. Its participants are not concerned that bureaucrats be sensitive and warm, but that they be reticent and limited, less imposing, less intrusive than they often are. Insurgency is a demand that bureaucratic services make possible, instead of replacing, local decision-making. Or rather it is the acting out of a new dialectic, which denies conventional definitions of good behavior and seeks to make the "helpfulness" of the welfare bureaucracy into the

---

*It is one of the odder features of political life that we characterize the common forms of oppression and domination with euphemisms and use words with the most violent connotations to describe modest acts of individual and popular self-assertion. In an article in *Dissent* some six years ago I used the term "resistance" to suggest the sorts of activities presently called insurgency by various New Left writers. Their word will do as well, though they are no more guerrilla fighters than I am.

starting point of a new politics of popular resistance and self-government.

In the long run the issue for socialists is not state power* but power *right here*, on this shop floor, in this university, in this city. And the central assumption of insurgent politics is that such power must always be won "from below"—which is also to say, against all odds. For the triumph of benevolent bureaucrats in virtually every local society has been one of the results, not so much inevitable as overdetermined, of the entrance of masses of men into the political world. It is a function of integration.

Most of the previous forms of radical politics have involved demands for wider and wider systems of integration; every successful revolution has produced such a system. But insurgency is different from revolution (more limited, more immediate) precisely in that it seeks no more extensive unity, but calls instead for the multiplication of diverse and independent unities. And it begins this process with a modest but urgent demand for a share *right now* in the management of *this* community.

Whether this can actually be won and the victory sustained is another matter. It is not difficult to imagine a kind of permanent insurgency, generating marginal but never major disturbances in the welfare state, always asserting its claims, never able to enforce them, capable of staging riots, never capable of building a movement or a new community. Newspapers provide us daily with intimations of such a pattern. We do not know if local organizations of rebellious citizens can displace entrenched officials, sanctioned and supported by the central state; nor do we know if they can win any substantial allegiance from their own members, establish some more or less effective control over the local politics of work and culture, and generate significant cooperative activity. Above all we do not know if they can create new patterns of democratic responsibility so that the militants of this or that rebellion don't simply become a new elite. That success is possible

---

*Nor is it corporate power: the problem of counterbalancing, regulating, or destroying the power of private corporations is primarily a welfare problem; it concerns the most immediate interests of workers and consumers. But its solution would not necessarily even raise the question of democratic decision-making.

must be the socialist's faith, or better, the wager that sustains his commitment.

The politics of insurgency and the politics of welfare obviously overlap, both in time and technique, and their different purposes are sometimes confused. Insurgency has been a prominent feature of every struggle for recognition: the sit-in strikes of the 1930s are the classic example. Oppressed groups must always win enough power either to threaten those who refuse to grant their demands or to threaten the general peace and so compel state intervention on their behalf. And "enough" power always means power in some particular place, sufficient to inflict some particular injury.

But so long as the goal of the oppressed is (as it ought to be) membership in the greater society rather than autonomy for the smaller one, such power is largely a means to an end, and it disappears when it ceases to be a necessary means. It gradually seeped away from local unions, for example, once bargaining rights were granted at the national or industrywide level—and while this was certainly a democratic loss, it must be admitted that what the workers wanted could only have been won at the national level.

Something like this will probably happen in the civil rights movement also, since the problems of the black community cannot be solved until its activists transform such local power as they may win into national recognition and full admission into the welfare state. And this suggests a lesson which is not easy to learn: that political power must always be twice-won. It must be won first with the help of the state or through the creation of parallel bureaucracies against established local or corporate elites. Then it must be won again by new popular forces against the state. In the U.S. today blacks are still fighting the first battle; Americans who have already won national recognition are, let us hope, ready for the second.

SOCIALISM, it has often been said, requires decentralization. But that is not quite accurate, for it implies a process that begins at the center and is, just for that reason, inherently unlikely. It suggests that socialism awaits the triumph of a national movement whose leaders are ready to sponsor the fragmentation and dispersion of the power they have so recently won. Once installed, however, won't they be driven to realize how much good might be done with their power if only it is kept intact . . . for a few years more? (And they may well be right.) We ought, of course, to insist that state officials do as much as they can to encourage the growth of secondary associations independent of themselves, not forming wheels within wheels of their welfare-producing machine. But the vitality of such associations depends finally on those who associate.

Socialism then requires insurgency, that is, self-government within the welfare state and against it whenever necessary. And it is the great paradox of socialist politics that the state toward which we must always remain tense, watchful, and resistant is or will almost certainly become the most legitimate, rationally purposive, and powerful state that has ever existed.

Erazim V. Kohák

Possessing, Owning, Belonging

THE future of socialism, I am convinced, depends more on its ability to provide a new conception of ownership than on its ability to redistribute property or secure social benefits. Those traditional aims retain importance even in a technologically mature society, but now have less power to inspire than they did in the past. For once ownership is coupled with the awesome ability to bring large-scale, irreversible changes in our physical and social environment, the question "Who shall own the world?" becomes distinctly secondary to the question "What shall it mean to own?" The urgent task today is the humanization of ownership.

I like to believe that this indeed was the concern of the pioneers of socialism, and there is some evidence to that effect. But as a matter of historical fact socialist movements have seldom risen above a Robin Hood model of socialism, concerned more with the distribution of property than with its definition. With a few exceptions socialists, like capitalists, have conceived of ownership as a formal relation, independent of practice: regardless of who tills the soil or uses the tools, the "owner" is the person named in a deed or is the state agency specified by law. Both these "owners" conceive of the essence of that relation as the "right" to derive benefits from the object owned, whether in the form of rent or dividend, or of appropriation of profit by the state, with the corollary "right" to determine how the object shall be used, and in both cases without reference to the persons who actually till the soil or use the tool. In collectivist and capitalist countries alike the definition of ownership given by the Austrian civil code of 1811,* as the right to use, abuse or ignore, destroy, transfer, or abandon, remains uncomfortably accurate: ownership continues to be conceived of as the "right," formally defined and independent of practice, to dominate and exploit.

Certainly the Leninist conception focuses on the question "Who shall own the world?" As in politics so in economics, the dominant concern of Leninism has been not with the nature of power but with its possession. The Leninist prescription, summed up in the slogan "All Power to the Soviets!" has been the transfer of power into the "right hands" rather than its transformation—and this held true in economics as well. The bureaucratic collectivism to which Leninism gave rise effectively transferred ownership from an economic to an ideologico-political elite; but it gave ownership little meaning beyond the traditional one of domination. Not surprisingly the collectivist owners have matched their corporate counterparts in the ability both to exploit labor and to despoil the environment: the "socialist" pollution exuded by the paper mills of Český Krumlov differs from its capitalist counterpart only in its greater immunity from protest by the disenfranchised labor force. Bureaucratic collectivism can provide little inspiration for the technologically mature societies—including the Soviet Union.

Nor has the social democratic attempt to civilize ownership by holding it to social responsibilities provided a model of a liberated society. The welfare state has probably given its citizens a greater degree of personal freedom and social security than any society since the Industrial Revolution, but it too retains the idea that domination is the content of ownership. Tenant vandalism in public housing duplicates the effects of slumlord neglect, while Britain's "socialist" trade unions sometimes wield their power with as much regard for the public weal as did Commodore Vanderbilt. The achievements of welfare-state socialism may be less ambiguous than those of collectivism, but they are hardly

---

Common Civil Code, Register of Judicial Laws, no. 946, paragraph 354. The code remained in force in Czechoslovakia until 1950.

inspirational. Taking from the rich and giving to the poor is a noble and even necessary activity, but historically it is the merest beginning. If socialism is to make a unique contribution to both the developing countries and the technologically mature societies, it must offer a vision of a liberated society that would not simply transfer formal ownership or compensate for its inequities but would break the bond between ownership and alienation.

THE recognition of this bond is perhaps the distinctive socialist contribution to the making of modern political consciousness. The mere recognition of alienation as a basic trait of modern social existence is itself more Hegelian than Marxist, and it remains so in spite of the recent cult of "the young Marx." Nor is a stress on the importance of the social as against the individual dimension of human experience uniquely socialist. The socialist contribution has been a recognition that alienation is not simply a spiritual phenomenon but also an experiential one, acted out not only in the subjective relations of the ego but also in the tangible relations of human beings to each other and their material world. More specifically it is the recognition that the modes of ownership inherited from an earlier age are no longer adequate for mediating the relationship of human to human and to their social and material world. The alienation of the human in postindustrial society cannot be overcome by moral exhortation to love and stewardship, whether we call it moral rearmament, Consciousness III, or "a new socialist morality." Something more is needed: a transformation of the rationale and forms of ownership that underlie alienation.

Socialist attempts to achieve this end, however, thus far have done more to discredit than to realize it. From the start socialist theory and practice were marked by a basic contradiction in the socialist analysis of ownership, its diagnosis of what precisely makes ownership alienating—and so also in its prescriptions for transforming ownership. It is easy to oversimplify, but there is considerable justification for interpreting this contradiction within socialism as the difference between interpreting alienation as the effect of *being deprived of property* and of interpreting it as the effect of *possessing property*. In his "Critique of Hegel's *Philosophy of*

Right" Marx sees the impoverishment of the German proletariat —that is, its freedom from property—as the quality that will enable it to carry out an apocalyptic revolt against a system that exploits it and deprives it of property. This difference in turn is reflected in social strategies as contradictory as distributing large estates among the peasants and expropriating small holdings for state farms. Ultimately it is the difference between the strategy of welfare-state socialism, which seeks to liberate workers from poverty, and of bureaucratic collectivism, which seeks to liberate them from property. The roots of the contradiction may lie in the radically different and socially conditioned experience of property among socialism's founders. The socialist movement, after all, has always been an alliance of outsiders, the specially privileged and the specially deprived—"the progressive intelligentsia" and the proletariat. Intellectuals and proletarians can pledge allegiance to a common ideology and share a common abhorrence of exploitation. But the stereotypes of property that appear obvious to the one are, to the other, radically different.

Marx may have written of and perhaps for the proletariat, but he was the son of an affluent upper-middle-class family. Most of his life he derived his sustenance not from wage labor but from private means—in large part the largesse of a factory-owner friend, Friedrich Engels. Similarly, Lenin was anything but a proletarian. By contrast the mass of their followers had little experience with private means. For the most part they were workers for whom the wherewithal of daily existence was not a trivial distraction from work but its very content and goal.

Speaking of property as "theft," like Proudhon, or as "soulless commodity," like Marx, reflects the condition of the privileged. The lived bond between a human and his world is forged in labor: tilling the soil or wielding a tool is what makes an object genuinely "mine," not an accidental possession analogous to the object of theft. It is the labor a subject invests in the object that makes the object an extension of his being rather than a soulless commodity. The privileged, no matter how "progressive," inevitably lack this experience. Intellectual work may be no less valuable and productive than that of a laborer, but by its very nature it is experientially distinct from the intellectual's income and the objects he can buy with it. A man of private means or a salaried professional may well "deserve" his reward, but he understandably experiences his sustenance as autonomous and as a distraction from his work. To be sure, such work still has its objective counterparts: the opportunity to write and publish is as real a part of it as tilling the soil and reaping its harvest. Yet the modern intellectual's sense of freedom from immediate material concern—from property—is real. On the level of socially conditioned forms of experience, it is quite understandable that many socialist intellectuals speak of liberation from property, or insist that the forms of property simply do not concern them.

Quite understandably, however, the demand for liberation from property makes as little sense to a worker as a demand for liberation from the freedom of the press would to the intellectual. While frequently supporting demands for expropriation of large productive units, the workers have usually done so in the name of *appropriation* of property. In a laborer's experience property is anything but a soulless commodity. The soil he tills is a part of his very being; the tools he uses are extensions of his muscles. This is no less true of the industrial worker than of the individual craftsman or the small farmer. There may be "property-less classes," but there can be no "property-less men" as there are no disembodied souls. The industrial worker may detest the factory where he has spent the major part of his life, but as with a bad marriage, it is still an intrinsic part of him, his home and his extension in the world. The oldtimers hanging around the shop after retirement provide a painful reminder both of the need to belong and of the very basic sense of belonging that work forges between a human and the tools he uses, even when that tool is a steel mill. The worker's wage has to be reduced to the status of bare cash nexus—experientially it is the tangible bridge between his work and the objects that manifest his care for those who share his immediate world: the warm house, the clothes, the food on the table, even the garish plaster dwarf in his garden. A worker's burden is precisely the lack of property: it is deprivation which seems to hinder his self-realization. His appropriative demand for the ownership of his land or tools, for higher wages, or even for the product of his labor is no fetishism of property at all—it is a demand for recognition of his identity, strictly analogous to a writer's demand for the freedom to publish.

I have stressed the analogy between the two sets of experiences, since on the level of the primary relation of the human and his world that analogy is real. But on the level of socially conditioned forms of experience it is the difference between the experience of the laborer and the experience of the intellectual that counts the most. For the one ownership holds out a promise of freedom from care and a place in the world; to the other it suggests the bondage to objects. One set of experiences quite naturally issues in a demand for appropriation of property, the other equally naturally in a demand for liberation from property.

THIS is the contradiction Karl Marx sought to resolve, valiantly and in vain, by interpreting the protest against deprivation and the demand for freedom from property as two stages of a continuous socialist development. The formula resolved nothing, but it papered over the contradiction, and as long as socialists were in opposition this was all that was needed.

When revolution in Russia and electoral victories in the West confronted socialists with the responsibility of creating an alternative to capitalist ownership, the compromise broke down. The demand that all humans become owners and the demand that all humans be freed of ownership issued in radically different alternatives to capitalist ownership, both legitimate yet fundamentally incompatible.

In semifeudal Russia, with its diminutive working class and long tradition of elitist autocracy, the revolutionaries set themselves the task of "abolishing property"—and since even Russians are not pure spirits but incarnate men with material needs, they settled for an attempt to make property anonymous, collective: property without individual owners.

Successive Soviet civil codes distinguished three forms of property. The first category, socialist property (owned by the state or the collective), includes all means of production—land, tools, factories—on the assumption that a tool is not something a human uses but rather something he hires another to use. The second category, personal property, is restricted to goods that a person consumes rather than uses in his work, and that he receives from society (in effect from the state, as sole owner of the means of production) in recognition of his needs (health services, vacations) or of his contribution (wages, consumer goods). The third category, private property, refers to possession of means of production, at times tolerated in practice (NEP, private plots) but always condemned in principle as incompatible with socialism.

In collectivist theory only the means of consumption can be objects of individual ownership—the means of production belong to the collective. And so labor, which in experience belongs to a person perhaps more intimately than anything else, is treated as a means of production. An individual may use it in personal consumption (building a weekend hut, playing a sport), but he may not withhold it (having no job constitutes the felony of parasitism). Nor may he use it to produce a private income even when such use requires no ownership of tools (accepting a fee for guiding a tourist or for making a repair, though common practice, enjoys no legal sanction). The liberation from property is complete. With the exception of wages, which to some extent remain tied to individual effort, the system fulfills the vision of liberation from property.

Although ownership has become anonymous, it is still real. The state, in effect, becomes a holding corporation. Property is not "free"—a factory is not a spontaneous growth like a wild tree, providing fruit to all who pick it. It is controlled by the state. The collectivist approach to property is reminiscent of those monastic orders that combined the freedom of poverty with the security of property by having their chapter houses, lands, and flocks owned nominally by the church at Rome. A more ominous analogy suggests itself as well: slaves, after all, constituted a class free from all property, contributing according to ability and compensated according to minimal need. In the collectivist vision, however, the result was to be perfect freedom, because the owners would supposedly be the collective of the workers, peasants, and soldiers themselves. The owned would be the owners, thereby effecting a dialectical transformation of total bondage into perfect freedom.

The intent was pure, the result not. As the collectivist bureaucracy came more and more to exercise the prerogatives of owners, collective ownership became formal and abstract. By contrast, the breaking of the bond between individual humans and their most intimate embodiment, their tools and their labor, remained painfully tangible, and in contrast with capitalism, universal. In the U.S.S.R. and Eastern Europe, *socialist property* rapidly becomes not *ours* but *theirs*. The workers notoriously experience no living bond between themselves and their work and tools. Large-scale pilfering, abuse of property, and dismally low work morale on the job—in sharp contrast to the initiative and competence in the nonsanctioned afterhours enterprises and on private plots—testify to a high degree of alienation.

The abolition of private property—in the technical sense—in turn effectively destroyed the living bond that even capitalism had preserved, if only for economic rather than humanitarian reasons, between the small farmer or artisan and the most intimate counterparts of his being, the soil he tills and the tools he uses. The scars left by the forcible expropriation of small holdings, collectivization of cattle and small shops heal slowly if at all, as the perennial crisis of agriculture and services in the Communist countries testifies. Finally, the limitation of personal property —the only legally recognized form of identification between a human and his world—to objects of consumption has given rise to a consumerism that may well be the ultimate in fetishism of goods.

The achievements of collectivism are real, even though, given the grim realities of the Soviet police state, they are easy to overlook. In spite of virtually unanimous opposition to the regime in a country like Czechoslovakia, few Czechs or Slovaks would support the restoration of collective enterprise to private ownership. The failure, however, is no less real, and combined with the strong trade-union tradition of Western socialism, it left Western socialists with little appetite for experimentation with radical changes in ownership.

Social democrats in the West have largely become reconciled with capitalist ownership. What little nationalization they did carry out was predicated not on principle but on pragmatic consideration of public weal. Their strategy in power has focused largely on protecting workers from poverty by pressing the productivity of capitalism into service to relieve its victims. A wide range of social services, ranging from minimum guaranteed income to health care, have gone far toward providing some of the security and freedom of affluence for the nonaffluent, without demanding the bloody price exacted by communism. Despite the success of that strategy, continued social inequality and labor discontent since the first British Labour victory have shown that no matter how effective the social democratic strategy may be in coping with the ill effects of capitalism, it is not of itself a path to socialism. The idea of a socialist society that fired the imagination of an earlier generation is not, after all, simply of a society in which no one starves. It is the idea of a *liberated* society. It is the vision of a society that would in its economic as well as in its political aspects genuinely belong to the men and women who constitute it rather than to a handful of "owners," alienated from their fellow humans by the privilege of unearned income and in turn alienating them from their world by the claim to "ownership." It is a vision of a society without exploitation—conceived in a society in which a large proportion of the national product is appropriated by some 3 percent of the population in the form of unearned income, a society in which the wage-earner, no matter how well compensated, still is exploited.

It is this vision that makes even the victims of communism cling to the idea of socialism and makes idealists in Western socialist countries look—albeit utterly unrealistically—to the Communist model. But the relevance of socialism is contingent on its ability to offer a valid alternative strategy.

HERE now, I would submit, we have to start with a more careful analysis of the nature of ownership and the conditions that make it alienating than socialists hitherto have offered. One of the treatises on ownership, which appeared in Czechoslovakia in the years of Stalinism, illustrates the problem clearly: ". . . there is no ownership given by reason, God, or in any other a priori way [that is, natural law ownership] . . . the will of the owner moves within limits given by the will of the ruling class and concrete property relations are determined on a class basis. . . ."* The author states

---

*V. Knapp, *Ownership in the People's Democracy* (Prague, 1952), p. 35; cited by Rozenal, "Přeměna vlastnictví," *Proměny* 9, no. 1 (January 1972): 61.

the dilemma: ownership, which he regards quite traditionally as a formal claim to possession, must be derived either from pure reason, a priori—or be defined arbitrarily by the "will of the ruling class." Basically, ownership is presented not as a lived reality but as an arbitrary privilege that must be assigned to a particular individual.

On the level of social reality, from which both socialism and sociology derive their names, this conception simply does not correspond to experience. Here abstract possession is at best a consequence, but in no sense the ground of ownership. Ownership on this level is first of all the experience of a lived interaction between a subject and his world in the course of which meaning becomes actual and matter meaningful. Forms of ownership may vary in different societies and historical periods, but the mutual relation of belonging between a human and his world is more basic than the forms that express it. It is perhaps the basic fact of being human, as basic as "having-a-body," "belonging-to-a-context."

The experience of belonging precedes any formal assignation of property rights, whether by reason, God, or the will of the ruling class. It begins with the child's appropriation of his body as "mine." Perhaps the first step is the recognition of the wiggling toes as a part of myself. It is a process of appropriation of a material counterpart of my being: learning to use my body, making it an expression of my self. Nor is there any magic divide between learning to use my toe and learning to use a tool. In both cases the "I" is becoming actual—and the objects in which the "I" becomes actual, whether hand or tool, come to "belong to me," as extensions and expressions of my being in the intersubjective world. The acquiring of a body and of its extensions—tools, skills, familiar places, and the recognized place in a social world—is a process of self-realization.

It is important to note, however, that it is not only a process of individuation but a process of socialization as well. The "I" enclosed within my consciousness becomes a part of a social world precisely in the process of embodying itself in objective counterparts. As having-a-body I am individual, this and no other, but as having-a-body I am also social, since the body is not private but public, a member and a part both of a material and a social world.

On this level the ability to own and belong is neither theft nor privilege, but the indispensable counterpart of being actual. It does not alienate—quite the contrary, it is the basis both of individual identity and social participation. Property is in the first place the objective counterpart of my presence in a social and material world. It becomes alienating under special circumstances, and our task is to isolate those circumstances.

For the purposes of political theory it is crucial to note that collective ownership can similarly be either the basis of individual identity and social participation or a source of alienation. Children habitually speak of "our house": here the ownership is collective, expressing a collective experience. We live in this house together, together we work on it, keep it up, enjoy it: it is ours, and in each individual case the house is no less my own for being ours. As with individual ownership, there is nothing prima facie alienating about collective ownership when it is an expression of lived experience.

The disruptive element again enters with the formalization of the claim of ownership. When a child expresses the claim "This is my house; (I need not work on it, help keep it clean, but) I have a right to it (for instance, invite friends here) because it is mine," that claim is rightly resented by her siblings. Conversely when parents appoint themselves the vanguard of the family and pre-empt the right of making decisions concerning "our" house, the collective ownership becomes alienating and evokes an individual-istic, appropriative response: "(This is our house, but) this room is mine—(I live in it, clean it, and) I'll decide what color wallpaper will go on the walls."

With this example we can formulate a provisional principle: the forms of ownership are liberating, sustaining the individual's freedom of identity and participation, if they express a lived relationship of belonging. They become alienating if they disrupt such belonging in the name of an abstract claim to possession. The basis of socialist ownership is belonging, the special reciprocal relationship that life and work forge between a human and a definite part of the social and material world—an object, a place, a right. In that special relationship a human defines his identity as well as his social participation. The institutions of a socialist society must respect and express that relationship rather than deny it.

I am not presenting this principle as a call for a subjective change in attitude toward property. Desirable though such change may be, it is more likely to follow from rather than lead to institutional changes. Rather, I am presenting it as an alternative rationale for the critique of capitalist institutions and for designing the institutions of a socialist society. Socialists have criticized past institutions and devised new ones (or in the name of humanity, refrained from designing new ones) on the assumption that ownership is alienating by virtue of being "private," and that, consequently, public ownership, simply by virtue of being public, would be nonalienating. On the principle "private bad, public good," they have created, in Eastern Europe, a system of ownership that is not private—and yet is no less alienating than capitalist ownership. Although this system has no "private" owners, the factory worker is no less excluded from participation in the direction of an enterprise and from sharing in the proceeds of production. In contrast to capitalism, however, on the level of small-scale enterprise, the principle "public ownership good, private ownership bad" led to the systematic elimination of ownership based on self-labor which survived in the capitalist economy—individual enterprise in small production, distribution, and service. Not the protests of expropriated capitalists but the staggering human, social, political, and economic cost of the dogmatic crusade against individual enterprise was the major factor inducing Western socialists to retreat to the humane but innocuous aims of a welfare state compatible with capitalism.

Yet institutions in the East did not fail because they were "too socialist." Nor did they fail because of an erroneous subjective attitude to property. They failed because the rationale in terms of which they were designed, "public good, private bad," did not identify correctly these characteristics of ownership that make it alienating. It led socialists to ignore the pressing problem of alienation in large-scale productive complexes—after all, once nationalized, such enterprises were public and in principle good, even if the workers did not seem to realize it.

Socialist institutions do not have to wait for a new subjective attitude to be effective—that would be a long wait indeed. They do, however, have to be based on a principle that correctly identifies the root of alienation—the divorce between work and ownership. Against the collectivist principle "public good, private bad," I would sum up the principle I am advancing as "self-labor good, hired labor bad," or in more general terms, applicable to large-scale production, "participating labor good, exploited labor bad."

Individual ownership of one-man and cooperative enterprises, essential in the primary and tertiary sectors of the economy, is entirely compatible with that principle. In such enterprise ownership is fully coextensive with the belonging established by life and labor. Yet collectivist ownership, vested nominally in "the people" at large but effectively exercised by a centralized state agency, both in the direction of production and in appropriation of the product, is just as incompatible with that principle as capitalist ownership. The state, even a state claiming to "represent the people," does not contribute labor and so cannot own. The only "owners" of a factory can be the women and men whose labor makes that factory a producing unit and transforms a soulless machine into a means of production.

Certainly a socialist factory, just as a capitalist one, must distinguish ownership and technical direction. The first is based on participation, the second on expertise. Directors and managers have to be hired on the basis of competence, not participation. The workers alone can be the owners: whether directly or through elected representatives, they alone can hire (and fire) directors and managers and decide how proceeds will be used and distributed. The basic socialist principle here is that those who work also own—both the tools and the product of their work—and that no one, whether individual, corporation, or state agency, whether in virtue of inheritance, stockholding, or a nationalization decree, can or need to possess tools he does not use or value he does not create.

IN this sense socialism is a direct continuation of the struggle for freedom that has motivated the social development of the West since the Middle Ages. In this struggle the enemies have been both the possessors—the individuals who claimed possession of the world—and the ingrained human fear of freedom.

The Reformation fought the first round in the struggle against the possessors—and against the need for possessors. Fitfully, gropingly, with many false starts and lapses, it has given us the conception of moral community as the *communio viatorum,* a community of free human beings, under God, who dare assume what in the jargon of another era was called "the freedom through which Christ made us free." It is the daring vision of humans who give up both the constraints and the comforts of a Vicar of Christ—or in Dostoevsky's image, of the Grand Inquisitor who would shoulder the ultimate responsibility; of humans willing to assume the freedom and the responsibility for decisions of faith and morals. It is the vision of a free church that belongs to the believers who constitute it—a community of believers without a human possessor.

The struggle for democracy was a continuation of this battle. The greatest obstacle to a politically free society has been the inability and unwillingness of men and women to imagine a state without a possessor, without a king or a prince or at least a class upon whom to shift the ultimate responsibility for social decisions. Cromwell's commonwealth failed because humans could not conceive of a state without a possessor and because humans were willing to give up their freedom in exchange for a king who would make the social decisions and bear the responsibility. The Marxist conception of the "leading role of the party" thrives on that lingering inability of men and women to conceive of a state that is the public servant of a community of free humans and so has no possessor. The "leading role of the party" thrives on the unwillingness of humans to assume the responsibility of freedom: it is easier to grumble about "them" than to assume the responsibility that belongs to us and to me individually when we are free. Democracy is the political equivalent of the Reformation: the conception of society as a community of free humans who accept the responsibility for governing themselves and dare do without masters on whom the blame can be shifted.

In retrospect the idea of a possessor in morals or in politics appears entirely fortuitous. Yet a century ago in central Europe it seemed no less self-evident that a village could not simply belong to the farmers who lived and worked in it—had to "belong" to this or that count or duke who had long since ceased to exercise any administrative function and who might simply have "bought" a group of villages he had never seen from another count—to whom they may have been "awarded" in turn by an emperor whose armies had conquered the land a hundred years ago. In the Austrian imperial army each regiment had its possessor—*Inhaber* —a civilian aristocrat with the honorary rank of a colonel whose sole function was to "own" the regiment—and that too seemed completely natural.

Democracy broke the old habit in politics: today the challenge is to break it in economics as well. The great, irreversible achievement of collectivism has been precisely that, as the Reformation in morals and democracy in politics, it has freed its subject —enslaved in every other way—of the pernicious habit of assuming that of course every industrial enterprise must have an "owner." No one who has lived in Eastern Europe can get over his first shock of incomprehension upon being told in the West that this or that factory complex "belongs" to the Smith family—who may live a thousand miles away, may have nothing to do with this factory, and yet is said to possess it and to claim a right to its proceeds. It is a shock analogous to the shock the Americans of a hundred years ago experienced on being told, in central Europe or in Russia, that a particular village "belonged" to a certain count. Collectivism did not liberate the workers—it could not do that— but it did demonstrate the utter absurdity of the claim that the investment of labor, capital, or effort does not only create a personal belonging and a right to compensation, but earns for a person's descendants a claim to perpetual possession.

As Marx recognized, corporate capitalism is teaching an analogous lesson, even if far more slowly and less painfully. By replacing the individual entrepreneur with a mass of anonymous stockholders, it illustrates the fictitious absurdity of the idea of possession—and at the same time makes the "possessor" superfluous. This is not a question of technical direction of an enterprise: certainly any working collective, especially one as complex as a modern corporation, must include experts and technicians charged specifically with the direction of an enterprise. What it does not need is an "owner," whether individual or private. The workers may not be able, in their spare time, to direct a factory, but they—and only they—can own it: directors can be hired by those to whom the enterprise belongs, whose labor makes it genuinely theirs—the employees, from the manual worker to the managers.

The Yugoslavs accomplished this with a system of Workers' Councils, elected by all the employees, which do not displace the expert directors but do displace the "owners." The Czechoslovaks moved in the same direction—until Soviet occupation restored central direction and state ownership. In America, despite isolated experiments, the idea of a Workers' Council made up of elected representatives of employees and possibly elected representatives of the public might seem too discontinuous with native development, but a system of issuing voting shares solely on the basis of actual involvement in the work of the enterprise—that is, the lived belonging—is entirely feasible. It would be even consistent with the use of nonvoting shares as a source of investment capital (though the sale of such shares, because of the pernicious social effect of unearned income, remains problematic unless it is restricted to other socialist enterprises).

The mechanics may differ but the principle remains the same: socialist ownership is not a legal fiction but a living relationship forged by life and work. No one can be denied the ownership he creates by his work—and no one, whether the state or an individual, can claim abstract "possession."

In the case of humans working individually—and even in a highly sophisticated economy such labor remains essential, especially in the tertiary sector of service and distribution and in some sectors of agriculture—that principle will result in "private" ownership. If the process of labor is individual, so is that of ownership. An individual clearly can, by his own work, "build a business"—and claim it as his own. What he cannot do within the limits of socialist ownership is to "hire" another to work "for" him. Such labor would again become alienating: the employee, by his labor, also builds a stake in the business. He can be a partner, whether on a straight cooperative basis or in proportion to the labor he invests, but he cannot be what earlier rhetoric aptly termed a "wage slave." To be sure, in practice it may well be necessary for economic reasons to permit the hiring of employees, but the point is that it is a matter of privilege, granted for reasons of common welfare—and always subject to revision. It cannot become a matter of right.

In the case of two or more humans working together, as in a three-man barbershop, a repair service, or a collective farm, the principle of socialist ownership—that ownership reflects labor —would take the form of cooperative ownership, since the work is done cooperatively. In the case of a factory it would entail a collective ownership, exercised by the collective through a Workers' Council. Finally, in the case of public service, whether in transportation, medicine, or basic industry, it would entail social ownership, exercised by a council of elected representatives of the employees and elected representatives of the public they serve. Throughout, however, the principle is the same: ownership follows labor; the only owner of a tool, whether that tool is 200 square meters of a backyard plot or a steel mill, is the human who uses that tool, whether individually, cooperatively, or collectively.

If socialism is to inspire and guide social change and not simply apply ideological smokescreens or patchwork remedies to assorted social ills, it must carry out in economics the liberation the Reformation carried out in morals and democracy in politics. The attempt to do this by retaining the conception of ownership as a formal "right" to dominate and exploit, but transferring that "right" from corporate to institutional owners has failed disastrously—just as the attempt to solve problems of faith and morals by transferring the "ownership" of the church from the pope to the presbyters failed in religion and the attempt to solve political problems by transferring power from hereditary kings to enlightened despots failed in politics, most recently in Russia. In both areas it was democracy that succeeded, by transferring responsibility to those over whom power heretofore had been exercised. Democracy might succeed in economics as well. The future relevance of socialism depends on its ability to extend democracy into economics: to substitute for the idea of ownership as a possessor's formal "right" to dominate and exploit the socialist democratic idea of ownership as a social formalization of the lived reality of belonging.

Robert L. Heilbroner

What Is Socialism?

BEYOND the welfare state lies the *terra incognita* we call socialism. It lies there more by assumption than by reconnaissance, for
no one has yet observed this socialism in reality: perhaps it will
turn out to be a New Atlantis, not a New World. But we assume
that socialism lies "beyond" the welfare state because what we
generally mean by Western socialism is a set of institutions and
cultural attitudes, of social structures and lifeways, that is qualitatively different from those we find under the prevailing state of
affairs. Socialism, as most of us think about it, is not just an
improved welfare state. It is another kind of society.

What kind? That is a very awkward as well as difficult question,
which most socialists, especially Marxists, have been reluctant to
examine. When looking at past or present, Marxists like to insist
on the necessity of emphasizing the "socioeconomic formations"
underlying each separate chapter of history. In so doing they force
an observer to pay special attention to the interaction of social,
political, and economic dynamics characteristic of each epoch. But
when socialism is mentioned, this tough-minded approach tends to
be abandoned, even denigrated as "counterrevolutionary." Socialism then becomes little more than a compass setting, an
imagined landfall over the horizon, and no effort is made to
discuss even the most basic characteristics that we would expect to
be associated with a new chapter of human history.

This failure of nerve—for that is what I think it is—carries
serious consequences. It enables us to use the word "socialism" in

a way that is purely talismanic and devoid of any operational significance. Worse, it enables us to evade questions and dilemmas that are posed by the analysis of socialism as a chapter of history that lies beyond the welfare state. These questions present painful, even agonizing, choices to those socialists who are devoted to political rights and humanistic culture as we know them in the West. That, however, is a matter for later consideration. For we cannot discuss the structure of the culture of socialism until we have reached agreement on the essential elements of the society that it is to displace. This leads us, as the first step in our argument, to consider the nature of the welfare state.

AT first blush that seems an unmanageably complex task. There is not one welfare state but many welfare states. The misery of a South Bronx drug "rehabilitation" center and the crude measures of American anticyclical fiscal policy are parts of the welfare apparatus. So are the humane open penal institutions and sophisticated employment policies of Sweden.

Nonetheless I believe we can discern a common element that allows us to place all these varied institutions under a single rubric. This common element lies in the relation of the welfare apparatus to its underlying socioeconomic formation, which is of course capitalism. Welfare institutions, I think all will concur, arise mainly to cope with the difficulties and damages that are brought about by the workings of a capitalist system. The welfare state, in a word, is a kind of apotheosis of capitalism—the form that capitalism takes in seeking its own salvation.

Whether or not capitalism will find its salvation, or whether it could survive its salvation, are questions we will disregard here. For if we are to contrast socialism as a socioeconomic formation with that of the capitalist welfare state, we must also agree on the difficulties and damages of capitalism to which welfarism addresses itself. And here again I think we can clearly identify the sets of central problems.

They are two. The first are the difficulties that emerge from the "anarchic" nature of capitalism. Anarchy does not mean an absence of any logic or order in capitalism—there is the famed, and indeed remarkable, "mechanism" of the market. The difficulty, rather, is that the logic and order of capitalism solves some kinds of problems only by imposing others. The market resolves the problem of "efficiency," for example, but it creates such problems as instability, unemployment, maldistribution, and social neglect of various kinds.

The anarchy of the market is of course a direct object of welfare redress. Fiscal and monetary policy, urban renewal, unemployment compensation, social security, antipollution controls, industrial regulation, and a long list of similar measures are typical welfare measures that address themselves to the repair, containment, or suppression of the anarchic ills of capitalism. If the remedies are often unsuccessful, the reason is that the anarchic malfunctions reflect the working-out of still deeper lying core elements in the socioeconomic makeup of capitalism—above all, the direction of productive activity by privately owned aggregates of capital. This is a fundamental aspect of capitalism—indeed, its vital center—to which welfare reforms do not penetrate or which they abridge only slightly. That is why welfarism is a development *within* capitalism and not beyond it, and it is why socialism must hesitate before it declares that it can gain its objectives within the boundaries of the welfare state.

There is also a second set of problems with which welfare institutions deal. These problems have to do with the culture of capitalism—its bourgeois "superstructure"—rather than its operational stresses and strains. Here we find such symptoms as the anomic quality of life, the much-discussed malaise and alienation of modern society, the degradations associated with commercialism, the decay of the communal spirit, etc. To alleviate or offset these ailments we find a second array of welfare measures that aim at restoring social morale, or at providing a sense of communality. The elaborate edifice of education is partly supported for this purpose. Services are provided to the sick or the aged not only for economic but for "social" reasons. Indeed the very presence of a government that declares its interest in the protection of the environment, in "law and order," and in the public weal, fills the need for an explicitly moral social concern to which the private sphere makes no contribution. The welfare state thus seeks to provide through the public sector a sense of communality that is absent from the attitudes normally engendered by a bourgeois culture.

To be sure, these attitudes of a bourgeois culture are themselves symptoms, not root elements. Just as the anarchic aspect of capitalism expresses deeper lying problems, so the familiar social ailments of modern capitalism also express more fundamental attributes of the system—in particular the profoundly individualistic ideology and morality of a system built on a universalized competitive striving for wealth. And just as the welfare state seeks to remedy the problems of the market while bypassing its core institutions, so welfare capitalism tries to undo the excesses of its culture while leaving untouched the acquisitive, privatized ethos that is inseparable from its economic structure.

This is not the place to discuss the limited efficacy of welfare reforms, either in the sphere of culture or economics. Rather what I wish to emphasize is that we discover the problems of economic anarchy and social alienation (to use catchwords) in all capitalist societies, from the crudest to the most refined. Whether we investigate West Germany or Norway, England or the United States, we see economic disorders stemming from the mechanism of the market, and disaffection, erosion of social morale, and a troublesome radicalism among students, arising from the cultural milieu.

My aloof tone may suggest a scornful denigration of the efforts of the welfare state to offset these problems. Of course once one sees the failure of welfare measures to grapple with the deepest roots of the malfunctions to which they are addressed, some critical stance is inescapable. Yet I am far from dismissing the achievements of the welfare state as hypocritical or insignificant. Indeed it may well be that the welfare state at its most advanced —as we find it in the Scandinavian nations or in certain policies of the Netherlands or Austria, for example—is the best we can do today to achieve humanist goals without jeopardizing key political and social rights. That too is a question to which we will return. Here I wish only to hammer home the point that the welfare state, adequate or not, must be considered as a form of capitalism—a conclusion that impels us to ask again exactly what we mean by socialism.

WHAT *do* we mean by socialism? Historical imaginations are notoriously poor. The response I shall hazard may be ludicrously wide of the mark from some future vantage point. Nonetheless one must do what one can, and my imagination yields only one answer to the question. *If socialism is to be a new socioeconomic formation—I must hammer home this premise—then it must depend for its economic direction on some form of planning, and for its culture on some form of commitment to the idea of a morally conscious collectivity.* These two elements seem to me to be the only alternatives to the anarchic character and alienated culture of welfare capitalism.

Let us begin with the economic issue. There are iron necessities that govern the economic activities of all societies. Provision must be made to satisfy needs for current consumption and to replace the worn-out capital of any period. Moreover a society facing technological change within, or environmental change without, will have to alter its patterns of inputs and outputs in order to maintain a steady state of final consumption and capital replacement. And last, a society seeking to increase its wealth must refrain from consuming, and must invest the resources and labor that have been saved.

These essential tasks require the coordination of activity, often on a vast scale. Speaking in stylized fashion, there are only three ways in which this can be done. Societies can trust to the guiding hand of tradition for the maintenance of a fixed configuration of activities; this is the "system" of tradition by which primitive societies secure their continuance. Tradition will not, however, arrange things when the environment changes, or when new technologies enter or when growth is sought (the two latter cases unlikely in a tradition-bound milieu). The coordinating mechanism then becomes "command"—the conscious direction of social energies by some individual or institution empowered to allocate effort, determine levels of consumption, etc. Finally, the integrating and directing economic task can also be performed by the market. The market is actually a form of highly decentralized command in which each person is trained by culture and impelled by self-interest (or at the extreme, self-preservation) to "obey" the stimuli of the marketplace.

Tradition is the operative system for nondynamic cultures; and it might in the future become the operative system for socialism. It conjures up the image of a socialist economy as a congeries of kibbutzim, each reducing to a minimum the "cash nexus" within its boundaries, and each affiliated in the larger economy by a web of long-established exchange relationships that would involve a minimum of either market dealings or command directives. Life would then follow a steady inertial course, presumably with a minimum of self-generated or externally imposed change.

However attractive such a vision, at today's juncture of history it is futile—worse, dangerous—to imagine that tradition could solve the problems of material reproduction and adaptation. The problem of change, stemming both from the continuous pressure of science and technology and from the tightening constraints of the environment, are aspects of our era that will not disappear with the advent of socialism. Society will have to alter its structure of production continuously whether or not it seeks growth. Moreover let us not forget that the stated purpose of socialism is to change the patterns of present-day income distribution and employment. Tradition cannot accomplish that.

Could the market system, under suitable guidance, accomplish these ends? Here the problems are twofold. The first is whether the conventional means of guidance for a market system would be sufficient to bring about the desired or needed changes. Would taxes, subsidies, regulations, and the like effectively alter income distribution, or would individuals following their acquisitive impulses (how else would a market system work?) nullify these intentions as they have been so often frustrated in the past? Would guidance by taxes and subsidies be powerful enough to overcome the profound inertias of occupational and industrial patterns of activity, or would these too persist, finding ways around the tax or subsidy structure to achieve ends at variance with those of the planners? I raise these questions in an apparent mood of skepticism, disillusioned with respect to the "reforming" powers of the market in the face of the wholesale cheating and evasion that seem to be endemic and irrepressible in a market system.

But that is not my deepest cause for doubt. Perhaps socialism can induce or legislate a high standard of law-abiding behavior.

There still remains another objection to the market as the "system" of socialism. If the market is to work, marketers must follow its dictates. Because we can assume that socialism will not permit individuals to suffer economic misery, we can assume that marketers will not follow these dictates by necessity, for survival's sake. They will follow them for gain.

Now comes the crucial question: Is this motivation compatible with the collective moral commitment that is to replace the self-centeredness of bourgeois society? Socialists have always railed against the invidious striving of the market that forces individuals to subordinate their full personalities to narrow economic roles. Moreover it is not only the motivations of capitalists that are at stake—perhaps under socialism managers could be trained to obey price signals simply as a guide to steering their nationalized enterprises, with no thought of personal profit. The issue is the motivation of working people. For the market mechanism is not merely a means to profit. It is also a means to individual betterment by the maximization of one's income. Without this drive the mechanism will not work.

But is the drive for private gain compatible with the goal of socialism? I do not see how it can be. The market system, in order to function, requires attitudes of self-seeking that are in direct conflict with the goal of an "other-oriented" society. If socialism seeks to avoid both the anarchy and alienation of capitalism, it must seek to break the hold of the market, not merely over the economy but over the mind.*

THUS the market cannot become the main order-bestowing system underlying socialism as a new order. Some limited reliance on a market mechanism may be necessary to achieve efficiency, for I doubt whether an industrial society could operate without price signals; some areas of market activity may serve as a vent for unwanted but insistent aspects of human behavior, much as do the

---

*This is the logic behind Marx's opposition to money itself. "Greed," he writes, "as such [is] impossible without money: all other kinds of accumulation and of mania for accumulation appear as primitive, restricted by needs on the one hand and by the restricted nature of products on the other *(sacri aura fames)." Grundrisse* (London: 1973), p. 163.

controlled red-light districts of certain countries. But I do not see how the market mentality can be encouraged within socialism *if socialism is to be distinguished from capitalism by a different kind of socioeconomic formation.* With much reluctance I am led to conclude that the market process, for all its flexibility, extreme decentralization, and self-regulation—indeed, ultimately *because* of these properties, all of which depend on market behavior—is not congenial to socialism as a new kind of social order.

If tradition cannot, and the market system should not, underpin the socialist order, we are left with some form of command as the necessary means for securing its continuance and adaptation. Indeed that is what planning means. Command by planning need not of course be totalitarian. But an aspect of authoritarianism resides inextricably in all planning systems. A plan is meaningless if it is not carried out, or if it can be ignored or defied at will. Some form of penalty must assure the necessary degree of compliance. Compliance need not be total, and penalties need not be Draconian. Incentives may succeed where punishments fail. But planning will not assure a socialist society of a capacity to endure or adapt unless the planning is a system of effective *command.* From that conclusion I see no escape.

This does not mean that socialism is doomed to repeat the disasters of central planning in the Soviet Union, where things are so bad that the system teeters on the verge of its own kind of anarchy. Perhaps associations of workers, long the ideal form of socialist "ownership," can replace rigid hierarchies of managership. Perhaps democratic and participatory procedures can break up the bureaucratic inertia of planning systems.

Nevertheless an inescapable necessity must be faced. The economy must be concerted. However democratic the internal organization of society, however much the principle of workers' control, or civil-servant stewardship, is carried into practice, the factories and stores and farms and shops of a socialist socioeconomic formation must be coordinated if socialism is not to become even more anarchic than capitalism. And this coordination must entail obedience to a central plan.*

*This general argument is given special urgency if we emphasize two historic problems that I have deliberately passed over in this essay. The first is the necessity

IT is clear by now that a great deal hinges on the determination that socialism be defined in terms of a distinct socioeconomic order, "beyond" that of welfare capitalism. Before we examine that question further I want to explore one remaining aspect of the idea of such a new socioeconomic order, an aspect on which my argument has repeatedly turned although it has not yet been placed at stage center. The issue concerns the culture that must characterize a social order deserving the name of "socialism."

Surely socialism will have its unique culture. Every major chapter of socioeconomic history—primitive life, "Asiatic despotisms," classical antiquity, medieval life, capitalism—has been identifiable by a distinct culture, recognizable not only in styles of art and philosophy and religious imagination, but in the habits and customs, folkways and moralities of daily life.

The culture of capitalism is "bourgeois." By bourgeois we mean a culture that celebrates, supports, encourages, and breeds the idea of the primary importance of the *individual*. Certainly that is the theme on which current ideology endlessly harps. If the culture of socialism is to be different, I presume that it must celebrate, support, encourage, and breed the idea of the primary importance of the *collectivity*. In addition I believe that the culture of socialism must depart from that of capitalism in a different way. Bourgeois culture is focused on the *material achievement* of the individual. Socialist culture must focus on his or her *moral or spiritual achievement*. A socialist society should be as suffused and preoccupied with the idea of moral purpose as capitalist society is suffused and preoccupied with that of personal gain.

I do not think there is much disagreement that some such collective morality is generally assumed to constitute an integral part of a genuine socialist order. Even the critics of socialism recognize this new moral commitment, and only doubt that it can be reached in practice. "You can't change human nature" is the standard dismissal of the vision of a society of heightened social concern.

---

to intervene deeply, and probably ruthlessly, into the economy in order to establish the socialist order in the first place. The second is the need to continue a policy of painful intervention to accommodate the socialist economy, once set into place, to the constricting limits of the environment.

I shall not examine that objection here. Perhaps at some very deep level it is true. Yet I see no reason to doubt that something resembling a socialist morality could be attained, however slowly and painfully and partially. Anyone who reflects on the difference between our own culture and that of the Aztec or Incan, Bedouin or Eskimo worlds, will be slow to affirm that a culture cannot be reached simply because it is so different from ours, so contrary to the way we see "human nature."

The issue I want to raise is quite different. It has to do with a problem that I believe to be as deeply embedded in a true socialist culture, *once that culture is attained*, as the necessity for a command form of economic organization is embedded in its socioeconomic structure. This cultural problem is the difficulty that a socialist culture will experience in accepting the tolerant political and perhaps social attitudes of bourgeois life.

I do not mean to exaggerate this tolerance in capitalist societies. There is a vast amount of repression in bourgeois culture. Yet one must ask oneself how it is that a magazine like *Dissent*, dedicated to the discussion—worse, the advocacy—of socialism can be permitted to exist. Why does capitalist society allow its subversive universities, presses, political movements to say and write and argue their seditious ideas? One answer of course is that bourgeois society is confident that the subversion of these ideas is negligible, that less harm is done to the legitimacy of the prevailing faith by ignoring than by persecuting these ideas. But that answer does not explain the relatively high threshold of psychological security (of complacency, if you will) that allows capitalist society to permit these *potentially* dangerous expressions to exist. Medieval society did not tolerate them. Classical Greek society did not. Soviet or Maoist society does not. Why then does bourgeois society find itself able to accept and ignore dissent to the degree it does?

The answer has two aspects. One, which we admire and like to advance, is that a culture founded on the primacy of the individual naturally asserts the rights of individuals to speak their minds freely, to act as they wish within reasonable bounds, to behave as John Stuart Mill preached in his treatise *On Liberty*.

I do not doubt that this is an important reason for the bourgeois tolerance of dissent. But there is another reason, less noticed because it consists in the absence of something, rather than in its forceful presence. This is the lack within bourgeois society of a *moral significance* attaching to most political or social acts or ideas. Dissenting thought appears within bourgeois society as a mere commodity in the "marketplace" of ideas, to use the common and illuminating phrase. Alternative lifestyles, departures in policies, new directions for individual or national activity are considered as "options" yielding calculable costs and benefits, or as "propositions" that can be considered in a detached and pragmatic light. Of course there is always a threshold of sensitivity. Attacks on property, on the legitimacy of government itself, on sexual or other prejudices are very difficult (although not impossible) for a bourgeois society to accept. But I must ask my readers to weigh the degree of bourgeois tolerance for revolutionary parties or "wild" ideas against their toleration in *any* nonbourgeois culture —primitive, despotic, religious, or "state capitalist."

The reason for the difference, I suggest, lies precisely in the divorce of bourgeois culture from a sense of moral commitment and concern. Dissident political and social beliefs in bourgeois society may be considered as erroneous, foolish, shocking, deplorable, or dangerous, but *they are not thought of as blasphemous*. Dissent is not intolerable because it does not breach a profound sense of what is good.

Yet if a socialist society is to attain the culture of moral commitment to which it aspires, it must view its politics and its social mores as guided by a desire to be good, not merely expedient. Dissents, disagreements, and departures from norms then assume a far more threatening aspect than under bourgeois society, for they hold out the possibility of destroying the very commitment to a moral consensus by which socialist society differs from capitalist.

Nor can we wriggle off this hook by asserting that, among its moral commitments, socialism will choose to include the rights of individuals to their Millian liberties. For that celebration of individualism is directly opposed to the basic socialist commitment to a deliberately embraced collective moral goal. Perhaps we get a sense of the tensions that are likely to trouble socialist society when we reflect on the difficulty with which democratic bourgeois society copes with those ideas or activities that threaten the democratic process itself. But under socialism every dissenting voice raises a threat similar to that raised under a democracy by those who preach antidemocracy. Because socialist society aspires to be a *good* society, all its decisions and opinions are inescapably invested with moral import. Every disagreement with them, every argument for alternative policies, every nay-saying voice therefore raises into question the moral validity of the existing government, not merely its competence in directing activities that have no particular moral significance. Dissents and disagreements thereby smack of heresy in a manner lacking from societies in which expediency and not morality rules the roost.

These conclusions will distress or even outrage many readers, because they seem to be nothing but the familiar conservative or reactionary warnings that socialism is incompatible with freedom, and therefore reprehensible. But I do not intend to join this chorus of admonishing voices. Instead let us ask what consequences follow from my argument that socialism, as a chapter of history truly beyond welfare capitalism, is likely to present structural and cultural aspects that are distasteful or unacceptable to many present-day socialists.

The first possibility is immediately evident. It is to avoid the difficulties of our position by undoing our original premise. Once we give up the insistence that socialism must be a new departure in history, we bypass many of the hard conclusions to which we have been forced. We can maintain the self-correcting, self-propelling mechanism of a market-oriented economy—a decision that vastly simplifies the organizational problem of socialism. We can retain an individualist, rather than collective, general orientation. Socialism can then be described as a *program* rather than a new social order. Its programmatic content is not hard to describe: a search for economic equity in society, for the constriction of property rights, for humanizing the work process, for democratic participation, personal cultivation, civil liberties, and the like. As I have mentioned before, I do not take such a program lightly; I repeat that it may be the best we can do to cope with certain present evils without jeopardizing the liberties we desire to defend.

Yet we must be clear about the consequences of this choice. Socialism then becomes a movement *within* welfare capitalism, not beyond it. The retention of the market system implies as well the likelihood of problems of "anarchy": the retention of an individualistic orientation probably brings many of the problems of anomie, malaise, "alienation." The idea of radical change would therefore be relinquished in favor of incremental change—a slow and uneven advance that would keep, perhaps indefinitely, some of the most important characteristics of capitalism. Socialism then becomes an unending and perhaps ultimately futile struggle to "humanize" a society based on the inhuman imperatives and ideologies of capital.

Revolutionary socialists will reject such a defeatist position. They must then accept the price of a leap into the future. There are respectable arguments for such a position. One can press for socialism as a new chapter beyond welfare capitalism because one believes that ills to which socialism would address itself are greater by far than those it will create. The anarchy of capitalism is after all an immense evil for millions of persons in the West, hundreds of millions or even billions if we widen our view to include the globe. The anomie, alienation, and purposelessness of an individualistic way of life extend far and deep under capitalism, robbing existence of the stabilizing certainties that have guided it under all other forms of social organization. Capitalism alone exposes its constituents to the anxiety of life without the succor of a collective morality. One can argue that the repair of these damages is worth far more than the curtailment of economic freedom or the diminution of personal liberty that socialism will require. And then too there is the thought that those who will live under socialism will no more regret the absence of vanished privileges than we regret those of earlier ages. We do not lament the vanished rights of aristocracy. A generation accustomed to the supporting discipline of socialism will not miss those of bourgeois individualism.

There will remain some socialists who cannot accept this rationale. There remains for them a third choice. Socialism can then be viewed as a direction of historic change whose underlying tendencies are those I have described. That does not require the conclusion that every socialist society must sink to the worst levels of tyranny and oppression, any more than the presence of anarchic and alienating tendencies in capitalism requires that every such society become a grotesque version of its latent tendencies. Rather, from this perspective socialism becomes a historical drift that can no longer be viewed uncritically as a deliverance, but must be regarded as a process that will bring unwanted changes as well as desired ones.

What is important in trying to think about socialism is to resist the delusion that history is so soft and indeterminate that we can have a socialist cake with bourgeois icing. A searching examination of the requirements for a truly new order forces us to recognize that deep qualitative differences must separate such a socialism from the society in which we live. The new order of socialism may display many surface variations and some vestiges of bourgeois ways, but at bottom it must differ from capitalism as capitalism, despite its variations and aristocratic remnants, differs at bottom from feudalism. This requires a much more sober estimation of socialism than is now generally to be found. Above all, it requires the bitter admission that socialism cannot be the best of all worlds, as we creatures of bourgeois society judge what is best. If we wish to bestow the name socialism on the next chapter of history, we must not expect it to be written in the vocabulary of a period that is finished.

Lewis Coser

A Response to Heilbroner

"SOMETIMES," says the protagonist in Robert Pirsing's novel *Zen and the Art of Motorcycle Maintenance*, echoing Montaigne, "it is a little better to travel than to arrive." The trouble with Robert Heilbroner's argument is that he is unwilling to consider this possibility. As in much of his previous writing, Heilbroner is so obsessed with what allegedly awaits us at the end of the road that he is rather unattentive to the benefits that may accrue to us as, hesitantly and stumblingly, we make our way on it. But it won't do to disdain the real gains in the human condition that have been made on the road from unrestricted capitalism to the welfare state.

Though he permits himself in places to say some nice things about the welfare state, the overall drift of his argument is designed to denigrate it and to characterize it as just another face of capitalist domination. He even argues that "the welfare state . . . is a kind of apotheosis of capitalism." This is about as useful as calling seventeenth-century absolutism a kind of apotheosis of feudalism. The social and political structure of, say, France in the seventeenth century, its culture and its lifestyles, were qualitatively different from those of the Middle Ages—even though certain key institutions of the ancien régime were only swept away by the French Revolution. In the same way an advanced welfare state, in which planned policy has partly replaced the unplanned operation of the market, and in which the unseen hand of God has given way in many sectors of the polity and the economy to the visible powers of regulating agencies, may be called an "apotheosis of capitalism" only in a Pickwickian sense. All of this is not to deny the enormous weight of the corporate giants that bestride many an industry and can exert inordinate sway in the economy as a whole. It is only to assert that in the advanced welfare state other powers have been able to contain and countervail them in major sectors of public life. I hold no brief for even an advanced welfare state, indeed I wish ardently to go beyond it, but I must still insist that to see in it the zenith of capitalism, rather than an indication that it might have reached its nadir, seems rather short-sighted.

To be sure the welfare state has not abolished capitalism and the profit motive—it still contains many of the evils that marked the preceding epoch—but it is emphatically a very different animal from classical capitalism. One may of course always argue that it is still "basically" capitalism, but this term is analytically so vacuous that it can hardly serve as well. As a matter of fact, "basic" breaks in human history are extremely rare. Powerful analysts, such as Tocqueville, have even argued that prerevolutionary and postrevolutionary France were "basically" more similar than dissimilar. Most transformations on the human scene proceed relatively slowly, gradually, and in an incremental manner, rather than through apocalyptic breaks. Is the New South "basically" the same as the Old South? Is the Germany of today "basically" the same as that of Bismarck? Is the role of women "basically" the same as it was in the Victorian age? Such questions really are no more enlightening than the famous dispute on whether the glass of water is half full or half empty. It all depends on your point of view.

Heilbroner's fixation on the "basic" continuity of capitalism from laissez-faire to the welfare state leads him to another mistake. He fails to see that the welfare state, far from developing "naturally" out of unrestrained capitalism, came into being largely through the continued struggle of labor and union organizations. It continues to exist and develop because of the unrelenting struggle of these forces. The welfare state, even though it has proved congenial to certain sectors of managerial and capitalist interests, is largely the result of continuous pressures on the haves by the have-nots. It is not a novel measure of social control, as Marcuse and his friends assert, but like the eight-hour day of an earlier time, a result of the assertion of power on behalf of the underdog. As Alisdair MacIntyre, in his fine critical appraisal of *Herbert Marcuse* (New York: Viking Press, 1970), says so well: "The notion that the ruling elite are now able to treat welfare as an institution of social control is at very best a quarter-truth, and a very dangerous one."

I suppose that others will address themselves in some detail to this part of Heilbroner's essay, and prefer therefore to deal in greater detail with what I think is Heilbroner's most powerful argument: the contention that socialism must necessarily enforce a collectivistic morality in counterpoint to the rampant individualism of the bourgeois age.

I cannot follow him when he characterizes bourgeois culture as one "that celebrates, supports, encourages, and breeds the idea of the primary importance of the *individual*." Individualism, however, emerged in courtly and aristocratic circles during the Renaissance and is by no means a bourgeois invention. It later was developed largely in struggles *against* bourgeois society. More important, I had supposed that if there was any basic agreement among socialist critics of bourgeois culture, it involved the notion that this culture rested on the enhancement of the individualism and autonomy of *some* individuals at the price of the repression of the individuality of most others. If that is not the message that is conveyed by Fourier or Proudhon, by Marx or Norman Thomas, then I have misread all of them through a lifetime of study.

The whole socialist tradition has centered on the criticism of bourgeois society as stultifying, thwarting, and stunting the capacities of human beings. What else did Marx mean when he talked about the alienating conditions of bourgeois life? Most of the classical socialist tradition maintained that socialist culture would for the first time allow the full flowering of individuality. Far from advocating, as Heilbroner claims, "the primary importance of the collectivity," it argued instead that only a fundamental restructuring of the conditions of collective life would permit the full development of human autonomy.

But no matter what the initial intentions of its founders might be, Heilbroner argues, a future socialist society, being necessarily built on the primacy of command over self-direction, will have to be antiindividualistic. It cannot, he asserts, permit the kind of laissez-faire attitude in the sphere of manners and morals that characterized the bourgeois age. But this laissez-faire attitude is, I think, mainly a creature of Heilbroner's imagination. In the period of bourgeois ascendancy, in the period of primitive accumulation, bourgeois culture was built on severe repression, even among its leading strata. The world of the Protestant Ethic and of Mr. Gradgrind was hardly a world of hedonistic pleasures, sensory indulgences, or assertion of unfettered human autonomy. Only the self-denying ordinances of Protestant and utilitarian culture allowed the accumulation of the capital needed for the emergence of capitalism triumphant. At later stages of bourgeois development such restrictions came to be progressively removed. And under late capitalism, and in the age of the welfare state, hedonistic enjoyment (to the sorrow of Daniel Bell) came to be a valid option in an increasingly pluralistic moral universe.

But if that be the case, why must we assume that under socialism such pluralistic options will no longer be available? I suppose that we are all agreed that a socialism of scarcity is a contradiction in terms. Given a relative abundance of resources there will be no need of excessive restraint. Heilbroner argues that a socialist society must enforce common uniform standards because it wishes "to be good, not merely expedient." But this is not, as they say, necessarily so. Richard Tawney answered Heilbroner over half a century ago when he wrote:

> It is obvious, indeed, that no change of system or machinery can avert the causes of social *malaise* which consist in the egotism, greed, or quarrelsomeness of human nature. What it can do is to create an environment in which these are not the qualities which are encouraged. It cannot secure that men live up to their principles. What it can do is to establish their social order upon principles to which, if they please, they can live up and not down. It cannot control their actions. It can offer them an end upon which to fix their minds.

It is not true, as Heilbroner says, "that celebration of individualism is directly opposed to the basic socialist commitment to a deliberately embraced *collective* moral goal." The society of which Tawney dreamed, and of which I dream, does not force people to be good, it simply removes some of the impediments that previously did not permit them to be good. It provides incentives for autonomous individuals, no longer driven by the compulsions of an acquisitive society, to choose paths of self-realization that do not conflict with the collective well-being. Solidarity and fraternity do not contradict the need for self-realization; they make it possible.

One last word: Heilbroner subscribes to the kind of "historicism" against which Karl Popper has directed his shafts for many years. He somehow assumes that a reified "history" drives people inevitably into some predetermined future. Against any such deterministic scheme one needs to insist that the future can never be predetermined since men and women in the here and now make it happen. If the future is in fact open (although partly bound by structural conditions and trends), then it behooves us to reject messages of despair such as those of Heilbroner since they might well turn into self-fulfilling predictions if they attract a wide hearing. The myth of inevitable progress served to emasculate transformative capacities by seemingly making voluntary activity supererogatory. The myth of the inevitable tyranny of the collective could serve to emasculate the prepotent desire of human beings to reach a society in which the free development of each is based on the free development of all.

Bogdan Denitch

ROBERT Heilbroner raises a cardinal question: Can *socialism* be democratic? Clearly it is not a question of whether socialists are democrats, or whether the various reforms of capitalism that socialists propose here and now are consistent with democracy. Heilbroner poses the more serious question: In a socialist society, the one presumably beyond the welfare state, the one in which socialists are no longer just adding one more reform to a pyramid of welfare-state reforms—in short, in a society in which the basic means of production, distribution, and exchange are socially owned, and no capitalist class is left as a class—can democratic institutions, as we understand them, continue to exist?

Part of the problem lies in the relatively mechanical definition of what a socialist society would have to look like. There is a commonly held definition, espoused not only by such economists as Paul Sweezy who have no problem with the question since their response is that socialism shall not be democratic, but also held by most of the Fabians and the more moderate social democrats who all had the notion that centralized planning was a feature that is indispensable to socialism, and that centralized planning would inevitably involve an enormous concentration of political and economic power in the hands of those who plan. In socialist critiques of the Soviet dictatorship, the formulation often used was: in a society where the state owns all the means of production, distribution, and exchange, the sole relevant question is who "owns" the state. Socialist critics of the Soviet Union concluded that since the political bureaucracy had a monopoly on the relevant decisions, it "owned" the state, and that the state therefore represented the interests of this class (stratum, group, or whatever) rather than those of the working class and the population as a whole.

In a socialist society where the monopoly of power would presumably not be as highly concentrated in a layer of top planners and bureaucrats and where parliamentary institutions and normal civil liberties would continue, this criticism would still maintain some force. It is after all a truism in modern political democracies that less and less power is wielded by the legislatures and more and more is transferred to bureaucracies. Granted, these can be selfless, well-wishing bureaucracies; but the notion is that modern society requires a level of expertise that can be mobilized at decisive points—and that for practical purposes makes the experts the rulers. This would be all the more so if the economy as a whole were in the hands of the same government experts who control the political mechanisms.

Heilbroner's second point—that a socialist bureaucracy would be more actively involved in governing because it is concerned with doing good and therefore more impatient with obstacles, disagreements, and inefficiency—all characteristic of the democratic process—is a separate and extremely interesting point, though I do not choose to pursue it at this time. If one grants the first assumption of bureaucratic planning at the center in a society fundamentally unchanged from the present one in terms of values and distribution of power, the second point does follow. But there is more than one tradition of socialism, and it is important to stress this diversity of socialist traditions. Whether one calls it socialism from above or socialism from below, refers back to the debates between Shaw and Wells among the British Fabians, or stresses the centralist versus the syndicalist strands of the socialist tradition in Europe, it is clear that on this question of centralized planning and control there is ambivalence. Heilbroner stresses only one tradition. It has an honorable pedigree, but nevertheless it has, in my opinion, little to do with what a modern, highly industrialized socialist society would or should look like. The socialism of centralized planning is, in one way or another, a socialism of scarcity.

There is another approach that could be called self-governing or self-managing socialism. It has an increasingly wide acceptance both among West European Socialists and East European dissident democratic Communists. The second have had direct and painful experience with the problem of centralization while the first are in part reacting to the dull welfare states established in Europe in the post–World War II period. Here the tradition is more syndicalist than centralist. It is based on a set of assumptions that have been submitted to prolonged testing in Yugoslavia, though under far from optimal conditions.

Whatever one thinks of Yugoslavia—and it is a one-party state—the economy has shown a great deal of autonomy from the center, and more to the point, numbers of previously uninvolved individuals have become successfully involved in running complex enterprises and institutions. The result is a more efficient and effective system than any centralized economy in Eastern Europe. While the Yugoslav experience does not tell us much about the political system appropriate to a democratic socialist society, it does posit an economy run essentially by elected bodies of workers and other employees. These elected bodies have had ever-widening powers. They have acted—and this is crucial—not merely as institutions managing sectors of the economy, but as organs of political socialization creating a new nexus of values and links in an industrialized society.

Two issues are involved. One is: Can elected workers' councils run an economy without prohibitive costs in terms of efficiency? The answer seems clearly to be, yes. To be sure there are problems. Sometimes wrong decisions are made, but apparently not more often than in centrally planned economies. What is remarkable is not that there are problems, but how sustained the rate of growth produced by such an economy was in the decade before the general European slump of the 1970s. During that decade Yugoslav growth figures approximated those of Japan. It is that, after all, which made the Yugoslav economic model so attractive to the liberalizing reformers of Eastern Europe. The second issue, however, is more interesting for the prospect of a democratic socialism, and this is the nature of institutions developing within such an economy. The economic enterprise also becomes a sociopolitical community. It is the place from which political and economic power is aggregated in the system as a whole. It is the place through which the newly industrialized peasants learn the rules of the game of an industrial society. It is the place through which the notion of individual and collective rights is taught and asserted. And it is a community in which a set of values consistent with the new socialist civilization will have to develop if there is to be such a civilization.

Here the problems are even more troublesome, for this means a society in which there is considerable pressure to participate and take responsibility. It means a society in which, since the work enterprise is one in which you expect to spend a good part of your life, one does not push differences to the knife. The mechanism, the style, is communitarian and consensual rather than conflictual. The pressures are toward egalitarian leveling, since in enterprise work councils the more skilled cadres are forced to argue *why* they should be paid more than other employees—sometimes a painful experience for surgeons talking to nurses and other workers in a hospital but one that I would argue has a good bit to do with socialist democracy.

There are two key elements that seem indispensable to a working decentralized self-managing economy. Again looking at the Yugoslav experience, it seems clear that without these the workers' councils become a sham, as they indeed have become in Poland and Hungary. The first is that the councils must have genuine economic power and must take responsibility for decisions they make, including bad ones. This had dictated the development of a socialist *market* economy for a very simple reason. Something, some institution or mechanism that at least appears reasonably impartial had to be developed to replace the bureaucratic planning center. The mechanism that seemed most adaptable was a limited market. Socialist theorists, with such rare exceptions as Oscar Lange and some of the more recent Yugoslav and Polish theorists, have had a dogmatic, almost puritanical attitude toward the market. Presumably harking back to the young Marx, the market reifies commodities and work and encourages the development of some kind of consumer sovereignty that socialist intellectuals all too often think is bad for ordinary mortals.

There are two sides to this aversion. One is a predilection of socialist intellectuals toward neat, organized plans run by experts not too unlike themselves; the other is a notion that if consumers of the lower orders are turned loose, they will not choose things that are good for them. Both are elitist conceptions and have only survived in the socialist movement for so long because of the association of the market with private ownership and great concentrations of wealth and power. But there is no reason why a modified market cannot be used on the one hand as a yardstick to measure the performance of enterprises, and on the other as a determinant of the consumer goods that the public wants. I have never found it a moral question that teenagers in Yugoslavia or in Poland yearn for Levis. Apparently centralized planners do. There seems to be a moral feeling that centrally designed, badly fitting pants are more appropriate for socialists than Levis. There, I suspect, the authoritarian bureaucrats of Eastern Europe probably have a good deal in common with the tradition in the Western socialist movement that parts of the British Labour party represented. I sometimes believe that Sir Stafford Cripps *preferred* to have rationing. A market economy in a socialist society may well lead to some hedonistic waste and frivolities for the plebeians; I believe it to be a good thing.

A more serious problem with a socialist market economy, at least in Yugoslavia—I am still using it as a model—is that various institutions other than plants are also run by workers' councils operating in a market setting. This has posed painful debates in the field of culture and in some service delivery institutions. Do the local cultural funds go to build more football fields or chamber-music orchestras? It is surprising how readily socialist intellectuals spring to elitist solutions. The truth is that within that particular market economy workers' councils dominated by blue-collar workers have proven more generous in subsidizing "high culture" than have their betters, either in state-run "socialism" or under capitalism. This is not to say that they have not made mistakes. It is simply to say that it does not follow that if blue-collar workers are given power over social and cultural expenditures, which presumably is what we mean by saying "to extend democracy into the economy and society," that an era of barbarism would follow. The Yugoslav metal industry, with two-thirds of the councils composed of blue-collar workers, has generously subsidized chamber music, avant-garde theater, operas, and the like—in fact somewhat more generously than the previous centralized system had done. The painful process involved was that various intellectuals were forced to go before the councils and argue their case for funding, an indignity they object to far less when it has to be done before a local equivalent of the Ford and Carnegie foundations.

This dwelling on what seems an almost peripheral issue of the democratic financing of culture in a democratically managed socialist economy is to lead up to my central point. Democratic socialists have had, all too often, far too mean and narrow an image of what a socialist democracy could look like. It is in response to this mean and narrow image that Heilbroner's polemic makes some sense. A socialist culture would, in my opinion, have to center on the process of production, the term being taken in its widest meaning. There is no reason to assume that history came to a stop with the development of liberal political institutions of the Anglo-Saxon peoples, that the end of history and the sole model of democracy is the multiparty polity based on geographical representation. After all a good case can be made for functional representation in geographically mobile societies, and whatever else the virtues of multiparty representation have been so far, they have been remarkably successful in keeping the lower strata from participation in governance other than in occasional elections. A democracy that will result in government by lawyers, or at best professional trade-union functionaries, seems to me a somewhat narrow definition of that term. And while Yugoslavia is clearly not the image of a democratic socialist society, at least it challenges our imagination in regard to ways that popular participation can be built into an economy and to the various possible social and cultural institutions. Without this participation, I believe that most of the talk about democracy in an industrial society of the modern type is a sham.

Nothing in the argument so far should be taken even as a hint that the classic civil liberties won in bourgeois societies (not "bourgeois" democracy but democracy won from the bourgeoisie) would not need to be maintained in a socialist society. What I am addressing myself to, rather, is the more troublesome question of how to create autonomous pockets of power in a society where the economy is socially controlled. The more serious critics of socialism have always picked on this feature of a socialist society as the one that facilitates the development of authoritarianism. Under capitalism, presumably, independent centers of power exist in the economy that can control what happens in the civil society or at least set limits to it. Therefore it is necessary in thinking about a postwelfare socialism to think of how in such a society centers of autonomous, legitimate, and institutionalized power could be created. This is far more important than the question of whether or not political parties, which would also exist, would be able to offer alternate platforms every once in a while. What institutions would have the capacity, politically and economically, to say no? This in turn means that there would be a continual tension in a socialist society between two goods—the autonomous, self-governing institutions and the need to coordinate these institutions for greater public good. Within this tension, continual debate and dialogue would continue.

My last point is that the underpinning of a self-governing economy requires a working population with capacities to utilize such an institutional framework. This problem has been grossly exaggerated by some critics because of a tendency to place too much emphasis on expertise and formalized training. The modern industrial working class is far better educated than was its nineteenth-century predecessor, and it is no longer willing to concede legitimate authority in the economy based on a supposed monopoly of expertise held by the owners and managers. This is so whether one thinks of the working class as limited to blue-collar workers or takes the term in its wider meaning to include the technical and white-collar strata who are often, if anything, better educated than their supervisors.

The rising educational level of the working population may not argue for the establishment of self-managing institutions in the economy, but it certainly does challenge the maintenance of rigidly hierarchical models that are prevalent under capitalism and state "socialism." Just as there has been a rising involvement of sectors of the middle class in local government, urban decentralization, and school management, it would seem that an analogous development is occurring in large-scale institutions and industries in Western Europe. Unions and workers increasingly show an impatience with the assumption that decisions affecting their lives cannot be made democratically within the workplace. I believe ultimately, therefore, that it is in this direction that the real answer to Heilbroner's argument lies. Can socialism be democratic? Yes; otherwise of course it will not be worth its name or worth supporting. But more to the point, yes—provided socialists do not permit their imaginations to be crippled by the limits of liberal democracy under capitalism.

Michael Harrington

I THINK it may be possible to have a "socialist cake with bourgeois icing." But I must immediately add that posing the issue that way obscures some of its essentials.

In saying this I do not dismiss Robert Heilbroner's argument out of hand, for he touches on a real problem. My objection is that

Heilbroner has somewhat simplified and mislabeled a complex trend in a way that, ironically, might contribute to the worst of his fears. There are, I think, two polar extremes that will define the social space in which the postcapitalist future will develop (is developing): authoritarian, bureaucratic collectivism, and democratic, communitarian collectivism. Heilbroner is quite right to warn us against that first possibility, but by giving it the name of its polar opposite—by calling it "socialism"—he unwittingly makes it all the more difficult to fight against it.

Bourgeois society, Heilbroner argues, gives primacy to the individual as part of its economic focus on personal gain. It tolerates dissent, and even revolutionary criticism, because it is in some considerable measure indifferent to ideals, even its own. Socialist society on the other hand will require "command" planning and, precisely because of its passionate moral commitment to the common good, is likely not to tolerate dissidence in the way its amoral, pragmatic, and cynical predecessor did.

To my mind, Heilbroner vastly overstates the tolerance that capitalist society *voluntarily* grants to its opponents. But it would be unfair to pursue such details, because he has obviously compressed his analysis into a small compass and would, I suspect, agree with most of my historical amendments to it. Even more to the point, I want to concentrate on the basic differences between us. They have to do with the relationship between political and economic power in bourgeois, socialist, and bureaucratic collectivist societies.

Capitalism is the first social-economic formation in which political and economic power are separated and the surplus is pumped out of the direct producers by economic, rather than political, means. This is an exceedingly complex reality, and I will here ignore aspects of it that would be important in a rounded analysis. I propose to focus narrowly on one strand of this phenomenon that is most relevant to Heilbroner's case.

I think that Heilbroner fails to analyze both the function and the (related) limitations of personal freedom within capitalism. It is not the "icing" of that system but a structural constituent of it. On the one hand Heilbroner does not give capitalism sufficient credit because he does not see how central democracy was to its development; on the other hand he does not recognize the profound limits of *bourgeois* democracy, limits that derive precisely from its functional necessity. And this failure to grasp the historic and systemic particularity of capitalist democracy keeps him from seeing the possibilities of socialist democracy.

It is the genius of capitalism that it presents its grimmest necessities as freedoms. The worker is not forced to pay a tribute established by tradition and exacted by the sword. He or she freely contracts to work or freely decides to starve. The role played by the various despots of precapitalism is taken over by the impersonal laws of the market, which impartially apply to the rich and the poor. And bourgeois democracy—political equality structurally limited, and sometimes vitiated, by economic inequality—is not only ideally suited to a system in which economic power is juridically private. It also reinforces the individualistic illusions that facilitate the growth of the most productive social system humanity has ever known. Capitalism needs democracy—but democracy of a certain, antidemocratic type.

Indeed the politicalization of economic power in late capitalism is, as Jurgen Habermas has brilliantly analyzed, one of the sources of a crisis of legitimacy in the system. As the invisible hand is replaced by the visible—groups, regions, and even nations begin to demand that the results be fair. The problem is of course that even though non-, and sometimes anti-, capitalist means are being used to preserve capitalism, the essential foundations of bourgeois power have not been disturbed. This is why the welfare state normally follows corporate priorities.

What is the socialist response to this situation? The socialist essential, it must always be remembered, is not the plan: it is the democratic power of the people over the plan and the planners. The very core of capitalist power is the domination of a tiny minority over the basic investment decisions that shape the future of society behind the backs of the people and perpetuates the maldistribution of wealth at the same time. When that structure is transformed, the "icing" of bourgeois democracy is not placed on top of the socialist cake. Rather the possibility of democracy *tout court* is established for the first time.

Fine words. But isn't Heilbroner right that planners' decisions could lead in the direction of authoritarianism? Of course he is. My objection is not that he identifies that very real possibility —but that he tends to treat it as the *only* possibility. This narrow focus becomes quite apparent in the choice of a critical word: "some form of command" is necessary to the socialist order. The term "command" predetermines the judgment that will be made by anyone who uses it. What must be done—in theory and in practice—is to counterpose democratic planning to command planning. Obviously that counterposition is easier said than done. But it is a possibility, and one that Heilbroner ignores.

All possible forms of postcapitalism will see the reintegration of the political and the economic, a trend that is already in furious motion in every country in the world. But there is a wide variety of political structures and—this is the great lesson that Stalinism should have taught us—they will determine who holds economic and social power. If I can use a distinction that I find misleading and dangerous in most other contexts, in the consciously directed societies of the future it is guaranteed that the "superstructure" will control the "base." The critical question is, whose "superstructure"?

One example: As society continues to develop its planning mechanisms, will there be formal, legal provisions and subsidies for counterplanners and counterplans? If not, the dictatorship of some or another bureaucracy on the basis of monopolizing the means of decision-making is likely; if so, there is the possibility of new forms of genuine democracy, which would be as central to a socialist system as skewed democracy is to the bourgeois system.

So I would not reject Heilbroner's argument. I would amend it. Specifically, I would rewrite the last sentence in his next-to-last paragraph in this way:

> From this perspective collectivism becomes a historical drift that can no longer be viewed uncritically as a deliverance, but must be regarded as a process that will bring unwanted changes as well as desired ones. Socialism is the movement for the democratization of that collectivist trend which points in the direction of, and struggles for, the desirable changes.

Michael Walzer

ROBERT Heilbroner's argument about "moral culture" can be summed up in this way: capitalist laissez-faire makes for toleration and liberty, if only because it leaves us utterly indifferent to each other's opinions, while socialist solidarity would give us new reasons to worry about dissent and incline us toward repressive policies. It is a serious argument, and I do not think it is wholly wrong. But one might tell the same story in a rather different fashion.

When men and women are cut loose from every kind of communal support, conceived as rational egotists, encouraged to think only of themselves, they are in a certain sense, not an unimportant sense, set free. But they are not set free in ways that encourage political activity. They have more room in their private lives, but their lives are overwhelmingly private. They live in the narrow circle of family and business. They have friends, but not comrades. And partly for these reasons, they are radically exposed to the pressures of the market. To some extent these are pressures to conform, and surely the ability of the market to shape the tastes and opinions of masses of people ought to be disturbing to anyone who loves liberty. "They like in crowds," John Stuart Mill wrote, not of socialist but of bourgeois society.

But market pressures work also to exploit and trivialize, rather than eradicate, our personal, religious, and political differences. Heilbroner makes this point in explaining the range of contemporary tolerance, but it is relevant also to the issues of depth and seriousness. I am indeed free, let's say, to celebrate a black mass in my living room; and if I am unlikely to escape television coverage, my neighbors will complain only about the cameramen on their lawns—they won't say a word about my "religious preferences." But what is the point of a black mass that everyone finds *interesting*? A similar argument holds with regard to secular and political forms of dissent. Dissent is parasitic on belief, and a society that privatizes and trivializes belief takes much of the meaning out of dissent. And then toleration is too easy.

I have no doubt at all as to the value of religious freedom, or of political freedom. But I am not sure that either can be sustained for long without the experience of conviction, solidarity, and struggle. Within bourgeois society this experience has been provided, above all, by the effort to create a more just and egalitarian social order. Conceived ideally, however, the private lives of individuals-as-egotists do not generate enterprises of this sort and therefore do not test the seriousness of toleration. Private men and women are shaped instead by those patterns of inequality and passivity central to capitalist organization, into consumers and spectators, perpetually excited, sometimes satiated, often frustrated, but fundamentally dependent and acquiescent. Meaningful freedom depends, by contrast, on the existence of an active public life. Here again I am following Mill: "The spirit of a commercial people," he wrote, "will be essentially mean and slavish wherever public spirit is not cultivated by an extensive participation of the people in the business of government in detail. . . ."

Now extensive participation of that kind is, I think, the core of socialism. The moral culture of socialism is rooted in a shared citizenship, the fellowship of the forum. We seek a remedy for passivity and privatization in a radical democracy, opening new opportunities for collective decision-making so that the beliefs of ordinary citizens become important. Men and women acquire dignity and strength by taking a stand among their peers. But taking a stand can also be dangerous: it invites disagreement and conflict, and it can in certain circumstances breed political fierceness and intolerance. If politics is serious, it cannot be entirely without risk.

But Heilbroner is wrong to suggest that socialist democracy requires everyone to take the same stand or that it involves the triumph of a single idea of the good. It involves something very different: the creation of a new forum in which ideas about the good can be disputed. Or better, a series of forums: since we are not primitivists and do not intend a return to undifferentiated social structures or preindustrial economies, social politics is entirely compatible with pluralism. And if arguments go on within different and overlapping organizations, there must also be, and there will be, negotiation and compromise. Value attaches to the arguments themselves, not to particular outcomes. Some disagreements will be expressed in moral language, others in the language of expediency. It is not likely that a proposal, say, to reorganize the steel industry, though it may well be called erroneous, foolish, dangerous, and so on, will be denounced as blasphemous. Indeed I see no reason to think that the formal structure of disagreement will be so different from what it is in bourgeois democracies. It is the participants who will be different.

But perhaps I have not confronted the strongest feature of Heilbroner's argument. I am assuming that the deep morality of a socialist society will be self-respect and mutual respect, and that these will provide a better basis for freedom than can possibly be provided by mere egotism and indifference. But this may be true only for political freedom. The fellowship of the forum may encompass only those committed to the forum. One can imagine socialist democracy generating a kind of political highmindedness, intolerant of people without strong opinions and public interests. Perhaps this is what Heilbroner means when he speaks of "the primary importance of the collectivity." Socialist citizens would expect one another to think about and to work for the common interest. It would be more offensive in socialist society than it is in bourgeois society to evade jury duty, cheat on your taxes, stay home from critical meetings. Certain forms of withdrawal might be harder to manage, private interests harder to defend. Every solidarity, I suppose, produces a new set of strangers. But I am not inclined to view this problem in the ultimate terms that Heilbroner sets. As bourgeois society has adjusted to a certain level of commitment among its citizens, so socialist society could adjust to a certain level of apathy. Of course we will have to make sure that it does adjust and find ways to accommodate individual waywardness. In socialist, as in capitalist society, vigilance will continue to be the price of liberty.

If we fail to produce an extensive participation of ordinary people in the business of government, then Heilbroner's collectivism would be very dangerous. A statist regime, controlling economic as well as political life, authoritarian in character, might well find it convenient to stir up among its citizens (or subjects) a new sense of moral purpose. It might encourage them to ask, for example, "not what your country can do for you, but what you can do for your country." It might use the language of socialist solidarity ideologically to mask an actual impoverishment of public life. And that impoverishment, together with the coercive power of such a state, would certainly reduce the range of personal and political liberty. But this would not represent the triumph of socialism, but only one more defeat.

Robert L. Heilbroner: A Reply

I THINK that Lewis Coser is out of sympathy with my purpose and therefore misconstrues my argument. My purpose is to examine the idea of socialism *as a new socioeconomic formation.* These italicized words do not seem to get through. Mr. Coser avoids the problems they pose, or insists that there is no such problem. Well, I must humbly repeat my conviction that welfare capitalism *is* capitalism, however much nicer than nonwelfare capitalism, and that socialism presumably means something "basically" different. I have spelled out the basic difference, which can be compressed into *planning* and *morality.* Coser's comment boils down to an insistence that we can have socialism with the same political and ideological constraints as in the best of capitalism. I do not think that history will be so obliging. Perhaps this is what makes me guilty of "historicism" in his eyes.

I must add a word of sharp disagreement about the meaning and origins of "individualism." By individualism I think we generally mean a conception of the relation between the person and society that puts the person first, society second. J. S. Mill's *On Liberty* is the most famous exposition of this view. We also imply, I think, a strong emphasis on the equality of persons: equality before the law, equality in voting, equality in economic life as "equal" parties in exchange. Of course these views are often cruelly betrayed in bourgeois society, but that does not detract from their bourgeois origin or their bourgeois identity. Show me the John Stuart Mill of

Greece or Rome, of feudal life or the aristocratic courts, or of socialism in any of its realizations to date, and I will cede the point.

Messrs. Walzer, Harrington, and Denitch *do* see what I am driving at, for which I am grateful. In one way or another they all think I overstate my case, and perhaps they are right. It is arguable that socialism as a new socioeconomic order would present a spectrum of variations, just as capitalism does and feudalism or the slave orders did, and perhaps some of these socialist societies of the future will tolerate the particular social relations that we celebrate. These relations remain, however, bourgeois in concept, however much they may use the "socialist" vocabulary of equality and democracy. For are not equality and democracy, as we define these terms, quintessentially bourgeois conceptions, as I have just argued against Coser? We can *hope* they will be compatible with socialism, as they are (in part) with highly developed welfare capitalism, but we cannot deny their bourgeois identity—to repeat, *as we define them.*

Bogdan Denitch's comment interests me because he goes the furthest in specifying the nature of an institutional structure that is not capitalist and that might admit the kinds of freedoms that we bourgeois-thinking self-styled socialists would like to see preserved. I have always felt it was a great pity that associationist socialism had to have its first trial in a country so burdened with history as Yugoslavia. I would agree with Denitch that this is a road many of us would like to see socialism follow, although whether that will be a historical possibility is difficult to say.

Philip Green

Social Democracy and Its Critics: The Case of England

AN American living in England after a while begins to notice certain events and institutions, trivial or profound, that seem to add up to a distinctive social pattern.

In American suburbs and even in many cities today the center of communal, group, and family life is the bowling-alley complex: hub of a multibillion-dollar industry that offers among its by-products food (fast and slow) and drink, equipment and machinery, clothing and other accessories, and associated or subordinate forms of entertainment (e.g., dancing, ice skating). In England that center is still the simple pub.

In England refrigerators are very small (an American visitor in an English kitchen can easily miss seeing the fridge altogether) and so are the milk bottles. Larger milk bottles would not fit into the standard refrigerator; milk thus does not come in larger containers, and thus there is no need for larger refrigerators. Thus also a great many low-paying jobs providing daily milk delivery to the population are kept available.

English workers do not strike much more often than American workers, but an astonishingly large proportion of their strikes turns out to be against fellow workers, to protect traditional lines of demarcation at the workplace, pay differentials, etc.

When the films of Marcel Ophuls are shown on BBC-TV, the dubbed-in English voices signal social class very carefully: officers, politicians (of the right or center), and businessmen speak in the poshest BBC accents, whereas "common" soldiers and workers speak in accents ranging from pronounced working-class to cockney. But when we are allowed to hear the original French and German voices the social class variations are not nearly so marked.

Street repairmen spend a lot of time sitting under tents drinking tea, or keeping out of mild rains.

Members of the very extensive royal family, who do absolutely nothing at all, are eagerly sought after to be the honorary heads of educational and scientific institutions, public-service bodies, and businesses. In that role they always receive considerably more publicity than the actual managers of the enterprise.

A majority of the top executives surveyed by the *Times* were educated at Oxford or Cambridge where, like most of their peers in British business, they received no training in business management.

Respondents to a nationwide survey, by significant majorities, expect life to be worse rather than better in the future, hope to maintain rather than to improve their social positions, and given a choice between more leisure or more income, would choose leisure.

No one (or hardly anyone) seems to try very hard to sell anything. Most shops and sometimes even large stores are open only at the hours most inconvenient for their customers; proprietors apologize for prices; clerks in expensive shops display attitudes verging on complete contempt toward potential clientele clothed merely in normal dress.

A merchant at a major street market, asked for a quantity of the fresh mint that is plainly visible on his stand, replies that the mint is available only to those who also buy Jersey new potatoes, which are eaten with mint sauce. No, he says sternly, no merchant on the street will violate that rule. But there is one old-age pensioner with a small stand around the corner; he is allowed by the other merchants to sell mint to people who are not buying Jersey new potatoes.

Everyone seems to be in some kind of uniform, even when

wearing ordinary clothes. Seeing Frederick Wiseman's film *Meat*, about the American wholesale meat industry, one notices that the union and management negotiators are dressed virtually alike, in semiinformal clothes.

THE picture that one finally begins to see (from an aggressively modernist and Americanist perspective of course) is that of a very class-conscious society in which the prerogatives and traditions of the past are jealously guarded, in which the personal and status satisfactions of the producer clearly take precedence over the multiplication of either production through hard work or consumption through a drive to growth. Thus the overall dynamic of the domestic economy seems to emphasize keeping things roughly the same, rather than changing and increasing them: Britain is a low-growth, low-productivity society, and clearly has been for a long time. A look at the history books and the data collections confirms this impression, moreover: Great Britain has been falling steadily behind the rest of the industrialized world throughout the twentieth century; industrial decay and urban blight were already a prominent part of the landscape of several of its major cities at the turn of this century. One remembers that George Dangerfield wrote a book about the Edwardian period entitled *The Strange Death of Liberal England*; little that one sees in 1977 seems to call for a reversal of that verdict.

What other Europeans call "the English disease," then, clearly antedates by some time the coming to England of the welfare state, which retrospectively was not so much an attempt to humanize a booming economy as to soften the cruel edges of a (comparatively speaking) declining one. The inadequacies of the British welfare state are therefore clearly visible, and defenders of unrepentant capitalism, who usually manifest no interest in the more (much more) successful social democracies of the continent, have always preferred to study Great Britain, the weak sister of the social democratic world.

Much as though an enemy of representative government had convened a symposium on "the political system that doesn't work: parliamentary democracy's failures in Italy," R. Emmett Tyrrell,

Jr., the editor of a new American journal called *The Alternative* (new in being but old in spirit) has brought together a group of American and English contributors in a book under the overall title *The Future That Doesn't Work: Social Democracy's Failures in Britain* (New York: Doubleday, 1977). None of these contributors seems to have noticed that in discussing Great Britain they are really discussing a *past* that doesn't work (or that works in ways not appreciated by those of us with other expectations). But that is because with two exceptions they behave as ideologues, not social scientists, dedicated to helping the editor prevent the coming of "the institutions of British social democracy to these shores."

Unfortunately the collection offers virtually no serious discussion of those institutions. There is an incompetent essay by Harry Schwartz on the British Health Service, which makes the points that the National Health is "threadbare and financially starved," that there are still "great inequalities in the health services available to the people of Britain," and that there is an excess of demand for medical services greater than that foreseen by the National Health's founders. Schwartz does not explain how a poor country could have a rich health service; nor does he explain that the remark about inequality, which comes from a Labour minister, is intended to ginger the equalization process in a health service already many times more egalitarian than that available to Americans; nor does he compare the crucial statistics of health care, namely those of life expectancy, time lost from jobs because of illness or accident, and infant mortality, for all of which Britain leads the U.S. even though it lags behind the continent.

By contrast, Leslie Lenkowski's scholarly description of the welfare state in Britain simply falsifies the stated views of the editor, although the latter seems not to have noted this fact. Lenkowski's summary is that the British welfare state has had a slight redistributive effect, and that "to the extent that [it] has promoted equality, it has done so by leveling up, rather than down." He also points out that in 1967, by which year there had been less than a decade of serious Labour party government in this century, the pretax distribution of British income was "already fairly egalitarian . . . by international standards": a condition again having nothing to do with "socialist" income policies but rather with Britain's position as a traditionalist and relatively nonaffluent capitalist society. The one serious criticism he makes of British social democracy is that though the "service state" succeeded quite well in fulfilling its intentions, it has grown too fast to do so any longer, without becoming a dangerous drag in the context of an otherwise declining economy. "As in Sweden and the United States," he notes, "providing services is now the occupation of a majority of the labor force, including the one out of six who work in the public sector. Britain differs from Sweden and the United States (and even more from other countries still moving in the same direction) in that industrial growth has been laggard."

Lenkowski does not go at length into the reasons for that situation, several of which I have already mentioned: a cultural bias against certain kinds of work, the excessive export of both financial and human capital during the imperialist period, a general social conservatism and comparatively strong class consciousness, an aversion to practicing the arts of modern salesmanship, all of which (and no doubt many other causes as well) have helped to produce an industrial sector that has become less and less internationally competitive in the course of this century. But he does conclude that *"the programs of the welfare state deserve relatively little of the blame"*: so much for "the alternative." (James Q. Wilson, in his serious though rather pointless study of crime in England, also gives little comfort to his editor, since it appears that the "socialist" Britons have much sterner attitudes than Americans about the prevention and punishment of crime, and that their less lenient institutions have not prevented a great increase in British crime during the past two decades, although its level is still much below the American level; his cursory attempt to assess causes turns up nothing about the impact of "socialism.")

Lenkowski's conclusion is that the condition of the British welfare state, for better and worse, is a legacy of Britain's past; this offers little support in principle to either the supporters or critics of social democracy, but is a helpful antidote to the shrieks of dismay that surround him. On the other hand it is when ideology breaks through the mask of social science that *The Future That Doesn't Work* actually becomes most interesting, for then at last we learn what really actuates this ideology. It is not, we discover, the "failure" of social democracy that upsets the *English* contributors to this volume at all. Rather, what dismays them is *the success of popular democracy in England:* the triumph of universal suffrage, and the achievement of civil liberty for organized workers. The tears they shed for social democracy are crocodile tears, because these men are not democrats of any kind. They are antidemocrats.

The "engagingly simple political philosophy" of free, competitive elections, writes Peter Jay, may have been a useful corrective to authoritarianism and paternalism, but "alas, it already has built into it the tension—historicists might say the contradiction—that lies at the root of our present troubles. . . . Indeed, the essence of democratic politics is a gigantic celebration of the fact that you *can* get something for nothing, or at least that *you*—the individual voter—can get something for nothing. . . ." In like language Samuel Brittan of *The Financial Times* points to "the generation of *excessive* expectations" (italics added), which "follows from the competitive nature of democracy. . . ."

More subtly, Patrick Cosgrave of the *Daily Telegraph* laments the "failure of the Conservative Party, 1945–75," by which he turns out to mean the success of its leaders in erecting "a somewhat superficially glittering rhetoric, which convinced the electorate that the more popular elements of the Labour program were accepted. . . ." And he castigates Edward Heath for having "pondered the spectrum of consensus and, like Mr. Macmillan, moved to the left." The unrepentant Tory intellect, a century late, discovers the real horror of universal suffrage and representative government: that once in a while the majority really does rule, and leaders really do what it wants. ". . . However difficult it may be to break with the consensus of the postwar years, this must be done if the British Conservative Party is not to go the way of its Scandinavian counterparts, reduced to impotent rumps following their pragmatic adoption of the nostra of socialism." These counterparts are not exactly impotent in either Sweden or Denmark today, of course, but presumably what Mr. Cosgrave cannot forgive them for is that they willingly participate in the management of economies that despite constant "intrusions" from the state and the general current decline of Western European capitalism are still two to three times as productive as Great Britain's. They accept without sufficient qualm, that is, the "engagingly simple" notion that what the great number of people think benefits them is what parties of the people should endorse.

Just which more sophisticated political philosophy is supposed to replace simple Benthamite liberalism? On this point ideologues of the new conservatism try to maintain a discreet silence. Peter Jay even refers to "the depredations practiced on mankind by authoritarian and paternalist regimes in the name of higher values." But on close inspection of his and the other essays in this volume, one begins to think that "authoritarian and paternalist regimes" are precisely what these Englishmen long for—regimes that will put labor unions in their place and undo a century's damage of painfully achieved liberal democracy.

Their reasoning also might be called "engagingly simple." According to Brittan, "union monopolies differ in an important way from other organized groups" in that only they "will normally withdraw output from the market until representatives of the public sign an agreement to pay more." He does not explain how this power differs essentially from that of business and farm monopolies to withhold products from the market until the offered price is "competitive"; or to cut back on the utilization of capacity because of "insufficient demand," even in the face of glaringly evident social *need* for their products. This kind of one-way reasoning is typical of the neoclassical economists and their journalistic followers, for whom the expressed needs of business (to raise prices, lower output, etc.) are always *determined* by impersonal market forces ("Drought conditions in West Africa have forced Tate & Lyle to raise the price of cocoa products 22 percent this year"); whereas the expressed needs of workers always appear as willful and arbitrary *demands*.

The deeper intellectual problem, however, is that the free-market theorist, having argued out of one side of his mouth that a rational price system necessitates the treating of labor as a commodity like any other, now turns around and refuses to accept the logical consequence of the one distinction on which, more than any other, market capitalism rests. Owners and managers of capital possess resources or skills that are carefully kept in short supply among a limited group of people; *their* withholding thus appears as no more than a short-run incentive to "rational adjustments" to the price of their goods in the marketplace. Moreover their situation as a class is never deeply painful or questionable, so that again they usually appear not as instigators of class conflict but only as hard-headedly rational economic actors: business monopolists or oligopolists are rarely seen willfully to "hold society to ransom" as a group.

On the other hand any attempt to bid up the price of labor collectively is seen as the worst kind of monopolistic behavior, as both Brittan and Jay put it. But it does not occur to these critics of trade-union "monopoly" that workers acting collectively are only acting as the capitalist market economy bids them act. Workers-as-commodities possess no capital and (except for the most skilled among them) they have been carefully trained (or untrained) to have only interchangeable capabilities. They are meant to be treated as averagely priced commodities, and how else can "commodities" act but collectively? The price of labor is a collective price; the price of management and entrepreneurship is (to a much greater extent) an individualized price. Neoconservatives heartily endorse this division of labor and then vent their fury or scorn on its victims. More: The strike is the only kind of action available to workers that gives them even a remote measure of the kind of market power that giant corporate structures routinely exercise. It is as crucial an aspect of universal suffrage as the vote itself, and repudiation of the strike weapon is again repudiation of democracy.

But then for the new conservatives "Labour" is not representing victims but predators, not the people democratic institutions should represent and protect but the people they should guard against (also for the old conservatives, who after all saw the working class as a dangerous beast before unions were even legal . . .). As Peregrine Worsthorne of the *Daily Telegraph* puts it, trade unions are the "new lads on top"; trade-union violence and "thuggery" are "tolerated by liberal squeamishness" though the police are held in disrespect; trade unionists are "the *nouveaux riches* and take home wage packets that make them the envy of professional people"; trade unions are always portrayed as "David fighting Goliath" in schools and in the mass media; working-class morale is high while middle-class morale is low; trade-union leaders alone are "in a position to exercise power without apology"; and tolerant, squeamish British management has "a wholly inappropriate reluctance to recognize that the paternalistic days of benevolent goodwill have long since passed in history."

Every one of those statements, however, is demonstrably false. In both respect and income trade unionists still rank toward the bottom end of the table. To be sure the wages of *highly skilled* trade unionists have approached or surpassed those of, say, schoolteachers or reporters since the wage freeze first took effect (and why not); but a cursory glance at the help-wanted section of the London *Sunday Times* will show that a systems analyst or sales manager or personnel "expert" earns almost twice as much as a spot welder—plus "perks." The differential in favor of media overlords is in the neighborhood of five or seven to one, and for company directors up to twenty to one (plus stock options, tax havens in the Caymans, etc.). Most professionals, furthermore, can hope for a *progression* in their income-earning powers as they get older that is denied to even the most skilled wage workers. (Comparisons that seem to favor the latter are usually between middle-aged workers and young professionals.) Once one drops from the ranks of the most highly skilled wage workers to those whose jobs are not advertised at all but who simply show up at the plant gate or union hall looking for work, these differentials become even more pronounced (although the major effect of the wage freeze in England during the past few years was to narrow differentials between segments of the wage-earning workforce themselves, much to the discomfort of skilled workers and to the destruction of trade-union solidarity).

Now that the wage freeze has been abolished under pressure from skilled workers, and now that, at last, high levels of unemployment seem to be an acceptable part of the landscape in Britain, all these differentials can be expected to increase. But it will still be the case as it always has been that if an American shops at Harrods, or eats at the Connaught Grill, or goes to see the American Ballet Theatre (sitting next to a man in a custom-tailored suit who might be Peter Jay or Peregrine Worsthorne and is volubly complaining about trade-union thugs during intermission), or is living in a house that is for sale in one of the better neighborhoods of North London, he will encounter a multitude of Englishmen and women who seem to be able to afford these relatively high-priced luxuries quite nicely, not to mention the relatively leisurely life that enjoyment of such luxuries implies. And none of them will be wage workers.

As for the "prestige" and "power" of trade unions, the major daily newspapers are almost 100 percent overtly antilabor whenever a labor–management or union–government conflict arises (except in the case when the government is Labour); and they are all covertly antilabor, in the sense indicated above, that the actions of workers are treated as willful and those of businesses as determined by market forces. The BBC indeed gives air time to strikers in notorious disputes, but it also tends to focus entirely on exceptionally inflammatory picket-line behavior, never looking at more commonplace strike behavior and also never taking a hard look at what happens inside factories—nor, especially, at the way in which employers use the National Front or the Special Branch to break strikes of immigrant laborers. An academic visitor to England will observe that the prestige of the "new lords" consists almost wholly in their having the privilege of being the subject of vituperative conversation wherever educated people or professionals (except the small band of genuine leftists) get together. The "power" of the Trades Union Congress too is greatly overestimated and misunderstood by conservative critics in both Great Britain and the U.S., for the sole use to which that power has been put in the life of the present government has been the employment of TUC officials as shock troops to subdue rank-and-file resistance to the tight-money, antiwelfare, proindustry policies of the Labour government. As to the alleged *class* power of the trade-union movement, suffice it to say that after a dozen on-again off-again years of Labour party government, labor legislation in Great Britain is still in a more primitive state in some respects than it is in the U.S., and the grounds on which courts can intervene in labor disputes are even more extensive. The political boundaries between the classes, in sum, are still strong, and the political influence of the average British worker or group of workers still feeble. The attack on organized labor remains an antidemocratic attack on fitful signs of the coming to equal power of what has long been a political underclass in Britain.

How to explain this attack is another matter. Peter Jay *et al.* cannot really be bemoaning the loss of class privilege, that combined horror of inflation and benign view of mass unemployment that all "informed opinion" now expresses is the essence of their own and their class's ideology. What rather gnaws at them, I think, is the fear that they are about to lose that privilege.

Why that fear? The question mires us in the ambiguities of national or class character. Any answer, though, must certainly point to the steady loss of national morale that has accompanied the long decline in comparative national productivity and the gradual surrender of Empire, and that was only momentarily and misleadingly arrested by the unifying experience of World War II. One can only speculate that the prolonged dirge unendingly played out by the residuary legatees of upper-class opinion comes from the sense of failed promise that a once-successful, now relatively backward economy produces. For British workers that sense of national failure results in a degree of class bitterness unrivaled elsewhere in the capitalist world, combined with an exceptional degree of political and economic conservatism: fear of collapse leading most often to a desire to preserve rather than to change. The same is true, in reverse, of intellectuals and professionals. Fighting their way upward through the still-oppressive class structure (a structure for which Peregrine Worsthorne, significantly, reserves his most passionate denunciation), they find that their hard-won privilege seems feeble and chancy in comparison with that of their American counterparts. To them too change seems frightening, preservation necessary. Unwilling to turn on the enduring structure of privilege that (even while they excoriate its excrescences) gives shape to their careers, they attack instead the only other available opponent: democracy, however weak its institutionalization and limited its growth has been and can be in the future the instrument of change in Britain.

Advanced social democracy, meanwhile, as practiced (for example) in Scandinavia and the Low Countries, is a political economy beset by severe contradictions. The richest nations in the world (per capita) are social democracies (the U.S. having dropped off the lead), but their affluence depends on the continuing exploitation of scarce resources, many of them subject to other people's sovereignty. (This is also true of the U.S., of course.) Their legislation is the most egalitarian anywhere in the "West" (and in some cases anywhere at all), but the progressive income taxes that support this legislation more and more come under sustained assault from the middle classes, who work for the incentive of social superiority only to see the promised reward taken away to produce more equality. These are, in short, societies that are trying to be vaguely socialist and egalitarian without abolishing the basic institutions of capitalism ("private" control of the means of production, and hierarchically structured market incentives to work). As such they are interesting and important experiments that may ultimately show either that the contradictions and limitations of capitalism are insurmountable, or that a different and better social system can be generated out of capitalism by peaceful means.

But such "new conservatives" as the editor of, and some of the British contributors to, *The Future That Doesn't Work* appear to have no interest in such possibilities. The only slight hope they see in the future is for a more capitalist America that will avoid the "ills" of social democracy. It will also, if they have their way, continue to be the advanced capitalist society in which the average person, white or (especially) black, has the best chance of being born poor, of staying poor, of receiving inadequate or no medical care, of dying in an industrial accident, of being excluded from participation in the management of one's workplace, or of being cast on the scrap heap by an ailing corporation without any attempt being made by anyone to nourish and reward his or her potential productivity. What makes that an attractive prospect must be left to these authors to explain in some future symposium.

Ulf Himmelstrand

Sweden:
Paradise in Trouble

FOR over forty years, ever since Marquis Childs wrote that bestselling book, Sweden has been known as the land of the Middle Way, which was slowly but consistently moving from a backward state toward its present position as the most developed of all welfare societies. Praised by progressive liberals, at least outside Sweden itself, its gradually achieved social reforms have been discussed contemptuously by dogmatic revolutionaries who profess to be true Marxists. However "pure" this Marxist criticism may be, armed as it is with the powerful if not flawless analytic tools of historical materialism, the "purer" fact remains that these critics simply bungle the whole story.

Even when critics have got the facts straight about this land of the Middle Way, their image of Sweden has been incomplete and superficial. In place of understanding we have stale "profundities" about Sweden's being a country that is stagnating morally and culturally—affluence corroded by boredom and drift, and by a loss of incentive for work and innovation—so "profound" that once again President Eisenhower's statistical nonsense about suicide is becoming fashionable. The conservative opposition, in the nature

Most of the research underlying this article was financed by a grant from the Bank of Sweden Tercentenary Foundation.

of things, always leveled these accusations. With the defeat of the Social Democratic Labor party in the Swedish general elections of 1976, they could not be so easily dismissed. The election results rocked progressive confidence that Sweden was on the right road to utopia.

Marxists, whether supporters, critics, or merely observers, have been less concerned with moral and cultural decay and the loss of incentives than with the amazing stability of capitalism in a country that for more than forty years was ruled by a mass labor party. In Sweden to this day 94 percent of the means of production in manufacturing are privately owned. Private gross investment (housing excluded) is 57 percent, and private investment in machinery 78 percent. Swedish exports, which constitute nearly a third of GNP and hence are a crucial factor in the welfare of the country, derive almost completely from private enterprise.

From what I hold to be a more genuine Marxist standpoint, it would seem possible, however, to argue that Swedish social democracy, by helping capitalism to develop and mature, in fact (if not in a conscious and deliberate manner) has brought Swedish society closer to a socialist transformation. Socialism is supposed to spring from the internal contradictions, problems, and crises generated within the capitalist order precisely where it is most highly developed. If Marx's prediction about the "bursting asunder" of capitalist social relations of production should be borne out in any highly industrialized nation, Sweden is a natural candidate. Admittedly this "dialectical" interpretation is rather unusual among Marxists commenting on contemporary Sweden. Nevertheless it deserves closer scrutiny. Even those who reject deterministic prognostications about the socialist transformations of capitalist societies as propounded by orthodox Marxists might possibly find in this interpretation of the socialist potential of late capitalism a basis for a theoretically and empirically meaningful analysis of the Swedish situation.

I do not for a minute accept ideological propositions about the inevitability of socialism as a result of the mobilization of the working class in response to the decay of capitalism. But after many years of research and political experience I do believe that

Sweden is far from being a stagnant society. It is indeed a country at a crossroad, with an enormous potential for qualitative and structural change, beyond the slowly incremental, and moving in the direction of socialist innovation within the framework of democracy.

Problems of Late Capitalism

Problems abound in Sweden today, but they are the problems of late capitalism, not of democratic socialism. As seen from the "commanding heights" of a capitalist economic policy, several problems are obvious: the loss of incentive, if you wish, since the whole capitalist *cum* welfare system is approaching its limit of growth in consumer demand as well as in fiscal measures; the absence of innovative impulse and far-sighted investments, which lead to dwindling competitiveness and diminish the profitability of industrial production. Or as seen in the perspective of the man in the street: the acceleration of the work tempo; an improved but still quite inadequate work environment; poor job satisfaction with spillovers into impoverished and depersonalized use of leisure time; air, water, and traffic pollution; rapidly rising prices for food and services; threats of unemployment and the terror inspired in whole communities dominated by single, crisis-struck, dying industries.

Such lists of problems could be established for any advanced capitalist country. Sweden may exhibit some of them to a lesser extent than some other highly developed capitalist countries, but that is not crucial. The crucial fact is that Sweden, in spite of its extensive efforts to tackle most of these problems, is still unable to achieve real success in solving them—except perhaps in a few areas such as water pollution. It is the gap between aspiration and performance that generates a disappointment perhaps more intense in Sweden than in other societies even though the latter exhibit the same problems of late capitalism to an even greater extent.

Since Sweden is probably one of the most politicized countries in the world, these problems are the object of intense political debate. Comparative sociological surveys—most notably by the Finnish sociologist Erik Allardt and the British sociologist Richard Scase—support the conclusion that the Swedish citizenry, beneficiaries of a high level of social welfare, remain more aware than most others of the continuing problems of inequity, injustice, and class contradiction. It would therefore seem that the stage is now set for political action to solve these problems and so change society. But it is not that simple.

Problem-Solving in Business and Government

For several decades the Swedish business community collaborated reasonably well with the Social Democratic government. Until it lost power in the 1976 elections that government was the driving force behind our ambitious but largely piecemeal social-welfare and monetary policies, while the basic problem-generating structures were left very much intact. This social policy imposed certain costs on private enterprise, but also earned it substantial benefits. During the long postwar period of economic growth, private enterprise could depend on a predictable labor market, favorable credit conditions, and an expanding domestic market. The purchasing power of the public grew while inflation was contained at a reasonable rate. It was not of course a "free" ride for wealth. The business community demonstrated its perception of self-interest by supporting bourgeois political parties, which eventually displaced the Social Democratic government. Business reacted swiftly to the new political situation. In bargaining negotiations with the trade-union movement in the spring of 1977, the Swedish employers confederation (SAF) took a harsh and rigid stand, unprecedented since the late 1920s, not only with regard to wage demands but also on issues that had been legislated rather recently in parliament. Traditionally these matters had been outside the accepted range of collective bargaining. Among other things SAF demanded revisions in the legislated system of income benefits during illness, and of legislated provisions on working and vacation time.

The new government is not taxing the business community as severely as the Social Democratic government did. It is in a general way trying to improve the market situation for free enterprise and shows little taste for applying selective regulations on business. Yet these new policies have done little to improve the business climate. In addition to the impact of the abnormally prolonged international recession, the domestic situation has deteriorated a great deal, particularly in respect to relations between labor and capital. Gloom and disenchantment were obvious at midterm of the new government.

The solutions proposed by increasingly hawkish business leaders would ultimately dismantle some still significant welfare institutions. They would increase incentives for private capital accumulation and investment, allowing the market to operate with more complete freedom. Such a policy may indeed strengthen the position of capital. But the increasing strength that Swedish business may be gaining through further capital concentration, through the growing influence of investment companies and through investment abroad rather than in Sweden, may prove to be hollow. In its net effect this strategy exposes the basically antisocial nature of capitalist relations of production, particularly at a time of prolonged recession when the most attractive asset of capitalism—its capacity for economic growth—is left in doubt.

Some less hawkish and more pragmatic business leaders may be aware of the hazards in allowing business criteria to show themselves in this naked and brutal manner. They may also anticipate the forceful reprisals to be expected from the powerful Swedish trade-union movement, and from the Social Democratic party if it is returned to governmental power in the 1979 general elections. But such pragmatism leads nowhere—except perhaps to a strategy of muddling through, which may work for a while in politics but will breed further stagnation in economic life.

When a crisis situation has deteriorated to a point where problems no longer are seen as exciting challenges but as a depressing tedium—as an occasion to find irrelevant scapegoats —then it is time to reconsider the very terms in which our problems have been perceived and defined. The pervasive chain of gloom and stagnation cannot be broken unless we discover that our problems no longer can be dealt with efficiently one by one, but only by tackling the social structures that have generated these problems in the first place, and that must be transformed in order to release new forces of social development. This may sound forbiddingly abstract or theoretical, but there is no way around it if we wish to escape what seem to be intractable difficulties and social boredom.

Structural Contradictions

Let us pause here to restate some of the aspects of Marxist thought in terms that can readily be understood by nonbelievers. The Marxist perspective recognizes a basic contradiction in that the industrial forces of production become increasingly societal, while the decision-making machinery implied in capitalist relations of production virtually exclude consistent and effective considerations of the wide-ranging societal responsibilities of production.

What is implied by an expression such as "the increasingly societal character of productive forces"? Industry depends more and more on society and state for infrastructural, productive, regulative, and planning inputs. Yet it manages its own internal decisions in a manner primarily conditioned by the narrow and often short-term needs of single-firm profitability. Simultaneously the growing transnational market of commodities and capital significantly reduces the ability of society and state to influence and control the effects of their intervention. As productive forces grow they become increasingly international in character. "Outcomes" of industry in activity such as variations in productivity, capital-intensity, and related employment levels, and in the production of negative by-products (such as environmental effects) impose wide-ranging consequences on society as a whole.

The resource-accumulating, decision-making, and resource-allocating processes within capitalism—that is, the social relations of capitalist production—cannot match this increasingly societal and international character of the productive forces. Most of the piecemeal problems mentioned earlier derive from this basic problem of modern capitalism. They are generated by the structural contradictions of capitalism. But these contradictions of capitalism could be examined not only with respect to the incompatibility of two overarching structures—the forces and social relations of production—but also in some other respects.

There are also more specific processes of internal and external contradiction unfolding as we take a closer look at concrete aspects of the modern capitalist economy: the competitive market, the interventionist state, and the incentive behavior of investors and labor.

A competitive market, in practice if not in the idealized models of neoclassical economic theory, operates in a self-destructive manner. The market is "self-contradictory" over time. The success that bred further success in what was originally a strictly competitive market succumbs in time to oligopolistic or monopolistic structures. These in turn reduce or eliminate the very competition that is supposed to be the unique vehicle of optimal resource allocation in a free-enterprise economy.

This contradiction, coupled with recessions and crises, and the inability of capitalism to resolve them quickly, has promoted the demand for state interventions in all the advanced capitalist countries. Sweden was one of the first to introduce state intervention, first to fight the business cycles and later to mitigate market imperfections. It was the Social Democratic party that was responsible for these early attempts to improve the functioning of the capitalist order, and it did so with the support of such liberal politicians as the leader of the *Folkpartiet*, Bertil Ohlin.

But even when the capitalist order, intelligently controlled by the state, operates reasonably well both in terms of growth and of distribution, and by improving the standards of living for most of the population, as it did for many postwar decades in Sweden, new contradictions emerge. The growth of affluence hurts the very mainspring of the capitalist system: its reliance on monetary incentives and rewards.

Several studies have suggested that a majority of Swedish employees, including the lesser paid, just a few years ago were less interested in increasing their private consumption than in improving the quality of working life and safeguarding an environment threatened by industrial pollution. This new attitude found an expression in demands for monthly salaries instead of backbreaking piece rates, despite the fact that monthly salaries frequently meant less money in the pocket by the end of the month. Wildcat strikes, as well as regular union activities, have now brought about a shift from piece rates to monthly salaries for large groups of Swedish workers.

Trade unions that have operated within the parameters of the capitalist order still demand higher wages of course, since that is the job they have learned to do. But they have increasingly asked for other things as well: legislated authority to control health hazards at work, workers' codetermination, and worker-controlled capital funds that would give labor an increasing power over capital accumulation and investment. Monetary incentives are no longer seen as sufficient. No wonder that capitalist spokesmen complain about the loss of incentive to work. The only incentive they offer—monetary reward—no longer functions quite the way it did; and they are unwilling to offer the incentives of codetermination and power over capital now in demand.

As the unprecedented postwar years of economic growth and widespread affluence are grinding to a halt, other contradictions of the capitalist order emerge, especially as the puzzle of stagflation remains unsolved. Distrust in the system infects not only employees but also investors—see, for instance, an illuminating article by former President Ford's advisor Allan Greenspan in the *Economist* of August 6, 1977. Incentives for speculative and unproductive investments in art collections, diamonds, luxury houses, and idle land are often displacing productive investments in industry. This trend is as discernible in Sweden as elsewhere.

Liberal vs. Socialist Perceptions

Leading liberal economists in Sweden have arrived at ideas that roughly, but far from completely, correspond to Marx's concept of the contradiction between the forces and the relations of production under capitalism. Progressive liberals are not unaware of what Marxists call the increasingly societal character of the productive forces, as contrasted with the narrow focus of business decisions.

Progressive liberal economists make an important distinction between the concept of business economics that emphasizes only private costs and benefits, and a broader concept of economics that embraces social or societal costs and benefits. These liberal economists are quite aware that there is no longer an "invisible hand" that will bring about an automatic harmony between private and social economic considerations. Though this perception may resemble Marxian theory, it differs significantly from a socialist conception based on a Marxist diagnosis of capitalism.

In Marxist terms the structural contradiction of capitalism is not only a theoretical construct guiding the best informed decision-makers in government and private enterprise but also a reality that expresses itself in the exploitation of those who have nothing to sell but their labor. Some Marxists realize that this exploitation no longer can be defined exclusively, or even predominantly, as an appropriation of surplus value; it is an exploitation that defines the quality of working life and also the quality of leisure since both have been shown to be closely correlated. Problems of family life and childrearing, alienation of working-class youth in school, work, and leisure are all manifestations of exploitation in the contemporary capitalist order.

There is to be sure a precise class content in Marxist analysis that is absent in corresponding liberal notions. In effect it points to a third actor on the stage beside the interventionist state and private enterprise—namely the *working class* as organized in trade unions and not only in political parties. The formation of social classes, which act out societal contradictions through measures of strike activity, political action, and so forth, is an element missing in the liberal understanding of the divergences between private and social economies. Of course the existence of working-class organizations as *social facts* is obvious to everyone. What matters is that social-liberals cannot relate effectively to this "social fact," evidenced by the deteriorating relationship between labor and government in our present bourgeois regime. Nor do they seem particularly interested in theoretically considering the possibility of mobilizing this class under a liberal banner, since class action cannot be accommodated within the individualist framework of liberal theory.

The failure of Swedish social-liberal politicians to relate at all to organized labor (in contrast to the experience of the U.S.) has left them in a predicament where they have access only to one actor to tackle all the problems gnawing at capitalism, namely the interventionist state. This predicament is all the sharper because these Swedish social-liberals, during the long era of Social Democratic government, relentlessly attacked the role of the state and the actions of the central governmental bureaucracies. Now that they are themselves in government, they cannot avoid using far-reaching state intervention, just as in other European states run by bourgeois governments. This is part of the internal inconsistency of bourgeois social-liberalism. Another inconsistency may be found in its refusal to make use of specific government interventions proposed by the Social Democratic opposition, limiting themselves instead to generalized measures supplemented by appeals to the "social responsibility" of private enterprise. But by definition private enterprise cannot be socially responsible; in fact it is not.

Though the policies of the Social Democrats in their forty-four years of governmental power also were essentially social-liberal —i.e., the use of state intervention within the context of a so-called mixed economy—their "social-liberalism" could be pressed much more consistently and energetically than the bourgeois social-liberals would have dared undertake, given their ideological hang-ups regarding the role of the state.

Furthermore the Social Democrats, because of their close collaboration with the trade unions, could involve more than the state in coming to grips with the problems of capitalism. The voice of organized labor was clearly heard in Social Democratic headquarters, and unions were usually willing to collaborate with the Social Democratic government. Now that this combination of capitalism, state interventions, and union collaboration seems to have reached its limits in negotiating the uphill stretch of economic policy, it is not too difficult for Social Democrats to change gears. The largely unused reservoirs of power, knowledge, and drive in the trade unions will be able to assert themselves in a new combination of labor and state collaboration once the Social Democrats recover their government posts.

But would not a political incorporation of the new issues of working-class power recently introduced by trade unions lead to more serious class confrontations, and thus threaten the creative national effort needed to get Sweden out of its present impasse? This has been suggested, for instance, by a leading management expert, Ulf af Trolle, who recently said: "We have created problems that cannot be solved in an atmosphere of confrontation." This statement is typically liberal in its idealistic belief that "confrontations" based on objective fact can be dissolved by wishes and good intentions. Policy formations based on mere goodwill are likely to intensify the contradictions they are meant to soften. There is no alternative to squarely facing the issues at stake, and allowing them to be articulated in political debate. As this is written we are in the midst of such a debate in preparation for the next general elections in September 1979. Who will win that election, and those that follow, and on what platform? What is the likelihood of structural transformations in the relationships between capital and labor in the near future?

Who Is Losing Ground?

On the stage of social change there are several other actors besides the political parties formulating state policy, the business community and the trade unions among them. I will limit myself here to the relative strength of the political parties and the prospects of a Social Democratic comeback.

Seasoned political commentators are already predicting a Social Democratic victory in our next elections, with another relatively long period of Social Democratic government. The three bourgeois parties now represented in the government have been unable to deliver on most of their campaign promises. Inflation in 1977 was twice as high as before, taxes have not decreased except for certain higher income groups, private enterprise has not shown itself more capable of improving its performance, and the nuclear power program, which the Center party promised to abolish, is still being pursued, even if at a somewhat slower rate. Important and urgent decisions in this and other areas where the three parties in government could not agree have been postponed, and thus have given the Social Democratic opposition an opportunity to argue that our present government is incapable of ruling. In the one area where the present government admittedly is following the policies of the previous Social Democratic government—in fighting unemployment—they have been somewhat more successful. All in all it is not surprising that public-opinion polls show a decline in support for the bourgeois parties.

However, all this could be a passing phenomenon. Viewed in a long-term perspective, it could be argued that a Social Democratic party deriving most of its support from the working class will inevitably lose ground, since the working class is diminishing in size. Certainly the percentage of industrial workers is decreasing; today the proportion is only about a third of all those gainfully employed. But at the same time lower white-collar strata are being "proletarianized," which may compensate for the decreasing proportion of industrial workers. Operating machinery as "unskilled" labor, and performing routine tasks without access to the privileged knowledge embodied in this technical machinery, has become increasingly common among so-called nonmanual white-collar workers. Furthermore the position of white-collar employees is more vulnerable than it used to be; unemployment is as much a threat to them as to blue-collar workers. It seems necessary then to redefine the working class, as many have proposed in Europe and the U.S.A., to include clerical or service operations which require no intellectual labor in the true sense. Under this definition about three-quarters of all those gainfully employed in Sweden would be counted as part of the working class.

If the numerical strength of this working class were sufficient for constituting an electoral majority in behalf of a party prepared to initiate structural reforms leading to the abolition of the capitalist system, then Sweden would already have taken giant strides toward socialism, which it has not. The Swedish Social Democratic party in recent years has been receiving only between 43 and 52 percent of the electoral vote, and the small Communist party has obtained no more than about 4 to 5 percent. Not all members of the working class, as I have here defined it, vote labor. Factors beyond class position obviously affect the electoral vote. One such factor is the degree of unionization. Whereas more than 90 percent of all blue-collar workers in Sweden are organized in LO, the central federation of blue-collar unions, unionization until recently has been much lower among white-collar employees. The trend, however, is clear: whereas only about 50 percent of white-collar employees were unionized in 1950, about 70 percent were unionized by 1975. Moreover the collaboration between TCO, the federation of white-collar unions, and LO has become more and more intimate in recent years. Though TCO is careful to indicate that it is unattached to any political party, its stand on several crucial issues with regard to workers' codetermination, labor-controlled capital funds, etc., places it very close ideologically to the LO.

But Swedish labor is not only very highly organized and unified it also has tended to become bureaucratized and centralized. The spread of wildcat strikes in the late 1960s and early 1970s can be interpreted as directed against this "centralistic" trend in trade unions, and not only against management. The fact that quite a number of wildcat strikes have been fairly effective in attaining their ends plus the emergence of demands for a more responsive trade-union leadership has, in my judgment, and however paradoxically, increased the strength of organized labor. The same union leaders who officially condemn wildcat strikes have privately condoned them as significant reactions to underlying problems. They see in them, off the record to be sure, hopeful signs of worker mobilization and sources of strength, a collective resource to be tapped in future union work. The rise of a new generation of union leaders is significant in this respect.

To understand why the size of the working class and the strength of its organizations so far has not assured greater electoral support for a labor party committed to structural changes, we must take a closer look at the ideological components of class relations, and the subjective consciousness displayed by different strata within the working class.

I referred earlier to sociological studies by Allardt and Scase, which show that Swedes generally exhibit a stronger sense of conflict, inequity, and injustice than people in comparable countries—and this despite Sweden's superior welfare programs. The Swedish working class displays a higher level of such social consciousness than the population as a whole. According to these studies there is no evidence for an ideological "embourgeoise-ment" of the Swedish working class. Pursuing this theme Goran Ahrne and myself have carried out surveys probing the people's images of society, its threats and contradictions. We asked a series of questions regarding unemployment, inflation, nuclear power, and the like. These we called "piecemeal" threats. If respondents combine a perception of these threats with a perception of threats considered as systemic aspects of society—the influence of capital-ism, the increasing mechanization of work, the growth of big business, etc.—we classify such respondents as exhibiting an awareness of the structural problems that go beyond piecemeal issues. We also asked questions about more "traditional" working-class identification.

We found that clerical workers with lower levels of skill, these new entrants into the extended working class, do not identify themselves as readily with the labor movement and the working class as will industrial workers. But they do exhibit an awareness of the structural threats of capitalism as frequently as industrial workers; their increasing degree of unionization would seem to promise a continued expansion of this ideological perception, since the awareness of structural defects is correlated with unionization. It is also interesting to note that this ideological awareness extends beyond the working class far into the upper middle strata, al-though it is not as frequently found there as in the working class itself. Consequently the extended working class might be able to find a significant number of middle-class allies in support of structural reforms to reduce the flaws inherent in the capitalist order.

Finally, it is pertinent to emphasize that the emergence of this new type of structural social consciousness is not correlated with leisure-time consumption of mass-media and consumer commodi-ties. Rather it is linked to the objective nature of the work situation, as well as to the degree of unionization. Conjunctural swings in values related to leisure-time consumption are unlikely to affect this degree of social consciousness.

This social consciousness, however, merely sets the stage for the future. It implies no more than a certain definition of the problems of capitalism. The definition of a problem may be generally accepted long before adequate solutions come to be accepted by an electoral majority. But recently the process of defining such problem solutions, and making them acceptable, has picked up speed in Sweden. The speed of this process depends not only on the objective conditions of work and unionization mentioned above, but also on the responsiveness of political leadership and the tempo of political decision-making. Our assessment of the political forces that push toward more socialist solutions will therefore be concluded with a few observations about the Social Democratic party.

Three Stages

Looking back at the performance of the Social Democratic government during the 1972–1976 electoral period, when its position in parliament was rather weak, we find a quite remarkable list of legislative accomplishments on relations between labor and capital: capital for instance, acts on board representation for employees in joint stock companies, on management obligations to report on certain planning matters to trade unions, on greatly expanded powers for union-appointed safety stewards, on employment security, on the right of trade-union representatives to carry on union business at the workplace, and on the negotiability of most issues (which previously were the prerogative of management) within a scheme of workers' codetermination. The party was under heavy pressure from below, particularly from the trade unions, and it certainly proved itself responsive to these demands.

Sociologically speaking the most important aspect of many of these new legal acts is that they were intended to counteract the centralism that has been so pervasive in Swedish society, without destroying the power of the national federation of trade unions, LO. Genuine, not fake, local controls are being placed in the hands of workers in local unions. One possible effect of these laws, apart from somewhat changing the power relationships between labor and capital, is to create a new social climate that will encourage new ways of thinking and acting about the relations of production.

Among proposals for new legislation, one in particular deserves attention, since it may bring about more profound changes in the relationship between capital and labor, at least if the Social Democratic party is returned to power in 1979. I am thinking here of the proposal for worker-controlled capital funds, originally initiated by the Federation of Metal Worker Unions. This proposal explores the possibilities of gradually transferring company profits to a capital fund controlled collectively by the trade unions. This would not only give trade unions a decisive proportion of the shares in these companies over a period of time but would imply a corresponding transfer of decision-making power from the traditional holders of capital to labor. The Social Democratic party was not prepared to make this an issue in the 1976 election campaign but is presently on the campaign trail to promote such a reform in the near future. The original proposal is now being revised to take into account the results of further studies and debates within the party and the trade-union movement.

The limited laws now in effect already reduce the decision-making power of capital within the existing order of private or company property. According to a voluntaristic interpretation of power, which assigns power to the majority will of decision-makers, the legislation already in force, if pursued further, could lead to a more complete economic democracy even if it did not change the basic features of the capitalist system.

Those who hold a structuralist interpretation of power may argue, however, that even if labor hypothetically achieves majority decision-making power, under capitalist relations of production this could not significantly influence the movement of capital in the capital market. As long as there is a capital market the movement of capital will be subject to market mechanisms and not to democratic decision-making. The capital market is a structural arrangement that among other things separates capital and labor into different spheres of operation. Since the movement of capital in the present economic crisis is often geared more to profitable speculation than to production and labor, the dynamic of the capital market leads to a worsening of the predicament of labor. On the other hand the labor-controlled capital funds proposed by LO, TCO, and the Social Democratic party may significantly reduce the role of the capital market in capital accumulation and investment and may also help to reduce the contradiction of capital and labor. These funds will thus supplement the decision-making reforms provided in other laws at the point where these laws have shown their greatest weaknesses, and will make it possible to address more effectively the basic problems of capitalism.

Social Democratic historians now describe the development of the Swedish party in three periods. The first period was the struggle for universal suffrage and democracy undertaken together with liberal politicians some seventy years ago. In the second stage the main issues were economic growth and social welfare redistribution. In the third phase, which has just barely begun, the main issue is economic democracy, which implies a step-by-step but still complete overhaul of power relationships between capital and labor. From the point of view of professional academic historians, as well as that of Communist writers to the left of social democracy, this sequence of periods may seem a bit too neat to be historically true. Whatever the case, my point is that this "periodization" of Social Democratic history is itself an indication of a changing ideological mood within the party.

But is the Social Democratic party likely to become strong enough in electoral support and parliamentary votes to implement a program of structural reforms? Space limitation precludes here a thorough discussion of why the party lost in 1976 beyond a few observations buttressed by recent public-opinion polls.

Several statistical analyses of the 1976 election establish beyond doubt that the outcome rested on a single issue—the question of nuclear power. One of the bourgeois parties, the Center party, promised to abolish nuclear power, and its leader even went as far as to promise that he would rather give up a ministerial post than compromise with his stand on this issue. There were, to be sure, other issues—a negative attitude to state bureaucracy and "socialism," for example—but these had arisen in earlier elections that were nevertheless won by the Social Democrats. Slightly more than half the voters who shifted their allegiance from the Social Democratic party to the Center party seem to have based their switch on the nuclear-power issue. The party leadership, as it enters its "third phase" of development, seems convinced that raising the issue of economic democracy, the real problem of Swedish society, corresponds with the mood of the electorate. The forces moving in a socialist direction are certainly more articulate and well organized than ever before, though perhaps more visible through the prism of sociological analysis than in explicit political pronouncements. But that is the Swedish way, low-keyed and reformist rather than expressive and rhetorical.

Forces opposing or trying to constrain structural changes in a socialist direction are certainly also considerable in Sweden, but they are less united. Most important, they lack a comprehensive and consistent diagnosis of the obvious weaknesses of the present system.

The outcome of a struggle between these opposing forces within the framework of a democratic policy is by no means certain. Some Marxist commentators have voiced apprehensions that the Swedish capitalist class may turn fascist. This seems far-fetched to me. There is no evidence to support such a prediction; it rests purely on deductions from a highly simplified theory of class struggle, and on analogies of countries very different from Sweden, such as Allende's Chile. I keep my fingers crossed; it could still turn out to be at least partially true.

However, my own analysis—tentative as it is and relying on "fingertip" evidence—leads me to believe that Sweden, within a period of a decade beginning in 1979, will become the first country in the world to have taken decisive and virtually irreversible steps toward socialist relations of production in a democratic and reformist manner. I see the following scenario: The business community is torn between its dependence on an interventionist state and its internal needs to minimize private costs and maintain or increase its profitability. After further electoral defeats of the bourgeois political parties, they will pragmatically decide that "if you can't beat them, join them." Burnham-type managers, separated from the ownership of capital and primarily concerned with doing a good job, will become increasingly common in the business community and, to their surprise, will find it as stimulating to work for labor as for capital.

The greatest obstacle to taking these steps toward socialism will not be domestic. Our place in the international capitalist economy is not so easily resolved. Space prevents a full discussion of this point, but I would say it is very much a matter of timing and sequence. Certain changes, such as workers' control of capital accumulation and investment, can be realized while we still are part of this international capitalist order. Other, more far-reaching, socialist changes are virtually impossible without at least the initiation of change in this international economic order. Close collaboration with working-class organizations in other countries is therefore essential. The building of a full-fledged democratic socialist society is certainly not something to be accomplished within ten years.

Liberalism Under Socialism

If the bourgeois parties stay in government long enough, contrary to my predictions, we can expect more consistency in private interests and the economic policy pursued by the government. The conflict between labor and capital on the other hand could become more intense. However strange this may seem, the basic contradictions of Swedish capitalism would be dealt with less effectively by a bourgeois than by a Social Democratic government.

This does not mean that victorious return of a Social Democratic government would not have its problems. One particularly interesting problem concerns the future role of trade unions in a system of production dominated by worker-controlled capital funds and company decision-making dominated by trade unions. Under present conditions, where the interests of labor and capital stand in clear opposition, the direction of trade-union policy is plainly on the side of labor. However, under conditions of worker-controlled "capital-fund socialism," the unions would have to operate on both levels—on the side of management and on the side of the workers. This double focus within the trade-union movement will require organizational innovations yet to be formulated in a way that will satisfy democratic criteria, articulate opposing interests, and still assure efficiency in production.

Should such a situation arise, part of the solution may rest with progressive liberalism. Unable today to place itself unambiguously on either the side of capital or labor, it might demonstrate a less ambiguous role under socialism, because it can then concentrate on its classical function as critic and as defender of individual human rights. We have to recognize here that problems of bureaucratic ossification and neglect for individual rights will exist in a democratic socialist society—just as they exist in our present type of capitalism. In a society that has arrived at a socialist order through democratic means and parliamentary legislation, the liberal posture could be maintained with more consistency and less ideological confusion. Once economic democracy based on workers' control and self-management has been made constitutional, these controversial issues, which now divide and confuse the social-liberals, will be removed from day-to-day political preoccupations, just as political democracy stopped being controversial in Sweden long ago. Social-liberals can then concentrate on a creative concern for individual rights and related issues.

Our Social Democratic leadership has repeatedly proclaimed that the Swedish style of socialism would not impose a one-party political system. In a future democratic socialist system adjusted to the specific historical requirements of Swedish society, with new and better relations of production having been legislated, opposing interests would still have to be represented by different political parties in parliament. Liberals may even find a role to play in trade-union elections where today they are seen as completely irrelevant. Paradoxical as it may sound, progressive liberalism would be more relevant in a system of democratic socialism than it seems to be in what we now call a liberal democracy.

Michael Harrington

What Socialists Would Do in America–If They Could

LET'S pose a far-reaching question, without pretending to answer it fully. What would happen in America if we were able to make it come to pass? How would we move beyond the welfare state? What measures would be taken on the far side of liberal reform, yet well short of utopia?

These questions are not academic. In Europe today there are democratic socialist mass parties that are putting them on the political agenda. In America there is of course no major socialist movement yet. But this society is more and more running up against the inherent limits of the welfare state. We can no longer live with the happy assumptions of 1960s liberalism—that an endless, noninflationary growth would not only allow us to finance social justice but to profit from it as well. So, for instance, a Democratic president is told by key economic advisers that workers will have to bear the consequences of breathing cotton dust because industry "cannot afford" the cost of protecting their lungs.

In the United States at present the dominant reaction to such structural problems is to sound retreat. This may well strike cruelly at the poor, the minorities, women, and all other vulnerable people. But ultimately the forced march to the rear will not work. For there are limits to the ability of the nation to impose the social costs of late-capitalist production on those least able to defend themselves.

So I boldly assert that old-fashioned reaction is not, in the long run, a feasible way of dealing with our problems. There will either be a new-fashioned reaction—sophisticated, modern, planned —or there will be a socialist alternative. It is with this thought in mind that I undertake an attempt to define a socialist policy for the (still unforeseeable) middle distance. First, I will try to outline some of the general problems raised by such an imaginative definition of the future. Then there will be a brief sketch of that possible socialist future. And finally, I will try to relate these speculations to the immediate present, since I am convinced that projecting what should be must help us here and now in devising what can be.

Some General Problems

Capitalism is dying. It will not, however, disappear on a given day, or in a given month or even year. Its demise will take place as a historic process that could lead to democratic socialism—or to a new kind of collectivist and authoritarian society. And one of the key problems of locating socialism in this process is that it must emerge in a society that is not capitalist or socialist but something in-between, with elements of both.

Let me now hastily sketch in a few details to support the sweeping statements I have just made.

The way capitalism ends defines the terrain on which socialism becomes possible.* Present-day capitalism is more and more collectivist, that is, it increasingly makes its economic decisions politically. This happens because the inherent tendencies of the system subvert the always imperfect "free markets" of an earlier age and because in any case those markets could not organize a system of such interdependent complexity. Thus far this process of

---

*In what follows I have summarized the arguments detailed and documented in *The Twilight of Capitalism.* Readers who seek proof for my various assertions will, I hope, find it there.

collectivization within capitalism has been dominated by corporate priorities, even when the collectivizers have been liberals, trade unionists, or socialists.

This last trend is not the result of a conspiracy on the right or of betrayals on the left. It is a consequence of the fact that, as Claus Offe put it, the capitalist state is not itself a capitalist. The economic and political health of the government thus becomes dependent on investment decisions made in private boardrooms. Those decisions are critical determinants of the Gross National Product, the level of employment, and indeed of the government's own revenues. The rulers of the welfare state therefore must adapt themselves to corporate priorities—"win business confidence."

Those corporate priorities center on the maximizing of profits. This obviously is no longer done in an entrepreneurial or "robber-baron" way. The nonowning manager has a much more sophisticated calculus, and corporate collectivist that he is, takes political and even social factors into account. Yet even in this new guise capitalism remains dangerously and fundamentally antisocial. Capacity is expanded in good times as if there were no tomorrow—or more precisely, as if the ability of the society to consume were not limited by the very income structure that capitalist production enforces. In consequence there are periodic crises. At the same time the growing social costs of the system are imposed on those least able to pay—a fact cruelly visible in the devastated cities of the Northeast and industrial Middle West. Markets are rigged with increasing expertise, which is one source of inflation in the midst of recession. Inequality persists because under capitalism private wealth, personal and corporate, is the main source of new investment funds.

The welfare state reinforces these trends. Since the health of the entire economy is seen to depend on the will of those who control investment, "trickle down" becomes *the* ideology of late capitalism. Thus the political representatives of the rich are now demanding—in the name of the common good—that further tax privileges be conferred on the wealthy while government-spending for everyone else is curtailed.

This corporate collectivism is not, however, a stable system—as anyone who has lived in the 1970s can testify. The private, and antisocial, priorities that inform public action are becoming more and more destructive. The anticapitalist measures used to shore up capitalism create a crisis of legitimacy. And eventually the contradictions of "private socialization" will require basic structural changes. Those could move in the direction of a new class society, a bureaucratic sort of collectivism, or toward a new communitarianism, a democratic socialism.

This summary analysis points to a key assumption of all that follows and helps to define a central problem for socialists seeking to transcend the welfare state. *Socialism will have to define itself in the course of a contradictory transitional period in which elements of both traditional capitalism and corporate collectivism will coexist with, and threaten, socialist innovations.*

It is foolish to imagine a day, a month, or a year when society suddenly "leaps" from capitalism to socialism; the very complexity of modern society precludes that. Where, in some brief period of time, will one suddenly find a socialist cadre capable of taking over from the capitalist managers? How can new psychologies, and new ethics, be created quickly? Moreover one must have a due respect for socialist ignorance. We know the evils of the old order in great detail, but we do not have all the plans for the new order in our hip pocket. Even if we did, that would be of small help since a socialist society must be built democratically and cannot be proclaimed from on high.

After all, socialists do not simply propose a new economy. We realize that there must be a transformation of culture, of individual and collective values, if the new structures are to matter. As Antonio Gramsci rightly insisted, socialism is the work of an epoch and it has to do with an entire society, not just with property forms or tax laws.

But that fact creates enormous problems. How, for instance, does one avoid the cooptation of partial measures of socialization in an economy in which corporate collectivism retains considerable power? In a recent book, Serge Christophe Kolm analyzed what this meant in the Chile of *Unidad Popular*. One of the first measures of the Allende government was to increase enormously the wages of the poor while holding down prices. This meant, however, a reduction in the profits of the private sector—profits that had been the traditional source of new investment funds. At first the problem was not too serious since the wage policy set off a consumer boom. But eventually there occurred a slowdown and the corporations had to borrow, thereby setting into motion the inflationary spiral. The Nixon administration, the CIA, the copper companies, the world financial community (including the World Bank), all did what they could to make matters worse.

Still the relevant point here is that Chile demonstrates the inherent difficulties in introducing socialist measures in an economy still manifesting strong capitalist tendencies. So, alas, does the Tennessee Valley Authority. From its inception under the New Deal until the early 1950s the TVA managed to control floods and generate power in a way that enormously stimulated the region's economy. But from the early 1950s on this public property behaved more and more in a classic private way. It moved from hydropower to coal and in the process was a major initiator of the destructive strip-mining of Appalachia. Indeed it is possible to make a sad generalization: *Most existing nationalized enterprises in the world behave about as badly as private enterprises.* When one adds that those nationalized companies constitute more often than not the collectivization of private losses and inefficiencies, one gets a sense of the enormous difficulties of a transition toward socialism within the contradictory world of late capitalism. In that setting the danger of cooptation does not arise primarily because of the personal corruption of leaders or bureaucrats; it is a structural tendency of the society.

So in imagining socialism as it would emerge just the other side of the welfare state, the imagination must be realistic. How does one begin to create a new society in a world in which there will be capitalist striving for gain, socialist egalitarianism, and "communist" free goods in the libertarian sense of the word as used by Marx in his *Critique of the Gotha Program.* Under such difficult conditions, how is it possible to transfer the control of basic investment decisions from private boardrooms to the democratic process?

In facing up to these issues within the framework of a brief essay, much that is enormously important will be placed in parentheses. I will deal with a single developed society and ignore the international implications of socialism that are in other contexts decisive. I will posit the existence of a political movement capable of taking the lead in implementing the proposals I make, and I will focus on economic and social structures and present my illustrations as evocative symbols of a possible future, and not at all as a fully worked-out program.

Speculations and Possibilities

First, socialism proposes a national planning process in which all the people would have an *effective* right to participate.

Through a political process, the society would consider its basic options. Put in American terms, the administration would outline the needs of the next period and the resources available to meet them. Since the latter would not be infinite, there would have to be proposed "trade-offs." A crash program for the improvement of health might limit the growth of education; the decision to take the benefits of increased productivity in the form of more leisure time would mean that the same productivity could not be spent on more consumer goods. This last point is particularly important because one would hope that as socialist consciousness would rise, so would the tendency toward the decommercialization of life —toward communal, noncommodity forms of consumption, like neighborhood centers or public theaters.

Under such conditions there obviously would be debates over priorities. These would be resolved by a democratic process in which parties would compete with one another over conflicting programs. That, however, would not mean a mere extension of present-day "pluralist" theory, which ignores the way formal democratic rights, precious as they are, can be subverted by economic and social inequalities. In the period of transition there would not simply be a corporate sector striving to impose its values on the polity; the government itself would obviously be (and already is) a center of power. For democracy to work in such a context it would have to be much more profound and real than it is today. Let us imagine two quite unutopian aspects of such a deepening of democracy.

First, if the administration or even the administration and the major opposition have an effective monopoly on the machinery and personnel of the planning process, then the formal right to challenge the plan becomes almost empty of content. In French "indicative planning," for instance, the workers are legally guaranteed representation at every level of the system. But they, unlike business and government, do not have the expert staff, the computers, the "knowledge technology" so important in a modern society. Therefore they normally do not bother to participate in the exercise.

If, then, planning is to be a critical instrument of the assertion of popular control over the investment process, there must be effective provision for democratic participation. Any significant group of people—much larger than a coffee klatsch, much smaller than a majority—should be given the means to challenge the official plan(s). This could be done in at least two ways. Such a group could be given the funds to hire its own experts and computers; or it could be given the right to have the official bureaucracy work out the details of its counterplan(s). Within such a framework, when the administration and the Congress would go to the various regions and ask for popular inputs, there would not be the *pro forma* hearings that so often prevail today. The critics would be technically as well prepared as the establishment.

Second, the political process itself should be democratized. Here some of the West European countries now are far ahead of the United States. All television time available to candidates for federal office should be allocated according to a democratic formula. And each significant group should either get subsidies for its own press, or else—as is sometimes the case in this country with intraunion oppositions in campaign periods—have legally guaranteed access to the print media.

Let us assume, then, that truly democratic procedures could be established within the planning process, given a little imagination and a mass socialist political movement. What of the content of the plan(s)? How would it (or they) be rationally debated and worked out? How would it (or they) be implemented democratically without an enormous proliferation of bureaucracy?

It would be of utmost importance that everyone in the planning debates know the real costs of all the proposals. It was thus not an accident that on the few occasions when he explicitly referred to the socialist future, Marx spoke of the need for careful bookkeeping. Like Max Weber, he regarded bookkeeping as one of the great accomplishments of the capitalist era, and then added that it would be even more necessary under socialism precisely because production would be planned. And it is of course one of the central themes in a contemporary indictment of late capitalism that this system falsifies prices by imposing its social costs on helpless people and/or the government.

This point raises a technical question that should at least be noted before moving on to a basic issue. In the absence of capitalist-factor markets, can society rationally compute efficient prices? In a famous attack on socialism Ludwig von Mises argued that it would not be possible to do so. He was effectively answered by Oskar Lange, A. P. Lerner, and Joseph Schumpeter (the latter summarizes the debate in *Capitalism, Socialism, and Democracy*). To be sure, I do not accept many of the overly centralist assumptions of their imagined solutions, yet their central point about rational prices under socialism is persuasive. Schumpeter, brilliant Austrian conservative, held that socialist prices would be set by marginal costs; the late Anthony Crosland, a British Fabian, noted that *only* under socialism would such capitalist theories work; and some of the economists grouped around François Mitterand, like Philipe Brachet, have gone into detail as to how this might be done in present-day France. So I will assume that serious debate can take place on the basis of accurate information about "trade-offs."

But does this mean, then, that socialism will operate according to the criterion of profit? And if so, what of the claim that it entails production for use *instead of* profit?

Profit, I would argue on the basis of historical evidence, is the specific form that the surplus from production takes in, and only in, capitalism. Such a surplus exists in all but the most primitive of subsistence societies; it will certainly have to exist under socialism. Under capitalism the surplus is appropriated by the owners and managers of the means of production, and it is both a title to wealth and to the right to make basic investment decisions about the future of the economy. In precapitalist systems the surplus was appropriated by political and ideological, not economic, means, i.e., on the basis of "God's will" as backed by the human sword.

Under socialism there will be a social dividend to provide for those who do not (usually because they cannot) work, for depreciation, and for expansion (on the last count it should be remembered that I am speaking of the socialist transition when there will be many urgent needs for new investment, both at home and abroad). But that social dividend will not be a "profit." It will be appropriated by the society and allocated after democratic decision-making; it will not go to individuals in the form of wealth or elite power, as is now the case. Second, although a socialist society will have to create a surplus and will want to measure the return on investments as precisely as possible, the resulting "interest rate" will be an accounting device and not a flow of income to private owners. Third, socialist accounting will compute social cost and social benefit in a way that capitalism, for systemic reasons, does not and cannot do. For instance, mainstream economists today defend the ruin of the Northeastern and Middle Western cities as an inevitable—tolerable if unfortunate —consequence of making a more "efficient" use of resources. But efficiency, it must be understood, is not a mathematical absolute obeyed by technocrats; it is always defined in relation to the interests of different groups and individuals. Under capitalism this is done behind a veil of mystifying rationalization and in the interests of a minority. Under socialism the term will be democratically defined in public debate in relation to the needs of the majority.

LET us assume, then, that the democratic planning process has determined the basic priorities of the society. How will they be implemented?

There are two existing models, neither of them applicable to democratic socialism. In the Soviet Union and other Communist countries there is centralized command planning with the bureaucracy setting thousands of prices and production targets. The system is politically totalitarian and economically inefficient—two facts that are closely related to one another. I therefore reject this model because it does not satisfy basic socialist goals. The other model, that of indicative planning, is also not the way to democratic socialism, but it is worth examining more closely for a moment since it highlights one of the critical differences between liberalism (in the American sense of that term) and socialism.

Here is how Stephen S. Cohen described French indicative planning in a 1977 paper for the Joint Economic Committee. There is, he says, an economic "concert" achieved without the participation of the unions, consumers, or small businessmen:

> The economic concert is based on a simple political ideology and defines a simple political role for planning. The state needs a high-performance economy. This has come to mean a fundamental commitment by the state to the expansion and modernization of the big-business sector. Big business needs the active cooperation of the state. It needs the state to maintain a high level of effective demand and to socialize many of its costs. It also needs the aid of the state in managing its own affairs. The overarching organization provided by the state helps industry to regulate competitive forces. In brief, big business finds that it needs a cooperative economy and it needs the state to organize that cooperation. Most modern capitalist nations are doing some variant of the state–big business partnership model, but nowhere with such clarity and enthusiasm as in France.

The French planners assume that private corporate priorities are the pivot on which all decisions turn and that it is therefore the role of the plan to facilitate, and sometimes humanize, the work of big business in the name of the common good. This, it will be noted, is the tacit assumption of much of American liberalism. However, it should be emphasized that in technocratic, *dirigiste* France, what is implicit in America has achieved the status of an ideology. I insist on this point for a political reason: the American liberals (including labor liberals) who unconsciously accept the corporate premise are often also hostile to corporations and in the future could become socialist. This is not true of a principled French technocrat or, rather, the conversion required in the second case is much more profound. One of the hopeful aspects of American liberalism is its contradictory character.

In any case we have come to a fundamental divide, one that marks off socialism from all variants of capitalist reform. The latter believed that liberal goals can be limited to a late-capitalist economic and social structure, while socialists define that structure as the core of the problem. What then is the socialist alternative? How will socialists actually implement the lovely choices made in the democratic planning process?

Not by command of the Soviet, or any other, model. However, in rejecting indicative planning within a late-capitalist society that is economically and politically dominated by corporate power, one is not ruling out indicative planning in an utterly different milieu. For in imagining a socialist transition from capitalism toward the good society, I hypothesize two different motivations for working to fulfill the democratic plan and see them as operating within three different kinds of enterprises.

The first motive is individual gain. The goal of socialism clearly is to transcend greed as far as is possible, and to act on the basis of "to each according to his/her need, from each according to his/her ability." This lies in the distance, although approximations of it should begin on the first day of socialist transition. But as socialism emerges from capitalism, there would be differentials in wages within an enterprise and even differentials between enterprises within the same industry. At the same time there would be a progressive, egalitarian tax program to reduce radically the outrageous spread between executive and worker pay in capitalism today. Managers receiving hundreds of thousands a year—and setting their compensation for themselves—are not being paid wages, but if I may speak in an old yet useful language, they are appropriating surplus value in the guise of wages.

The wage structure then would be infinitely more progressive than it is within capitalism and would follow the biblical injunction by exalting the lowly and making plain the high ones. Yet there would be differentials related to skill and output and these would be tolerated, precisely as an incentive for individuals and enterprises to produce more efficiently. Moreover the differentials between enterprises, even though carefully limited, would be the basis of a certain competition between them. It would obviously be preferable if moral incentives alone would guarantee efficient cooperation with the planned priorities. But in this transitional stage there is simply no realistic reason to suppose that this would be the case.

The second major motivation would be moral. It would not

suffice, in and of itself; but it is absolutely essential as the growing edge of socialist possibility. The point, however, is not self-evident. In the United States moral incentives have played a role during wartime, but only then. Moreover the American labor movement has been particularly hostile to "work enrichment" schemes, regarding them as artfully designed programs to get more work out of fewer people. More often than not this judgment has been accurate. Why then assume that American workers as they are will be moved to change their attitudes in a socialist transition?

Surely it must be obvious—not simply the fact, but a fact plain for one and all to see—that the savings of productivity will primarily go to the workers who make them or to the society as a whole. If they go to the workers, then old-fashioned capitalist psychology would explain why this incentive would work. But what does it mean to say that the gains would go to the "society"? Why would that motivate the average worker? The answer to this question is best given in the form of a generalization about the socialist wage in a transition period.

Wage then will be composed of three different elements (I borrow some insights from Serge Christophe Kolm). It would be capitalist in the sense that there would be differentials based on performance; it would be socialist in that an egalitarian tax policy would severely limit the differentials and work toward a redistribution of income and wealth; it would be "communist" (in the libertarian sense) in that an increasing part of people's incomes would take the form of "free" goods, i.e., collectively paid goods and services, such as health, education, transportation. So a part of the wage would be received collectively, as a social dividend from heightened productivity.

Far-fetched? Not at all. Right now the socialist parties of Sweden and Holland are moving in the direction of such collective payment, proposing that corporations pay a portion of their tax in stock placed in a worker-controlled mutual fund. And one of the reasons for this development is precisely to give workers a communal stake in productivity. This is not, it should be noted, a traditional stock-sharing device where the individual workers get shares in lieu of certain wage increases. In Sweden this is the conservative alternative. It is a proposal for the *social* sharing of productivity gains.

One last point on wage structure. The capitalist component would be settled by collective-bargaining negotiations. That issue, and the more general question of working conditions, would provide one of the bases for the continuing existence of a trade-union movement. The socialist and "communist" components would be determined by a political process in which unions, parties, and other voluntary institutions would be involved. Here again I am positing the necessity of conflict among organizations that would interpret the common good in terms of the particular good of different strata of the citizenry.

So individuals would be motivated to cooperate in the work of the plan on the basis of capitalist, socialist, and "communist" incentives. What about enterprises? Given the previous analysis I assume that there will be three main types of economic organization: socially owned, privately owned large enterprises and cooperatives. There will also be a stratum of privately owned small businesses, but these will function primarily in the area of consumer markets and are not likely to play a decisive role in fulfilling the society's democratic priorities for production.

In all three of the major sectors there will be elected worker representation at every level. This is not merely desirable as a way of dealing with alienation. It is a practical necessity if the sense of communal solidarity—the socialist motive—is to grow. And that in turn increases productivity. It is also essential to the antibureaucratic aspect of the socialist program, institutionalizing as many local, face-to-face controls on authority as is possible.

So far this may sound like the socialist version of apple pie. It is much more problematic—and important—than that. Contemporary capitalist technology, Harry Braverman persuasively argues in *Labor and Monopoly Capital*, did not evolve in a value-free, technical way. It had, and has, social and even ideological functions. Specifically, it is not an accident that this technology worked at every point to expropriate the skills of the workers, to dispossess them of all decision-making, and to try to turn out automatons. Therefore, as a technology incarnating capitalist values is extremely difficult to run on a socialist basis, one of the goals of the transition will be to build different kinds of factories—and offices.

I make the last point about offices for an important purpose. Most socialist language and imagining is focused in terms of plants. But what about the "postindustrial society"? Without going into all the complexities of that question, it should be noted that a major part of the "tertiary sector" is made up of service workers in large, anonymous, factorylike settings, e.g., typing pools, supermarkets, the middling and lower levels of the information industry. Moreover the skilled and educated reaches of this sector —engineering, universities—often in themselves require collegiality. So I am not projecting workers' control as an exclusively blue-collar proposal.

But then neither can workers' control operate as an absolute. In the socialist transition, as many functions as possible will be located on the most immediate level, where the majority of the people work. But individual enterprises or industries cannot be given the right to veto the democratic plans of the entire nation. It is possible, as the Yugoslav experience shows (and the authoritarian character of that country's political structure is not relevant to this point), for worker-controlled enterprises to develop a collective egotism. The Yugoslavs, for instance, have found it difficult to convince the more affluent collectives to invest their surplus in high-risk underdeveloped areas. So workers' control is not a panacea, and it will require democratic political checks on the part of the society as a whole. It even demands the redesign of technology and economic organization, in the postindustrial as well as in the industrial sectors.

WORKERS' control will function in all the enterprises of the society—but those enterprises will have different structures.

First, there is the social property sector. I say social, not nationalized, property for a reason. Any fool or charlatan or dictator can nationalize a plant. In and of itself nationalization is neither good nor bad. Or rather, to the degree that nationalization suggests centralized state ownership it is bad. It is not necessary to argue the almost self-evident point that such ownership is politically hostile to democracy and economically inefficient. "Social property" stresses both the direct participation of the actual producers *and* democratic control by society rather than administrative control by bureaucrats.

It is painfully obvious that it is simpler to stitch together such harmonious formulas than to realize them in practice. As John Kenneth Galbraith emphasized in *The New Industrial State*, elected bodies either lack the competence to oversee the managers of public property or, if they acquire that competence, they create a second bureaucracy to regulate the first. Galbraith was thinking of existing nationalizations which do not involve workers' control, but still his point is a substantial one. As I mentioned earlier, in the very first stages of the transition it will be difficult to impose participatory socialist values on an antiparticipatory capitalist technology. Therefore I do not see socialization as an act, a law, or a charter, but as a *process* in which democratic forces will have to struggle during an entire historic period to give real content to their legal rights.

In this same spirit, social property will obviously not be operated as departments of the state run by civil servants. They should be constituted on the model of the TVA, as authorities with relative independence but ultimate responsibility to the elected representatives of the people. Another check on their power will be economic. There will be a multiplicity of such authorities within each industry. The size of American enterprises, as Robert Lekachman has pointed out, is not determined by the technical requirements of "economies of scale" but is the result of the drive of major corporations to control markets, politics, and consumer taste. Within a framework of democratic planning there would not be an antitrust utopia of Adam Smithian competition among tiny economic units in a perfect market, but there could be a rational policy on corporate size and a consequent decentralization of economic power.

With certain carefully defined exceptions, social enterprises would be required to pay their own way and return a surplus for depreciation, new investment, and the social dividend. Obviously there would be cases when, in full consciousness of the cost, society would want to continue subsidizing production for "noneconomic" reasons (in the callous, capitalist sense). That, it should be noted, is the case in most nationalized industries today, and although it might also be true under socialism, it would hardly be the dominant model. The point would be to locate social property in surplus-yielding activities. For example, the present private energy industry is completely unwilling to develop alternative sources of energy without huge government subsidies. If it gets that money from Washington it will surely develop a socially inappropriate technology. This, therefore, would be a prime area for society to invest in socially oriented research and development, which it would implement through socially owned enterprises.

Social property would also be a key element in a full-employment policy that would emphasize the growth of all regions rather than a competitive struggle between regions as in the current "beggar thy neighbor" situation in the United States. Instead of providing private corporations with multimillion- (and billion-) dollar bribes to go into the South Bronx or Appalachia —which are always collected and often dishonored—locating new and vital social industries in such areas would do that job much more directly and efficiently.

The second tier of economic activity would be a profoundly modified private sector.

You cannot, I have stressed, *socialize* an economy overnight. It is possible to nationalize the "commanding heights" at a stroke, but that would have the negative consequences I have already described. So we must anticipate a corporate sector in the socialist transition. But if that is a necessary fact of life it is also a problematic one. A major private company, Oskar Lange argued in one of his classic discussions, is not likely to behave responsibly if it operates within a socialist political environment and feels that it is working, so to speak, on death row. Part of that problem might be met because of developments that postdate Lange's fears: the emergence of a Galbraithian "technostructure" that except at the very summit will hire out to anybody as long as the pay is relatively good. But precisely that summit is the controlling factor in today's economic world.

This is why workers' control and public participation in the corporate structure are so important. The private title to corporate wealth and a limited profit have to be recognized; but many of the existing functions of corporate power can be socialized. For example, the worker and public representatives on the board of directors should routinely reveal all company secrets to the public. Secret debate and decision-making with regard to plant location, pricing, new products, hiring and firing policy, etc., are today considered to be "managerial prerogatives." In the private sector during a socialist transition such matters would be made as transparent as possible and would be subjected to social controls within the planning process.

Still, a transitional socialism would have to tolerate private profits from this sector. One of the reasons why people would invest in such undertaking would be in order to make money. (I speak here of investment in new physical assets—real investment —not of the shuffling and dealing of stock certificates in the great gambling house on Wall Street, a parasitic, near-functionless waste of resources that could simply be abolished.) The deleterious social consequences of the continuing existence of profit would, however, be moderated by a highly progressive tax policy and above all an inheritance law that would effectively end the possibility of transferring large concentrations of wealth from generation to generation. By now the Ford family has been more than compensated for cantankerous old Henry's genius.

Finally, there would be a major cooperative sector, an idea much stressed in nineteenth-century socialism.

In the United States cooperatives account for less than 1 percent of GNP; in Finland their share is 10 percent; in Israel, 30 percent. There is then enormous room in this country for expansion of the cooperative principle. During the socialist transition we might make great use of one of the Rooseveltian reforms: the Rural Electrification Administration. Under that system the government has supplied cheap (subsidized) credit to cooperators and thereby accomplished a decentralized, locally controlled electrification of the countryside. (The private sector opposed the program in part on the grounds that farmers did not need electricity!) That strategy could be a major level of socialist policy in the future. It would allow for a proliferation of locally controlled, face-to-face under- takings, including community corporations. In this sector, the capitalist motivation would be most attenuated, the socialist most emphasized as the "associated producers" would actually run most of their own working lives.

THE goods and services of these three tiers of production would be distributed in two ways. There would be free goods and services collectively paid for by various levels of government. How would one control waste and overuse in this area? A New York *Daily News* dispatch on the thirteenth anniversary of National Health in Great Britain suggests that the problem itself might be somewhat exaggerated. Not only is British medicine superior in some important indices to its American counterpart, it is also less costly as a percentage of GNP and has a lower rate of patient utilization. Even so, there obviously should be some checks on the provision of free goods and services. An idea that is already partly at work in the United States might be generalized well beyond its present use. Health-maintenance organizations now provide lump-sum payments for the care of an entire group. If the providers can maintain set standards but reduce costs, they are able to get some of the savings from their own productivity. This principle might be tried out in other areas, e.g., in transportation.

Second, a transitional socialist society would make full use of the virtues of the market mechanism in the areas where consumers would choose, and pay for, their goods and services. To be sure, there is no point in investing markets with the mystical powers claimed for them by their capitalist advocates—advocates who love to ignore the essential. Thus after Charles Schultze devotes a lyrical hymn to the power of the "unanimous consent arrangement" within markets, he adds, "if the income distribution is grossly unfair, the concept of voluntary decision and unanimous consent is a charade. . . ." Since this is the prelude to a book that praises markets in the extreme, Schultze never so much as bothers to ask whether the data show that his argument is a charade.

Socialists, however, can do more than probe the question that Schultze sidesteps; they can create a new answer to it. That is, if an egalitarian tax policy has enormously reduced the discrepancies in income *and* if public control of the private corporation has severely limited, or even abolished, monopoly pricing—*and* if the engineering of consumer taste is replaced by straightforward information—*then* markets could really function as they are supposed to. They would operate within the broad limit of the democratic plan, and alongside the free sector, in order to communicate the desires of the people and to maximize their choice. The existence of such a market would not determine the basic priorities of the economy—but it would provide more real consumer freedom than capitalist society has ever offered.

Fine, someone might reply. Sitting in a study, socialist writers can conjure up all kinds of glowing dreams. But who will pay for all these utopian proposals?

The largest single source of corporate investment funds in the United States today is found in retained profits. Within the limits already discussed—relative autonomy of the enterprise, but under the ultimate control of a democratic society—that could well be true under socialism. For as Marx foresaw before anyone else, capitalism has more and more "socialized" itself within its private framework. Horatio Alger and the individual stockholder long ago ceased to be that important to the investment process. Moreover as the Meidner Plan of the Swedish trade unionists and similar proposals by the Dutch socialists indicate, a democratic sharing in an essentially social surplus could provide the basis for higher rates of capital formation than are now possible under capitalism.

Second, a useful if somewhat capricious book by a corporate apologist, Peter Drucker's *Unseen Revolution*, helps to focus on a socialist solution to the question of "Who pays?" Private-sector pension funds, Drucker said in 1976, own 25 percent of the equity capital today, and the pension funds of the self-employed, public employees, and teachers account for another 10 percent of the total. By 1985, Drucker calculates, the pensioners will "own" between 50 percent and 60 percent of equity capital, and 40 percent of debt capital. I put "own" in quotation marks for a reason. Most of those funds are employer-controlled and are invested, as required by law, in an utterly capitalist fashion. The workers cannot sell their pension interest during their working life, borrow on it, etc. It is only available on retirement and since some of those claims are not fully funded, there are even questions about payoffs.

However, the point here is not the inadequacies of the existing pension system; it is to take Drucker's rhetorical fantasy—that "pension-fund socialism" now exists in the United States—and try to turn it into fact. Roughly two-thirds of domestic welfare expenditures today are for people over 65, and there are in addition the private pension claims Drucker cites. Socialists, I suspect, would want to create a single and uniform system, since current practices give government support to enormous inequities. But the point here is that societies committed to the decent care of the aging—as all the welfare states, to one degree or another, are—will indeed have to set aside or provide for huge sums of money.

In Sweden some of those funds are already used for investment in housing. Here the AFL–CIO has a program to attract union funds, where possible, into similar undertakings. Why not generalize again? An intelligent and socially motivated investment of pension funds would provide an enormous pool of capital for all three sectors of the economy in a socialist transition.

Third, some individuals might want to save more of their income than others. Within the constraints of a socialist commitment to wealth and income redistribution, that could be accomplished by the revival of an old American institution: the post office savings system. And there is still another source of savings: the people would pay for the nonfree goods in the society and the cost would include, as it now does, funds for depreciation and new investment —but not, as now, under the control and to the benefit of wealthy individuals and their hired managers.

Finally, there is another important source of savings in the elimination of some of the outrageous waste inherent in American capitalism. Business today spends about $38 billion (in 1977) on advertising. A little of that money provides the public with useful information about products people truly want and need; a major portion of it is employed in a corporate disinformation program to gull the supposedly sovereign consumer. Strict standards for private advertising and public support for a variety of (competing) consumer services could free much of those outlays, and a fully employed economy could find useful work for the people now living off them.

I mentioned earlier the parasitic character of a great deal of the activity on Wall Street and in the financial industry as a whole. A portion of the American legal profession thrives on the pervasive venality of the society. A radically progressive income and inheritance tax law, to take but one example, could free the graduates of many of the elite schools from essentially wasteful and antisocial lives. There are other activities—antiunion consultants, managerial psychologists, etc.—which are a cost of capitalist production but not of production itself. Here again socialism, even in the confused period of transition, could offer a more efficient system (always on the premise of a social, not a corporate, definition of efficiency).

It would thus be possible in a socialist transition to plan democratically, to effectuate that plan realistically, and to finance the entire process. In making this point I have not tried to be complete and detailed in my analysis, only to evoke the direction —and the problems—of socialist solutions. Moreover I have been "economistic" on purpose and not indulged in the poetry of socialism. This is not to suggest that the culture and personal dimensions of socialism are unimportant. On the contrary the economic programs are only means to the noneconomic end of human liberation. But the cynics impugn those ends by saying that we socialists cannot realistically present a program of means. And that is what I have tried to do here, in briefest outline.

A Vision of That Socialist Future

I am writing this essay during the summer of discontent of 1978. Proposition 13 has just passed in California and polls in that state show that the voters want welfare to be cut, first and foremost. There are many other signs of a growing social meanness. The hope and good feelings of the first half of the 1960s seem to lie a century or so behind us. Is, then, this description of measures that go far beyond the welfare state a simple exercise in social fantasy? I think not.

First, there is the reason I have already given. The problems of American society today are structural and they require deep-going changes. Those, I noted, could be undertaken by sophisticated and modern reactionaries—or by democratic socialists incorporating the best of liberalism in a movement that goes beyond the welfare state. If it is thus necessary to project the middle-distant future in an open-ended way, with both rightist and leftist possibilities, it is certain that incantation, conservatism-as-usual, or political temper tantrums against our complexities will not work. The ideas I have described here are, I believe, more realistic than most of the popular panaceas of the late 1970s.

Second, all utopian anticipations of the future are also descriptions of, and prescriptions for, the present. This effort at imagining socialism is rooted in—and more important, relevant to—the America of the late 1970s. In the briefest and sketchiest fashion, let me simply list some urgent and possible contemporary approximations of the more distant hopes whose realization and beginnings I have just imagined. Here and now the democratic left should:

Challenge corporate control of the investment process by insisting that public policy concern itself with what is produced, and how it is decided, instead of confining itself to Keynesian "aggregates" and leaving all the details to the private sector. This would include public controls over private investment decisions, such as specifying the conditions under which corporations can leave a locality or oligopolies can raise prices, as well as such public undertakings as a democratically owned and controlled gas and oil company;

Demand national economic planning for full employment, with the implementation of the Humphrey–Hawkins bill as a first, but only a first, step;

Suggest public cost-conscious and accurate definitions of economic alternatives in which corporations are charged for their use and destruction of social resources;

Propose sweeping tax reform aimed at a redistribution of income and wealth, and in particular at the unearned income of rentiers and the untaxed wealth of successive generations of the rich;

Suggest a rethinking of the entire American pension system, public and private, with emphasis on using such funds, theoretically "owned" by the people, for social purposes as determined democratically by the people;

Urge employee and public representation on the boards of

*directors of all major corporations and a radical increase in
democratic decision-making by primary workers in factories and
offices;*

*Propose federal support for a vast expansion of producer and
consumer cooperatives, including funds for community corporations.*

Some of these proposals are more difficult to imagine in the near
future than others, yet none of them requires a commitment to
socialism and most have been approved in principle by major
institutions of the mass of the democratic left. But why burden
such empirically justifiable ideas by relating them to an ideology
called "socialism"? There are two reasons why I do that. First,
time is running out on the very American creed of utopian
pragmatism, i.e., the religious conviction that all problems can be
solved in the middle of the road by a process of bumbling along.
The ills that afflict our society—which, to repeat the most obvious
and appalling of current examples, are laying waste entire cities as
effectively as a rocket attack—are systemic. They are the product
of a late capitalism that collectivizes on the basis of antisocial,
corporate priorities. Either the democratic left will find a systemic
response to that challenge, which is fairly called socialism, or the
undemocratic right will.

Second, America—Western capitalism, the world—desperately
needs not simply a legislative shopping list, but a vision. Not a
religion, not a secular salvation, but a new sense of purpose. And
so in the details sketched out hopefully here there is not only a
rational response to immediate issues but also the intimation of
some tentative steps in the direction of a new civilization.

Kenneth J. Arrow

A Cautious Case
for Socialism

THE discussion of any important social question must involve an inextricable mixture of fact and value. The fundamental impulse to change, and especially to great change, is a perception of present wrong and a vision of potential right. The initial impulse must still be checked for feasibility; we live in a world of limits, and what we desire may not be attainable or it may be attainable only at the expense of other high values. There is an ancient warning, "Be careful what you dream of when young; your dreams may come true!"

With the painter Braque, then, I can say, "I like the rule that corrects the emotion." But that presupposes a strong emotion to begin with—and it is there I would like to begin.

Values and emotions are best apprehended personally, and I will speak of my own attitudes and their development. This does not mean that my values are all that matter, even to me. I hold that others are free and autonomous human beings, each capable of developing his or her own value system of equal worth and respect to my own. But by that very token, the values of others must always retain an element of mystery. The equal but different emotionally based axiological drives of others can never be fully communicated. This is not to say that they cannot be partly understood; historical study, sociological inquiry, intellectual debate, and the many dimensions of the political process are all ways in which we do communicate values. But my own values are the starting point, though not the terminus. In the oft-quoted words of the sage Hillel, "If I am not for myself, then who is for me?" to which he immediately added, "and if I am not for others, then who am I?"

This methodological preface is by way of apology for the extent to which this essay is an intellectual autobiography. Notice the adjective "intellectual." Anyone who knows me will not be surprised; I have always preferred the contemplative to the active life. I prefer the freedom to see matters from several viewpoints, to appreciate ironies, and indeed to change my opinion as I learn something new. To be politically active means to surrender this freedom. I say nothing against activism for others. It is only through the committed that necessary changes come. But each to his own path.

The great issues of socialism and capitalism became alive to me, as to so many others, in the Great Depression. My own family was severely affected. A precocious high-school boy, brought up with excellent newspapers and a family very interested in world events, could hardly help reflecting on the system and its failures. They seemed obvious enough. The long queues of unemployed at the soup kitchens shown in the newspapers and the newsreels, the waves of bank failures and the personal tragedies of the depositors, the gasping struggles of relatives who tried to run small businesses, and the ominous connection between unemployment and the rise of Nazism were convincing evidence that the current economic system was a disaster. The idea, sometimes bruited about then, that unemployment was the fault of the unemployed —that they were lazy or incompetent or whatnot—struck me as laughable. I regret to say that this concept has been revived by some of my fellow economists.

I was impressed not only by the personal tragedies of unemployment but also the clearly anomalous coexistence of desperate needs with keeping idle the resources, men, and machines which could meet those needs. I was of course economically illiterate, though considering the standard pre-Keynesian textbook economics this may have been an advantage. One day I remember working out to my temporary satisfaction an explanation of why the capitalist system could not achieve full employment; it was in effect a Keynesian explanation except that there was no investment at all. I realized, however, that it was a little too powerful, since there could never have been any prosperity.

WHAT gave bite and impetus to these reflections on the rottenness of the times was the presence of an alternative possibility. It has become a truism that a scientific theory, however incapable of explaining the facts, will never be displaced except by another theory. It is even more true that a social system, political or economic, however bad its consequences, will be replaced only if there is a vision of a better system. The idea of socialism was easily available. One read about it even in textbooks and newspapers, as well as in that major source of education, the public library. Here we did seem to have a resolution of our difficulties. Surely a rationally organized, centrally coordinated economic system could avoid the instability of the capitalist economy and the terrible human and material costs of unemployment.

Further, there was such an economy. The Soviet Union was building and expanding: there was no unemployment at a time when the advanced capitalist economies were spiraling downward or at best stagnating. The *New York Times* was the source of this favorable information, much more to be believed than the Communist party pamphlets passed out on the streets. To be sure the Hearst newspapers were telling us about famine and repression in the Ukraine, but who would believe them? My family was hardly radical; indeed they changed from Republicans to New Deal Democrats only under the influence of poverty. But the Hearst newspapers were not respectable; my unwillingness to trust them as against the *Times* had perfectly respectable middle-class justification.

I have spoken so far as if efficiency were the main value. Indeed it was true that the apparent sheer irrationality of the workings of capitalism was a basic condemnation. But as I observed, read, and reflected, the capitalist drive for profits seemed to become a major source of evil. Clearly the individualistic profit drive had something to do with the uncoordinated inefficiency of capitalism. But, more, the drive for profits had other manifestations. The Nye committee, a congressional investigating committee, was engaged in a major investigation of the munitions industry; its influence over governments in creating the fears that improved its sales seemed to be well documented. The economic explanations of imperialism were virtually standard. Charles Beard and other historians had accustomed us all through their books to seeking an economic explanation of all political actions. The Constitution represented a certain set of economic interests, the Civil War a conflict, sometimes called "irrepressible," of different profit-seeking groups. Most serious of all, World War I, a tragic living memory, was clearly caused, at least in great measure, by competition among the capitalist interests of the different powers.

It was in this area of political-economic interactions that Marxist doctrine was most appealing. I was never a Marxist in any literal sense, unlike a great many of my fellow students at the City College in New York. Irving Kristol has written an evocative article on the intensity of intellectual life among the anti-Stalinist Marxists who foregathered in Alcove One and listed the many eminent social scientists and literary critics who emerged from this training. It would appear that a Marxist background is an essential prerequisite for the development of a neoconservative thinker.

I could not follow Marxist doctrine very literally for a number of reasons. The labor theory of value was a stumbling block even before I studied economics with any seriousness; there were too many obvious phenomena that it ignored. Nevertheless the insight Marxist theory gave into history and particularly as to political events was striking: the state as the executive committee of the bourgeoisie, the class interpretation of political and social conflicts, and the interpretation of war and imperialism as the conflict of competing national capitalist interests were illuminating and powerful. It appeared more profound than the alternative versions of the economic interpretation of history; they seemed to be mere muckraking, the behavior of venal individuals. Marxism put the system rather than the individual into the foreground.

What I drew from this thinking was an argument for system

change. The basic criterion for change was moral and ethical. I did not accept ideas of historical inevitability. What the Marxist analysis did say to me, at least then, was that the system of production according to profit established vested interests in destructive activity, most especially war and imperialism, but also oppression of workers and destruction of freedom. I do not believe I ever accepted the theory that racial discrimination was the result of capitalist endeavors to divide the working class, but I certainly accepted the general belief that the capitalist class would over-throw democracy rather than lose its power, as it had done in Italy and Germany and was then striving to do in Spain.

Thus beside the efficiency value, the values of freedom and the avoidance of war were vital in my attitude toward socialism. The two were and are intimately linked in my mind. Being killed is, after all, a rather extreme form of deprivation of freedom, and in a typical modern war the killer is subject to as much compulsion as the killed. I tended therefore to a rather pacifist position. This position, to be sure, began increasingly to separate me from a revolutionary socialist position.

On the value of freedom, I don't think I ever thought it through; it was just a value that was taken for granted. Obviously an American education inculcates such a value strongly. However, I was naïve or conscientious enough to take it very seriously and to be shocked at examples of its denial. Discrimination against blacks—denial of their political rights, segregation in housing and employment—was the most blatant case domestically; remember that lynching still existed. Imperial control of the United States, as in the Philippines, and much more extensively by Great Britain in India and Africa, served to demonstrate that political freedom had narrow limits under capitalism.

The freedom of workers seemed to me much restricted. Strike-breaking by fairly direct and brutal methods, as well as more subtle forms of economic pressure, was a common event. Even apart from overt conflict the regular operation of the factory appeared as a form of regimentation and a denial of individual freedom—an implication then widely accepted, expressed in such movies as Chaplin's *Modern Times* and René Clair's *A Nous La*

Liberté, and more subtly and profoundly in Lewis Mumford's *Technics and Civilisation*, then very famous and still worthy of rereading.

A BROADER and less direct form of control flowed from the concentration of control in American industry, indeed capitalist industry everywhere. The importance of relatively few large industrial and financial corporations did not need much documentation, and numerous investigations documented their scandals. But massive support for the more scholarly minded came from Berle and Means's *The Modern Corporation and Private Property*, which established not merely the concentration of the productive sector into large firms but also the concentration of control within those firms. Even the capitalist stockholders were deprived of power, if not wealth.

The absorption of the economy by a small elite implied that the formal democracy and freedom was increasingly a sham; the major decisions on which human welfare depended were being made by a few, in their own interests. The same process had another implication, as Marx had argued long before: production was in effect already being carried on in socialized enterprises, so that the shift to a completely socialist economy would be that much easier.

As some of my examples indicate, I did not find any sharp line to draw between the values of freedom and of equality. The typical example of lack of freedom was a great inequality of power. Much is made these days of the alleged opposition of freedom and equality, but I would have regarded the two as close to identical in many contexts. As for inequality of income, I took it for granted that it would be reduced under socialism by the abolition of the income category of profits.

Finally, there was a strong antipathy to an economic and social system based on selfish and competing motivations. I eagerly sought confirmation in the works of contemporary anthropology, such as Margaret Mead's *Sex and Temperament in Three Primitive Societies*, for the proposition that cooperation was at least as natural as competition.

My pacifist views coincided in a natural way with these broader motivational assumptions. Like many others of the time I was strongly attracted by Gandhi's nonviolent campaigns against British rule. The underlying assumption was the common humanity of ruler and ruled; the appeals to cooperative and altruistic motives seemed to have at least some success as against the simple selfish exercise of power.

To sum up, the basic values that motivated my preference for socialism over capitalism were (1) efficiency in making sure that all resources were used, (2) the avoidance of war and other political corruptions of the pursuit of profits, (3) the achievement of freedom from control by a small elite, (4) equality of income and power, and (5) encouragement of cooperative as opposed to competitive motives in the operation of society.

From the perspective of greater education and experience and with forty years of history, my understanding of the relation between these values and the desirability of socialism has altered. Many countervailing considerations have been raised by further analysis and knowledge of the facts.

One problem that I did not face was highlighted by history almost immediately. If capitalism was to be reprehended for its concentration of control and consequent inequality of power and lack of freedom for the average man, what would happen under socialism? Did not state ownership imply or at least permit overwhelming concentration of power in the hands of a political elite? Soviet Communism pushed these questions into our consciousness. For me the Moscow trials of 1935–1936 were a dramatic, even traumatic turning point. It was clear that the old Bolsheviks were unjustly convicted, and their confessions only increased the horror, since it spoke of barbaric pressures. I reflected too that in the improbable event that the charges of treason were true, the Stalin regime was equally condemned; for what could induce those who had risked all under the tsars to create this new world to turn against it save a deep sense of its evil? However the facts were interpreted, they were not compatible with the idea that the Soviet Union was a democracy or was even moving in that direction. Differences of opinion, even among socialists, were not being tolerated. I had not believed that the Soviet Union was a genuine democracy at any time, but its political backwardness could easily be explained by history and the ring of quite genuine enemies it had. But now it appeared that as the generation raised under socialism came to adulthood and as the Soviet Union grew stronger vis-à-vis its enemies, the repression grew greater, not less.

The true enormity of the Soviet tyranny was revealed only in time. But from my point of view the challenge to socialism was already reasonably clear. At a minimum the socialist economy did not guarantee democracy and individual freedom. I had the naïve idea that in the absence of a profit-making class there would be no class interested in achieving power over others. It became clear that this point was hardly adequate. The worse problem was the possibility that socialism, by concentrating control of the economy in the state apparatus, facilitated authoritarianism or even made it inevitable. I return to this vital challenge below.

I BECAME seriously interested in the study of economics only after beginning graduate study around 1940. Needless to say, learning something of the workings of the economic system and of the logic of neoclassical economics had a considerable effect on my attitude toward socialism. George Stigler remarked once that the study of economics is a highly conservatizing force. To some extent this is true, but only to the extent that any increase in knowledge may lead to greater realization of limitations. The inner coherence of the economy, the way markets and the pursuit of self-interest could in principle achieve a major degree of coordination without any explicit exchange of information—in short, the valid elements in Adam Smith's doctrine of the invisible hand—became important possibilities that qualified a simple view of the inefficiency of markets. Similarly the facts of long-term economic growth in spite of the contemporary economic debacles had to register—though, to be sure, one could scarcely ask for a greater testimonial to the creative power of capitalism than was already contained in the *Communist Manifesto*.

My immediate reaction was to interpret neoclassical economic theory and particularly the then new and rapidly developing discipline of welfare economics as pointing to an ideal efficient economy rather than the actual one, marked both by massive unemployment and by monopolistic distortion. Socialism was the way in which the ideal market was to be achieved. This doctrine was held by many, including especially the professor here at Columbia to whom I owe so much, both intellectually and personally, Harold Hotelling. Graduate education in economics at Columbia at that time, just before our entrance into World War II, seemed curiously designed to emphasize the ideal nature of neoclassical theory. The dominating voices, Wesley Mitchell, J. M. Clark, and Arthur F. Burns, held that neoclassical theory had little descriptive value. Though Clark and Burns, at least, certainly had no support for socialism, their views, when taken into conjunction with the theorems of welfare economics, resonated with my convictions that socialism could yield a more efficient economy.

Finally, the development of Keynesian economics, and after the war its gradually increasing application, changed the nature of the efficiency discussion. In true Hegelian fashion capitalist instability and the socialist counterattack seemed to be synthesized: it seemed possible to have an economy that retained much of capitalist drive and initiative and yet gave room for the government to intervene to avoid at least the worst inefficiencies of unemployment and the idling of other resources. I accepted provisionally what seemed to be a widespread consensus in the euphoria of postwar economic growth. The state had an active role to play in maintaining effective demand and in dealing with the many imperfections of the market system revealed by theoretical welfare economics—the overcoming of market failures and monopoly and the realization of economies of scale. These interventions should take the form of relatively impersonal measures, taxes and expenditures, rather than detailed controls and direct regulation. The higher taxes meant that the government was automatically engaged in redistributing, and some of us felt that it should go much further.

I have spoken of a provisional acceptance. I still felt it important to explore more deeply the possibility that socialism was a superior possibility. I was more aware of the complexities of operation of a socialist system and sought to develop more deeply the theory of such a system. I also sought to explore more fully the criteria for a democratic social organization. These matters could be thought of as matters for slow reflection and long-term analysis, so long as the economy seemed to be performing so well and the political process seemed to be responding, however slowly, to demands for improvements in efficiency, redistribution, and the overcoming of market defects. The apparent pause in economic growth, the crisis in stabilization policy occasioned by the current inflationary threats and realities, and the loss of purpose in redistributional measures all combine to raise anew the question of alternatives to capitalism. In many of our sister democracies the issue is much more closely on the agenda than it is here. Beyond that there is the large fraction of the world where socialism and authoritarianism coexist in varying degrees of comfort. And then, since, to twist a phrase of Marx's, every historical phenomenon appears as both tragedy and farce, we have the widespread solemn use of the word "socialism" to cover some of the most absurd travesties of that term.

Let me spend the remaining time in reexamining briefly the case for socialism from the viewpoint of the five values mentioned earlier: efficiency, separating political decisions from selfish economic interests, freedom, equality of income and power, and the stress on cooperative as against individualistic motives. These are not balanced remarks; only the favorable side will be presented. Perhaps on another occasion I will present the contrary case. The case for socialism from each value viewpoint is much more refined and complex than I originally thought, and there are many qualifications that must be made. But I still consider that the argument can be made.

For reasons of time I will deal only briefly with the last two points. With regard to equality of income, let me first remark that I am taking it to be a good, other things being equal. It can be objected that the drive for equality may dull incentives, and the net result will be a reduction in everyone's real income. This is a legitimate instrumental objection but not an objection to the value presumption in favor of equality as such. Many current thinkers object to distributive equality on principle, on the grounds that it contradicts freedom of property. This is a large subject; I simply state my conviction that property is itself a social contrivance and cannot be taken as an ultimate value, indeed that institutions that lead to gross inequalities are affronts to the equal dignity of humans and can only be accepted as necessary evils.

It certainly seems as obvious as can be that a socialist economy can achieve much closer income equality than a capitalist economy. The category of profits is absent. While we now understand that most inequality in income is due to inequality of so-called labor incomes, it is certainly true that the ability to acquire profits increases inequality. Further, the higher end of the income of professionals and executives is largely a rent in the economic sense and would be unnecessary in a socialist society. One need not ask for utopian dreams of virtually complete equality of income.

In a world of any complexity there must necessarily be both antagonistic and cooperative elements. The model *laissez-faire* world of total self-interest would not survive for ten minutes; its actual working depends on an intricate network of reciprocal obligations, even among competing firms and individuals. But the capitalist system is structured so as to minimize cooperative endeavor. The worker is a factor of production, a purchased item, not a part of a team. The attempts to handle externalities in recent years have led to interesting resistances: antipollution regulations are perceived as a threat to profits, not a social gain. Again socialism is far from a magic cure. Each suborganization, for example industrial plants, will have its own proximate goals, which will not mesh completely with those of others. But the system should permit a greater internalization of broader goals. It should be easier for a plant to regard product safety as one of its socially valued outputs.

The comparative economic efficiency of capitalism and socialism remains one of the most controversial areas. The classical socialist argument is that the anarchy of production under capitalism leads to great wastage. An appeal to the virtues of the price system is in fact only a partial answer to this critique. The central argument, which implies the efficiency of a competitive economic system, presupposes that all relevant goods are available at prices that are the same for all participants and that supplies and demands of all goods balance. Now virtually all economic decisions have implications for supplies and demands on future markets. The concept of capital, the very root of the term "capitalism," refers to the setting-aside of resources for use in future production and sale. Hence goods to be produced in the future are effectively economic commodities today. For efficient resource allocation the prices of future goods should be known today. But they are not. Markets for current goods exist and enable a certain coherence between supply and demand there. But very few such markets exist for delivery of goods in the future. Hence plans made by different agents may be based on inconsistent assumptions about the future. Investment plans may be excessive or inadequate to meet future demands or to employ the future labor force.

The nonexistence of future markets is no doubt linked to uncertainty about the future. But this points to an even more severe shortcoming of the actual capitalist system compared with an ideally efficient economic system. The uncertainties themselves are relevant commodities and should be priced in such an economy. Only a handful of insurance policies, and to a limited extent the stock market, serve to meet the need for an efficient allocation of risk-bearing.

In the ideal theory of the competitive economy, market-clearing prices serve as the communication links that bring into coherence the widely dispersed knowledge about the needs and production possibilities of the members of the economy. In the absence of suitable markets other coordinating and communicating mechanisms are needed for efficiency. These come close to defining the socialist economy, although admittedly wide variations in the meaning of that expression are possible.

As I have already suggested the existence of idle resources is a prime example of coordination failure. The experience of the Communist countries bears on this point. With all their difficulties and inefficiencies, and they are not few, recurrent or prolonged unemployment is not one. A graph of economic activity in the United States is, under the best of circumstances, jagged and spasmodic, that of the Soviet Union much smoother. Fluctuations there are, as there must be in any complex dynamic system. But the planning, however inept, serves to keep the basic resources and their uses in line.

The sophisticated antisocialist reply to this argument is not to deny it but to emphasize that a socialist system is not an ideal resource-allocating mechanism either. Much is made of the obvious inefficiencies of the Communist countries, though the Soviet growth rate and technical development has on occasion caused fear and trembling and overall still averages above the United States rate. As all too frequently happens in the social sciences, no clear-cut dominance pattern of efficiency can be found either way. All that can be said is that socialism is clearly a viable economic system, contrary to what many would have asserted in the not-too-distant past, and it does not release energies and productivity far beyond the capitalist norm.

I have referred rather vaguely to the corruption of the political system by narrow economic interests as one of the evils of capitalism that might be avoided under socialism. More explicitly, a democratic polity is supposed to be based on egalitarian distribution of political power. In a system where virtually all resources are available for a price, economic power can be translated into political power by channels too obvious for mention. In a capitalist society economic power is very unequally distributed, and hence democratic government is inevitably something of a sham. In a sense the maintained ideal of democracy makes matters worse, for it adds the tensions of hypocrisy to the inequality of power.

My early assumption that only capitalists would have an incentive to influence democratic decisions was too simple. Everyone in an economy has an economic interest. It is also true that individuals have interests and attitudes that do not derive from their economic improvement and may even oppose it. But it is today a widespread doctrine, held by conservatives as well as socialists, that concentrated economic interests are more than proportionally powerful in the political process. George Stigler and his colleagues have maintained with great vigor that regulation of industries is usually carried out in the interests of the regulated and is not infrequently originated by them. The reasons offered are perfectly in accordance with ordinary economic principles; there are economies of scale in the political process, so that a small economic interest for each of a large number of individuals is less likely to get represented than a large interest by a small number.

So long as the state power can be democratically run, much of this distortion of the democratic process should be minimized under socialism. Income inequalities should be greatly reduced. Economic power deriving from managerial control rather than income should be less easily translatable into political power than under a regime of legally and practically autonomous corporations.

We come then, finally, to what is probably the most serious of all the concerns about socialism. Is it in fact compatible with freedom and democracy? It is the fear that socialism may bring tyranny that has inhibited so many of us from being more active advocates.

It is noteworthy that when Joseph Schumpeter wrote on *Capitalism, Socialism, and Democracy,* he affirmed that socialism, which he thoroughly disliked, was fully compatible with political democracy. It is only perhaps with Friedrich von Hayek's *The Road to Serfdom* that the association of capitalism and democracy became a staple of the procapitalist argument. The association itself, however, was not new; it was one of the standard Marxist views, though not held by all. The hypothesis was that the resistance of capitalists to the coming of socialism will lead to the subversion of democracy by them. At least the transition will require the "dictatorship of the proletariat," a phrase whose ambiguities have been only too well clarified by history. This Marxist view indeed gives credit to capitalism for the origins of democracy; it is an appropriate political form, a parallel to the ideas of free contract. So long as the "contradictions" of the system are not too sharp, the nominal equalization of political power offers no threat because economic power is so preponderant. But democracy will decline with the failure of capitalism. The experience of Chile, to cite only a recent example, certainly gives some credence to this theory.

Ironically the current conservative model explaining the supposed association of capitalism and democracy relates to the Marxist as a photographic negative to a positive. It too suggests that the political "superstructure" is determined by the "relations of production." The conservative model contrasts the dispersion of power under capitalist democracy with its concentration under socialism. Political opposition requires resources. The multiplicity of capitalists implies that any dissenting voice can find some support. Under socialism, the argument goes, the controlling political faction can deny its opponents all resources and dismiss them from their employment.

This theoretical argument presupposes a monolithic state. It is something of a chicken-and-egg proposition. If the democratic legal tradition is strong, there are many sources of power in a modern state. Adding economic control functions may only increase the diversity of interests within the state and therefore alternative sources of power. It is notoriously harder for the government to regulate its own agencies than private firms. Socialism may easily offer as much pluralism as capitalism.

The overpowering force in all these arguments is the empirical evidence of the Soviet Union and the other Communist countries, and it is strong. But the contrary proposition, that capitalism is a positive safeguard for democracy, is hardly a reasonable inference from experience. The example of Nazi Germany shows that no amount of private enterprise prevents the rise of totalitarianism. Indeed it is hard to see that capitalism formed a significant impediment. Nor is Nazi Germany unique; Fascist Italy, Franco's Spain, and the recurrent Latin American dictatorships are illustrative counterexamples to the proposition that capitalism implies democracy.

Further evidence can be drawn from the increasing role of the state in guiding economic activity. The United States, the United Kingdom, and Sweden, though not socialist as that term is properly used, have certainly greatly increased their intervention in the economy. Yet democracy and political and personal freedom have never been stronger in these countries. Indeed, Samuel Huntington has argued that an *excess* of democracy makes it difficult to meet the current problems of the United States.

The evidence, it seems to me, points to the view that the viability of freedom and democracy may be quite independent of the economic system. There can be no complete conviction on this score until we can observe a viable democratic socialist society. But we certainly need not fear that gradual moves toward increasing government intervention or other forms of social experimentation will lead to an irreversible slide to "serfdom."

It would be a pleasure to end this essay with a rousing affirmation one way or the other. But as T. S. Eliot told us, that is not "how the world will end." Experiment *is* perilous, but it is not given to us to refrain from the attempt.

About the Authors

IRVING HOWE, co-editor of *Dissent*, is the author of *World of Our Fathers* and other books. He teaches at the Graduate Center of the City University of New York.

MICHAEL WALZER, co-editor of *Dissent*, has written *Revolution of the Saints, Radical Principles*, and other books. He is now at the School of Social Science of the Institute for Advanced Study at Princeton.

KENNETH J. ARROW, who teaches economics at Stanford University, won the Nobel Prize in Economic Science, 1972. Among his books are *Social Choice and Individual Values, General Competitive Analysis,* and *The Limits of Organization.*

LEWIS COSER teaches sociology at the State University of New York at Stony Brook. Among his books are *Masters of Sociological Thought, Greedy Institutions,* and *Functions of Social Conflict.*

ROBERT A. DAHL teaches political science at Yale University. He is the author of *A Preface to Democratic Theory*, of *Who Governs: Democracy and Power in an American City*, of *After the Revolution: Authority in a Good Society*, and other books.

BOGDAN DENITCH, who teaches sociology at the Graduate Center of the City University of New York, is the author of *The Legitimation of Revolution: The Yugoslav Case*, of *The Legitimation of Regimes*, and of *Social Change in Eastern Europe.*

PHILIP GREEN, the author of *Deadly Logic: The Theory of Nuclear Deterrence*, teaches government at Smith College.

MICHAEL HARRINGTON, chairperson of the Democratic Socialist Organizing Committee, is the author of *The Other America* and *The Twilight of Capitalism*, among other books.

ROBERT L. HEILBRONER teaches economics at the New School for Social Research. Among his books are *Between Capitalism and Socialism, An Inquiry into the Human Prospect,* and *The Great Ascent: The Struggle for Economic Development in Our Time.*

ULF HIMMELSTRAND teaches sociology at the University of Uppsala, Sweden. He has published widely in the fields of political sociology, mass communications, and African development.

ERAZIM V. KOHÁK teaches philosophy at Boston University. He has translated works by Paul Riceur and Tomas Masaryk, and is the author of *Narod v nas* ("The Nation and Us"), published in Canada and distributed in his native Czechoslovakia by samizdat, and of *Idea & Experience: Edmund Husserl's Project of Phenomenology in Ideas.*

HENRY PACHTER, who died in 1980, was a frequent contributor to *Dissent* and *Salmagundi.* Among his books are *The Fall and Rise of Europe* and *Modern Germany: A Social, Cultural, and Political History.*

Index